"Jacques Lacan famously claimed that 'there is no sexual relation'. But wasn't psychoanalysis supposed to be all about sexual relations? From the primal horde to the mass society, from the lacking signifier to surplus enjoyment, from Lévi-Strauss to Marx, the investigation takes us through the complex texture of the psychoanalytic exploration of the social bonds."

Mladen Dolar. *University of Ljubljana*

"Despite so many attempts to claim Lacan's theory for the purposes of emancipatory politics, there has hitherto been no systematic take on his notion of society. Did he develop one at all, and if so, what is its critical value for the present? Here, we finally have a volume that fills in this striking gap, and it does this in an admirable manner."

Samo Tomšič, *University of Fine Arts Dresden*

"In this careful, insightful and immaculately researched book, Edgar Juárez-Salazar addresses and provides us with a much needed exploration of the Lacanian social, bringing to think again about well-worn aspects of Lacanian theory and key moments in his developing theory."

Calum Neill, *Edinburgh Napier University*

"Does society exist? If it does not, why are we so sure that it does? Proposing a 'sociologery', to match Lacan's notorious concept of 'linguisterie', Juárez-Salazar attempts a very ambitious high-wire act: to provide a new modus operandi for social research that grounds what we usually call the social. The right book, on the right subject, at the right time"

Timothy Appleton, *Camilo José Cela University, Madrid*

Lacan on Society

Lacan on Society is an exhaustive archeological and contingent review of Lacan's approaches to society throughout his work, seminars, and *écrits*.

Through a systematic and chronological analysis of Lacan's work, Edgar Miguel Juárez-Salazar highlights critical, structural, and divergent surfaces as they emerge within the concept of society. The book explores diverse manifestations of society to conjugate social and structural phenomena such as ideals, the metamorphoses of social enjoyment, the structural demand to produce social order, and the political economy of the signifier and its abstract circulation. Juárez-Salazar's work evaluates Lacan's critique of the notion of the family complexes, the relation between society and social modes of enjoyment, and the homology between Marx and Lacan, concluding with an invitation to subvert the understanding of society and its diatribes.

Lacan on Society will be of great interest to academics and scholars of psychoanalysis, critical theory and Lacanian studies. It will also be relevant to academics and scholars of political economy, cybernetics, post-Marxist thought, gender studies, and sociology.

Edgar Miguel Juárez-Salazar is a full-time researcher and Professor of Social Psychology at Universidad Autónoma Metropolitana–Xochimilco, Mexico. He practices Lacanian psychoanalysis and holds a PhD in Social Psychology. He has published several books and articles on Lacanian psychoanalysis and critical psychology and many translations of psychoanalysis from English and French into Spanish.

The Lines of the Symbolic in Psychoanalysis Series

Series Editor:
Ian Parker, Manchester Psychoanalytic Matrix

Psychoanalytic clinical and theoretical work is always embedded in specific linguistic and cultural contexts and carries their traces, traces which this series attends to in its focus on multiple contradictory and antagonistic 'lines of the Symbolic'. This series takes its cue from Lacan's psychoanalytic work on three registers of human experience, the Symbolic, the Imaginary and the Real, and employs this distinctive understanding of cultural, communication and embodiment to link with other traditions of cultural, clinical and theoretical practice beyond the Lacanian symbolic universe. The Lines of the Symbolic in Psychoanalysis Series provides a reflexive reworking of theoretical and practical issues, translating psychoanalytic writing from different contexts, grounding that work in the specific histories and politics that provide the conditions of possibility for its descriptions and interventions to function. The series makes connections between different cultural and disciplinary sites in which psychoanalysis operates, questioning the idea that there could be one single correct reading and application of Lacan. Its authors trace their own path, their own line through the Symbolic, situating psychoanalysis in relation to debates which intersect with Lacanian work, explicating it, extending it and challenging it.

The Origin of the Subject in Psychoanalysis
Rethinking the Foundations of Lacanian Theory and Clinic
Alfredo Eidelsztein

Decolonization and Psychoanalysis
The Underside of Signification
Ahmad Fuad Rahmat

Queer Theory, Lacanian Psychoanalysis, Sexual Politics
From Norm to Desire
Luiz Valle Junior

Taking Back Desire: A Psychoanalytic Approach to Queerness and Neoliberalism on Screen
James Lawrence Slattery

For more information about the series, please visit:
https://www.routledge.com/The-Lines-of-the-Symbolic-in-Psychoanalysis-Series/book-series/KARNLOS

Lacan on Society

A Radical Archeology of the Social Bond

Edgar Miguel Juárez-Salazar

Routledge
Taylor & Francis Group
LONDON AND NEW YORK

Designed cover image: © Edgar Miguel Juárez-Salazar, editing by Sandra Juárez

First published 2025
by Routledge
4 Park Square, Milton Park, Abingdon, Oxon OX14 4RN

and by Routledge
605 Third Avenue, New York, NY 10158

Routledge is an imprint of the Taylor & Francis Group, an informa business

British Library Cataloguing in Publication Data
A catalogue record for this book is available from the British Library

Library of Congress Cataloging-in-Publication Data
A catalog record has been requested for this book

ISBN: 9781032673820 (hbk)
ISBN: 9781032673813 (pbk)
ISBN: 9781032673837 (ebk)

DOI: 10.4324/9781032673837

Typeset in Times New Roman
by Taylor & Francis Books

Contents

Acknowledgments

First, I would like to thank David Pavón-Cuéllar, who guided the thesis that is now a book and wrote the prologue; without his teachings, this manuscript would not have been possible. I am also grateful for the enthusiasm of Ian Parker, who received and approved the proposal to publish the book in The Lines of the Symbolic in Psychoanalysis Series. Likewise, throughout my brief academic career, I have had the honor of meeting several fellow travelers who, in one way or another, have marked the modes by which I reflect on and discuss psychoanalysis. I want to thank the complicity, support, and comradery of Carlos Gómez Camarena, who has been a kind of Rosetta Stone that has clarified many of my doubts and reflections on the complex link between psychoanalysis and philosophy. He is also guilty that I have decided to publish my first book in English and not in Spanish. I would also like to remember here my comrades of *The Cartel Bucanero*. They have given me the libidinal force for the anti-academic resistance because, with their laughter and comments, we have built a friendship and a solid work team: Absalón Tavera, Rafael Delgado, Pamela Maya, and Diego Bernal have contributed to this from their concrete work carried out collectively. I also sincerely recognize Leobardo Jaimes, Laura Albarrán, Giancarlo Santano, Eduardo Zúñiga, Francisco Rocha and Christina Soto van der Plas. My gratefulness is extended to those who have been my students at the university: Planning for the lessons I teach, listening to their positions, being in the debates, making mistakes, and reorienting my postulates have deeply filled my Lacanian perspective of the world. I am deeply grateful, without any antagonism and with love, to my *partenaire* Andrea [*Si algún día me pierdo búscame en Zipolite, Costa de Oaxaca*], and to Broz-Tita for her feline anti-philosophy and because I wrote half of this book with her lying on my legs. Finally, I thank the Andrew Mellon Foundation for its financial and capitalized auspices through its Post-MA Scholarship within the *Extimacies. Politics from the Global South Project* allowed me enough time to devote almost exclusively to the rewriting and editing of this manuscript. And as Roberto Bolaño sang on his final passage to the death: *¿O es que acaso hay alguien más aquí?*

Series Preface for Edgar Miguel Juárez-Salazar's *Lacan on Society: A Radical Archeology of the Social Bond*

This book is a detailed scholarly explication of an irremediable disjunction, and a politically-charged argument about necessarily failed attempts to resolve it. The explication and argument revolve around a constellation of signifiers that conjure into symbolically effective existence the figure of "society," this commonsensically-understood and actually-experienced entity in which we are provided positions from which to speak and act. This "society" is so self-evident that to put it in question seems to threaten not only each and every imaginary "understanding" of it but also each and every attempt to analyze and transcend it.

The claim that "there is no such thing as society" is, of course, also a commonplace of neoliberal attempts to strip away social welfare support and to instantiate, instead, what bourgeois political economy has always insisted was the foundation of different kinds of societal illusion; that is, individual men and women and their families. This neoliberal claim was, in addition, anticipated and given an ostensibly more radical twist in the self-confessed "post-Marxist" descriptions of the social bond which, while showing allegiance to some Lacanian nostrums, dissolved the "society" they pitted themselves against into "discourse."

We are thus faced with a task that this book accomplishes with passion, to find a way of reading Lacan systematically in order to show how he excavated the historical production of the bourgeois individual without reducing it—a common trap in some forms of Marxist discourse—to "society." It is this social bond that is subjected to a radical archeological reading.

Here is the "explication" part of the book, something that will serve as an invaluable theoretical resource for Lacanian social-theoretic discussions of how we might conceptualize the symbolic and imaginary forms and functions of social bonds in psychoanalysis. The irremediable disjunction the book draws attention to is precisely between the apparently self-contained (and, it is hoped by apologists for capitalism, "self-satisfied") individual and the set of social conditions against which that individual is pitted, the kinds of "civilization" that they encounter and are expected to adapt to.

The argument which is then elaborated from this close reading of Lacan, and of Lacan in conversation with the "silent partners" that compose the discourse he himself is producing, brings us to an explicit engagement with one of the partners who became noisier, more present, more materially effective in the discourse of psychoanalysis in the 1960s—Marx. Here, in the realm of the Marxist critique of political economy, a critique that Lacan was keen to access, exploit, and pervert, is an insistence on what is real about the social bonds, forms of discourse, that make us into good subjects, adapted, and bad subjects, those who resist the repetitive machinery of capitalist "society."

Psychoanalytic clinical and theoretical work circulates through multiple intersecting antagonistic symbolic universes. This series opens connections between different cultural sites in which Lacanian work has developed in distinctive ways, in forms of work that question the idea that there could be single correct reading and application. The Lines of the Symbolic in Psychoanalysis Series provides a reflexive reworking of psychoanalysis that transmits Lacanian writing from around the world, steering a course between the temptations of a metalanguage and imaginary reduction, between the claim to provide a god's eye view of psychoanalysis and the idea that psychoanalysis must everywhere be the same. And the elaboration of psychoanalysis in the symbolic here grounds its theory and practice in the history and politics of the work in a variety of interventions that touch the real.

Ian Parker
Manchester Psychoanalytic Matrix

Prologue: Beyond the Incontrovertible Evidence of Society

David Pavón-Cuéllar

Society appears to us as incontrovertible evidence. We are in it. It surrounds us on all sides. We compose it by relating to other individuals. By joining together, we are together what society is.

Even what we are demonstrates to us the existence of society. By constituting society, we recognize ourselves as its constituent elements. We see each other as social and sociable beings. Our sociality and our sociability seem to condense our own reality as humanity.

The very idea of "reality" is inseparable from that of "society" in the human world. In this world, there seems to be nothing more real than the social. It is as if society were the reality par excellence for humanity.

Those who believe in reality will have no problem believing in society. This is the case for most of those who adopt the dominant empiricist and positivist perspectives of the social sciences, who are certain that their immediate experience of society corresponds to reality, allowing them to know reality and society as reality. In contrast to these naive scientists, there are those who distrust both reality and society, as is the case of the French psychoanalyst Jacques Lacan.

As Lacan represents it, reality is not even real in the strong Lacanian sense of the term. It is rather imaginary, deceptive, and superficial, deriving from a reification of the image in the mirror. This image, with its illusory depth, fills the empty space behind it, the emptiness of the symbolic, of the place of the Other in which we live. It seems then that the void of language is full, full of reality, of an intelligible and comprehensible reality. This reality is what is later specified as society.

The Lacanian conceptualization of society is that of something even more problematic and debatable than reality. On the one hand, society is a reality as imaginary as any other, a mirage in the empty space of language, in the emptiness left by the lack of sexual relation which is also a lack of social relation. On the other hand, society has no consistency other than symbolic, whether as a signifier or as a signifying structure, as a network of relations between signifiers that represent the subjects for other signifiers.

In reality, everything is even more complex in the Lacanian conceptualization of society, as Edgar Miguel Juárez-Salazar shows in this fabulous book. In it, the author not only sets out in depth the two Lacanian conceptualizations of society as something imaginary and as something symbolic. He also discusses them; explains them; goes back to their antecedents in Émile Durkheim, Claude Lévi-Strauss, and other authors; analyzes in detail how they are elaborated in Lacan's writings and seminars; examines their relations with culture, *jouissance*, and homosexuality; and reconsiders them through the homology between Lacanian theory and the critique of political economy in Marx.

Juárez-Salazar's work is, as far as I know, the only book entirely devoted to Lacan's approach to the concept of "society." This might seem understandable when considering that it is a concept that is neither properly Lacanian, like the object *a* or the surplus-jouissance, nor is it intensively used by Lacan or at the center of his theory, like the subject or the unconscious. It is no coincidence that there are so many books and articles devoted to Lacan's theorizations of the unconscious or the object *a*, while a work on Lacan and society can only be a curiosity, something quite rare, as well as something challenging, given the difficulty of reconstructing something as problematic and marginal as society is in Lacanian theory.

A book on the way Lacan represents society can also be considered something important when considering the centrality of the notion of "society" in modernity, as well as, obviously, in modern social sciences. These sciences, moreover, are increasingly interested in Lacanian theory. It is common for Lacan to serve sociologists, anthropologists, and political scientists in their investigation of society, but without touching the very notion of "society," as if it were something untouchable, as if Lacan had not touched it, as if he had not problematized it through the complex questions reconstructed by Juárez-Salazar in his book.

As we will see in the following pages, the notion of "society" conceals as much as it reveals for Lacan's perceptive gaze. What is revealed through society, behind the imaginary communion between human beings, is the disintegration of the culture held together by sublimated homosexuality, its disintegration between individual particles associated externally, without internal links between them. Modern society is thus a product of the dissolution of the traditional community, as Ferdinand Tönnies and other classic sociologists already saw, and as we can still see by comparing the social relations characteristic of modernity with the community ties established by indigenous peoples.

Although it reveals its own disintegration, society conceals something more fundamental, the aforementioned empty space that inhabits it, the emptiness of the absence of sexual relations. This emptiness has various manifestations, among them class division, the dissociation of society, which is therefore not as social, as associated, *as society* as it pretends to be. Instead of society, there is a dissociation between the dominant and the dominated class, a division between the exploiters and the exploited.

Class division is the very structure of processes such as exploitation and capitalist production. These processes presuppose dissociation more than society. The lack of sexual relations, in fact, is the basis of production under conditions of exploitation. It cannot be otherwise, since what is produced is what Marx sees in surplus value, what Lacan calls "surplus-enjoyment," conceptualizing it as the correlate of the lack of sexual relation.

The level of the critique of sexual political economy, the level of production and enjoyment, is where Lacan, guided by Marx, poses the problem unfolded by society. This is why Juárez-Salazar dedicates the last chapter of his book to political economy. It is perhaps also in part for the same reason that he has turned to the study of Lacan's reading of Marx, participating with Carlos Gómez Camarena, Christina Soto van der Plas, and myself in an ambitious investigation that recently led to the elaboration of *The Marx Through Lacan Vocabulary. A Compass for Libidinal and Political Economies* (Routledge, 2022).

Marx is an indispensable step in Lacan's approach to society. This approach could even be described as a continuation of Marx's approach to society. Marx contributes much to Lacan and Juárez-Salazar recognizes this more or less explicitly, thus distinguishing himself from many current researchers who absolutize Lacanian theory, representing it as a planet floating in the void, a self-sufficient sphere closed in on itself, without debts or dependencies or possible dialogues or insoluble conflicts with its surroundings, with no other link with the outside than refutation and overcoming.

Many Lacanians, in fact, are convinced that Lacan refuted and overcame all the scientists, philosophers, and writers before him or contemporary with him, especially those he cited and commented on. Of course, Lacan would have extracted the best from them, but only to overcome them. There would be no need, then, to read them directly, but to conform to their corrected and augmented version contained in Lacan. At best, Lacanian theory would serve as a filter for reading the authors he cites, to read them without really reading them, reading only what Lacan read. This is how many Lacanians, perhaps most of them, remain confined in the theoretical prison into which they transformed a work as open as the one Lacan left them.

Unlike those who show themselves incapable of seeing beyond Lacanian theory and of speaking any language other than a vulgarized and simplified Lacanese, Juárez-Salazar includes other registers in his discourse and uses them to dialogue with other authors and to consider the insertion of Lacan's arguments in various intellectual and political frameworks. Juárez-Salazar also resorts to authors other than those cited by Lacan, some of them astonishingly connected to the Lacanian theory of society, such as Friedrich Engels and the ultra-right politician Charles Maurras, who profoundly influenced Lacan in his youth. All this, combined with the decision to study an unpublished and marginal theme such as society in Lacanian theory, allows

Juárez-Salazar to say new and original things at every turn, thus offering us a tortuous and unpredictable discourse that is clearly distinguished from the loops of repetitive discourses of the Lacanians on Lacan's fundamental concepts.

Challenging many of the points of consensus of the gregarious Lacanian community, Juárez-Salazar reminds us both of the debts that Lacan contracted with Marx and of the Marxian-Marxist affiliation of Lacan's thought. Juárez-Salazar also shows us that this thought reserves important theoretical places for crucial and sometimes quite current themes that are generally considered alien to Lacanian psychoanalysis, among them ideology and specifically bourgeois ideology, capitalism and exploitation, the State and politics, patriarchy and its decline, as well as the cultural and historical particularities of the psychoanalytic questions of Oedipus, the unconscious, desire, enjoyment and the social bond. Suddenly we find ourselves before culture and history, economics and specifically capitalism, where Lacan's followers persist in listening only to an unconscious discourse, forgetting that the discourse is not of the subject but of the Other, that it is not individual but transindividual, and that it reveals a truth that is not singular but irreducibly particular.

It is as if the particular truth, incessantly repressed by Lacan's followers, returns in works such as Juárez-Salazar's book. This return is essential for the repoliticization of the Lacanian theory of the unconscious, of an unconscious that is itself politics, as Lacan recognized. Depoliticizing psychoanalysis neutralizes it and turns it into a simple psychology, while repoliticizing it is essential to save it by recovering it, by separating it from psychology.

Recovering psychoanalysis with its critical, subversive and revolutionary potential does not involve placing it in society, as the culturalists Erich Fromm, Karen Horney, and Harry Stack Sullivan wanted, and as Stephen Mitchell and other exponents of the relational psychoanalytic current continue to long for it today. These authors, who logically end up converging with the psychological currents of their time, do not realize that society, like psychology, is part of that which must be problematized in psychoanalysis. The blind spot of relational and culturalist psychoanalytic perspectives is precisely the one that is clarified through the Lacanian problematization of the concept of "society" that Juárez-Salazar examines in his book.

Juárez-Salazar gives us reasons why Lacanian psychoanalysis is incompatible with various psychoanalytic psychologies, including the culturalist and relational ones, which can assimilate the concept of society contested by Lacan. This concept is also the one that dominates current human and social sciences, as well as the common sense of modern subjects. To go beyond such a concept that is so functional for domination and exploitation in the capitalist system, I highly recommend reading a book that clears the way for the creation of a Lacanian social theory that does not cease to be political for being social.

Introduction

An Uncanny Antiquarian Work

In its unrestricted, plural, and contingent character, the exteriority of the psyche indeterminates the conditions of bonding between subjects. The subject's intimate voice is ingrained amidst the haphazard unfolding of cultural and social exteriority as an unequivocal manifestation of the differences that propel, consequently, diverse afterward effects [*Nachträglichkeit*], segmentations, repressions, and segregations at the level of the forms of distribution and management of societies. Likewise, in the particularities of the discourse and the cultural as signifier system, the nominal adaptation to social norms and its positivity is condensed in a sort of exploitation and banishment where the "discourse of the master" finds direction only in "segregation" (Lacan, 1971c, p. 90).[1] In this sense, society emerges essentially and succinctly from a problematic order and personalized exclusion, at times tenuous, at others more profoundly forceful or of direct oppression. In broad terms, society is instituted from the exchange axis with productive, fictional, enclosed, and sequential resolutions between discourses, social practices, and their directive demands on the subjects and their driving forces.

The book's leading orientation is the archeological exploration of Jacques Lacan's ideas about society during his teachings. The concern that emerges here is a re-reading of the Lacanian oeuvre that poses not only a critique of ideology but also its subversion in the face of the determinants of social and cultural existence that invariably affect the dynamics of encounters between subjects and, of course, the tensions structurally propelled by the destinies of drive and its vicissitudes. This archeological reading is a critique of knowledge in Lacan's terms. In his words, from the structure of knowledge and its subjects, "it happens that one interrogates a savoir on its outmoded usage, that one does an archeology of it. This is more than the work of an antiquary, this is in order to make its structure function" (Lacan, 1970b, p. 433).[2] Indeed, this implies examining the structural proportions of the social bond beyond merely historiographical determinations or a straightforward voyage into the past. In brief, it is a question of trying to understand the construction of the notion of society beyond a mere conceptualization and its supports and effects in the work of the French thinker.

DOI: 10.4324/9781032673837-1

In this sense, society in Jacques Lacan's teaching emerges enunciated and analyzed in a somewhat isolated and inconclusive form. It is a kind of theoretical foreignness, a conceptual randomness that ends up being drawn as a traversable hinge concept and, at times, is also enigmatic as a solitary signifier, not chained. This is why the concept of society in his oeuvre can be found as a symptomatic elucidation that is deeply uncomfortable at the limits of the social sciences. Furthermore, this symptomatic reading—borrowing Althusser's (1968, p. 28) locution where that which is not enunciated, or which reveals the un-veiled, is situated—also clearly explains the imperative of the psychoanalytic revision of society from a disruptive and subversive method at the cultural, political, and economic level. This critical thrust, undoubtedly, cannot be unanimously attributed to Lacan but has its first echoes in Freudian thought, in his libidinal economy, and in the essence of work that permeates his key concepts such as the joke work [*Witzarbeit*], the dream-work [*Traumarbeit*], work of mourning [*Trauerarbeit*], or working-through [*Durcharbeiten*], among other key social concepts such as identification, crowd, repression, and repetition.

Historically, psychoanalysis has had a unique relationship with elucidating society and its practices. Freud's vast oeuvre is often understood as a bipartite inner fracture. The first part of his thought is overshadowed—predominantly in *The Interpretation of Dreams* and his writings on infantile sexuality—by the false and apolitical reductionism of the novel clinical proposal of the allegedly inner sexual polymorphism. In contrast, is a second theoretical part in which Freud gives way to a social or anthropological thought of deeply pessimistic placements after suffering the ravages of the First World War. This generic division bluntly excludes that Freud (1900), from his earliest writings, gave rise to concepts of social and economic character, as in the work of "condensation" and "displacement" in dreams (pp. 279–309). As well as the power and support of the outer in the surrounding world as the "origin of all large amounts of energy" (Freud, 1895, p. 304). Indeed, Freud was never the same after these war events, considerably diminishing his optimism about humanity.[3] However, this repeated division seems to expel Freudian thought, the influence of the social sphere on his writing, and the scope of psychoanalysis in all its original extensions.

Beginning from this complex Freudian heritage, Lacan explored, from his first return to Freud—which not only implied restoring but also subverting his ideas—the power of the negative dialectic and the incidental that dislocates the organizational and positivity sets of society to cross, from the *au-sens*, the ideological subject's sequence and also his identifications and demands at the level of the diversification of the collective and the measure of the accumulation of pleasure and its surplus in social practices. These two elements make Lacan an astute and novel reader of society, for instead of being satisfied with the reading of social semblants, he placed Freud's energetic terms at the level of a political economy of exchange that is produced in the determination of the social modes of production.

This volume can be understood metaphorically as a staircase whose steps account for the theoretical appreciation of society in Lacan's teaching. A staircase that leaves gaps between each of its steps to incite revulsive conceptual understanding. A stair can be climbed but can also be descended or staggered down. As Julio Cortázar (2007) once recounted in *Historia de cronopios y de famas*, "stairs are climbed from the front"; climbing them upside down is a somewhat "uncomfortable" action (p. 24). Despite that, climbing a staircase from the front denies the pleasure of observing everything that goes unnoticed in those brief minutes or eternal moments when one turns back to the world to climb it. Consequently, we decided to start ascending the staircase of reading Jacques Lacan's archives by descending to the first step of his theoretical works: His doctoral thesis. Subsequently, we follow at times a partial though consistent chronological order by way of a decoy and in a strictly sequential sense, as this may avoid certain confusions as a result of the historical and retroactive construction of his theory and the elaboration and reorganization of his concepts throughout his teaching. Likewise, occasionally, due to the complexity of the concepts, sometimes chronological jumps are justified in an attempt to problematize logically the scope of their gaze.

If something has become evident from the reading of Lacan, resulting in the current book, it is precisely that the order of discourse is condemned on many occasions to nonsense, to misunderstanding, and, therefore, one cannot constantly follow an entirely continuous line in the conceptual interpretation of his production. Reading Lacan *in reverse* does not lead to going backward either in the chronological sense or for theoretical purposes only, but to opening up the possibilities of a concept such as society. Although conceptualizing may in itself be synonymous with containing, it can also allude to conceiving.

Here, we unravel and revisit Lacan by looking at society and its vicissitudes as that which summons the impasse. That is to say, reading what is written by proposing to explore Lacan's work from theoretical points that are rarely approached outside the exclusive clinical field of psychoanalysis. To read a concept is not to pigeonhole it but to understand it as an emergence of rewriting. This is the crucial point of the journey: To think of Lacan's teaching in a way closer to a reading of the social relations. This does not imply turning our backs on the clinic and its essential theoretical underpinnings, but instead seeking a re-reading of Lacan focused on a speculative, aleatory, and, above all, critical meaning of social grounds. The latter implies a confrontation between the totality and the indeterminate.

Lacan was an unconventional *anti-philosopher* by insistence and also, of course, a key reference in the post-war French intellectual movement. Controversial, disdainful, ironic, and cynical, Lacan has been the point where

Freud's psychoanalysis and so-called French post-structuralism converge. However, the French thinker was never a supporter of the latter.[4] Lacan, born in Paris in 1901, a year after Freud's *The Interpretation of Dreams* was published, grew up in a catholic and bourgeois family, a condition that would mark many passages of his work. He studied medicine and received his doctorate in psychiatry in 1932 in a thesis defense supervised by Henri Claude, which allowed him to lay the foundations of a first approach to psychoanalysis, even sending Freud his doctoral dissertation.

At the origin of this approach and to realize what Lacan traces around society, we must commence from several basic questions as guiding axes of this book: What does Lacan say about society, and, simultaneously, is there a concept or notion of society in Lacan's teaching? If such a concept exists and has been elaborated, what is its basis, how is it elaborated, and in what way has it transformed in the 50 years of development of Lacanian theory? The book's central objective is to elucidate what Lacan indicates about society in a way that contrasts with the reductionist views of psychoanalysis on an exclusively clinical spectrum. In this context, the paths of the labyrinth that represents society and its structure require us to remain attentive to the turns and argumentative consistencies, a question always complicated in the baroque Lacanian transmission. Likewise, the road is long and traversed by many collateral concepts when Lacan chooses to qualify—or further enigmatize—his approaches. We thus come to what refers to social practices and bonds in Lacan's thought, which constitutes a frontier elucidation of Lacanian enunciation.

Consequently, the book is a compass or sextant that attempts, to a large extent, to locate or suggest the detailed exploration of some passages, notions, and moments within Lacanian teaching regarding social keys. The first part of the volume could well be called Lacan, *the restless psychiatrist*, since we try to adjust, as already mentioned, the needle of the Lacanian *chemin de fer* in his first works of medical-psychiatric optics, concretely his doctoral thesis, and around the writing on *Family Complexes*, to then continue the journey through the rest of the stations of structural consistency where symbolic efficacy, ideology, the Other, and identifications converge, until the moment of concluding in the middle of which machines, ideals, and pleasures will appear in relation to the scope of political economy and Lacan's homology with Marx's thought.

The whole expedition, as mentioned, is positioned in its historical dimensions—uncomfortably chronological at times—since the writing and discourse of an author are always inserted in time and in the historical gears where they are enunciated: A strategy and descent in the train of history as Althusser (1992) affirmed in *L'avenir dure longtemps*. In fact, the above proposes that Lacan can also be reviewed in logical times as to confront his theoretical apparatus produces falls, gaps, and traumatic cuts. Not in vain, in his words and as a traversal, his only discovery is the *object a*—his little algebraic notation—and perhaps that was enough to give a structural revulsion to the determined modes of social relation and their encounter with political events. Lacan's historical position *stricto sensu* also appears, albeit to a lesser extent, as an adjacent element. His life and practical vicissitudes traverse crucial historical moments of great complexity in the history of humanity and in the social world, from the Bolshevik Revolution to the French May, passing through the Second World War and the Cold War. Lacan is a great reader of the world, a psychoanalyst who accounts for the vortex represented by the entire social and political moment that encompassed and preceded him and, more precisely, a subject who was topologically ahead of his time.

Writing about Lacan from a linear and univocal point of view would only stimulate elements that would reduce the power of the encounter and the theoretical distancing of his perspective. This entails proposing parallel, concurrent, and even divergent theoretical aspects to the interventions made by Lacan around the concept of society. We will address, from the above, his punctual references to the ideas of Maurras, Spinoza, Durkheim, Hegel, Lévi-Strauss, Marx, and in general those of several thinkers and psychoanalysts that Lacan reviewed and whom oriented his course—even though he did not even acknowledge that he had read them. This emerges as a function of continuing to explore the notions put forward by Lacan's planning to clarify the social structure's functioning and the direction of libidinal mobilizations within it.[5]

From the above, throughout the book, the quotations that elucidate society, the social bond, and the social in general, although also in other concomitant concepts, are essentially and strictly adhered to in Lacan's work. However, we also include several authors with whom we have directly and in our cutout served for the discussion. In the footnotes, there are various "silent partners" who qualify, question, transform, or amplify what Lacan says or the thoughts he uses.[6] More than evident, this is a politically inexcusable cause that, at present, Lacan's positions and contributions are a constant within the academic panorama of many authors in the social sciences and in the political scope of his work.

Thus, as elements at the bottom, the ideas of Lacanians who extend and discuss Lacan help to support the revulsive reading of psychoanalysis in capitalist society. They, in general, have managed to overcome the almost impregnable clinical oracle of Lacan—and also of the *right-wing* and *pure-strain* Lacanians—and to use their intuitions and even the impossibility of a conceptual translation of some elements of the psychoanalytic and Lacanian oeuvre in the social spectrum to open a novel and valuable path with which it is possible to question, stop, rebuke, and subvert the political forms of contemporary social and cultural organicity. In this sense, this manuscript also aspires to be a counter-response to the asocial puritanism of the psychoanalytic clinic that has forgotten that the function of psychoanalysis, and in particular Lacan's teaching, should not be summed up as a *psy- discipline* but as a subversion of the subject as a response to the subjective exploitation of pleasure and enjoyment from a political perspective.

To conclude this brief introduction, it is crucial to note that society as a concept deeply analyzed by the social sciences is, it seems, a kind of jumble that many try to understand, illustrate, or take for granted and that, to a large extent, usually remains as an idyllic love of meaning or as a product of normalized and unquestionable social exchanges. Society is, on many occasions, that relational cluster in which the subject moves and spreads. However, when the subject gives up those relations, that fragmented whole society can be thought of as a random and perhaps indefinable *thing*, one more signifier in the chest of signifiers. Is it not there where the acquaintance with which *there is no sexual relation* can become profoundly symptomatic? This watershed leads us to suggest that there is no social relation, and from there, maybe it is time for Lacan to seduce from the critical horizon to the social structure in a way that, *après coup*, the reader and the analyst can let themselves be overpowered by the revolutionary hysterical discourse with a *sociologery*. Last but not least, the reading of Lacan from a more plural plane than the psychoanalytic clinic is suggested here, which proposes new parameters of interpretation and implementation; new political formulas from Lacan are necessary to combat the orthodox academic and psychoanalytic praxis. Therefore, a reading of Lacan's social critique is welcome so that in the labyrinth of theory we may find an elusive analytical passage through the misfortunes and uneasiness of contemporary times.

As a final note, for the critical or conservative readers of *l'archive Lacan*, it is important to mention that we follow Lacan's quotations seminar versions published in English by W. W. Norton and Polity Press. In the writings and seminars not yet published in English, we have translated directly from Seuil's French versions, occasionally contrasting the translation with the English and unpublished versions by Cormac Gallagher and other translators, whose translations are available online. In some seminars, we also used and contrasted with Staferla's versions, and we utilized some *écrits* and conferences recovered and organized in French by the *École Lacanienne de Psychanalyse*; both are unrestricted on the internet. As a way of supporting the reader and increasing referential precision, the dates of the lectures are added after each seminar cited. In summary, the book that the reader now has in their hands can be a guide, perhaps a very light or brief one, to try to trace Lacan's position before the social bond or an excellent pretext to take Lacan to the horizons of social dynamism. It is based on the idea that one of the main differences between Lacan and other social thinkers is that, from his perspective, there is no social relation.

Notes

1 As Julia Kristeva (1988) pointed out, in consonance and with rampant clarity: "Otherness crystallizes in ostracism" (p. 39).
2 This praxis partially distances itself from archeology in a sense expressed by Foucault (1966) since it does not focus solely on "knowledge" as episteme, "discontinuity" or the "mutations" that give rise to an archive (pp. 13–14) but agrees on the way of "making appear the rules of formation of concepts, the modes of succession, chaining and coexistence of enunciations" that Foucault (1969) remarked as a question examined through "psychoanalysis" (p. 270).
3 This Freudian position is too similar to the "dialectical optimism" and "optimistic pessimism" with which Paul Beatriz Preciado (2016) identifies Marx's thought and his method. See also Wheen (1999).
4 Jean-Claude Milner (2013) wrote that Lacan "thinks" in a "strong structuralism" and a "weak structuralism." The former leads him to substantiate the thesis of the structured unconscious as a language. Nevertheless, this also causes Lacan to realize that "a language has nothing but properties of structure, but since there are no properties except in and by a structure, the circularity jumps out." This renders Lacan, according to Milner, a "hyperstructuralist," because he focuses on "the crack" that runs through the circularity of language as a system "from side to side" and that allows him to "discover particular properties by means of a method that denies them" (p. 147). In short, Lacan finds, in this traversal, the power of negativity as a dialectical method of inquiry and speculation, dislocating the traditional means of structuralism.
5 It follows, in these interconnections, what Jorge Baños Orellana (1995), in *El idioma de los lacanianos*, pointedly insinuates when he argues that "after thirty years of Lacanisms and anti-Lacanisms, it would be a gross simplification to disregard the fact that there is no one left who can approach Lacan casually and virginal" and, of course, "in this sense, any invitation that encourages a 'return' to a reading of Lacan restricted exclusively to his texts, thus disavowing everything produced around him, is little less than impracticable" (p. 28).
6 To borrow Žižek's expression.

Chapter 1

Displacements from Psychiatry to Family Complexes

First Turn: Towards a Science of Personality from Social Tensions

The advancement of the concept of society in Jacques Lacan's teaching must be analyzed, at first, from the theoretical perspectives on which he concentrated his proposals and around the psychiatrists, philosophers, intellectuals, and artists who influenced him or served as points of critique. Likewise, Lacan's theory has several approaches to social, political, and economic theory and elucidates society as an admittedly pragmatic notion. In his doctoral thesis, Lacan explores and proposes a critique of the metaphysical and reflective dimensions of the study of personality that are transcendental and profoundly radical.

Lacan (1932) assigns a primordial place to the "objective" and "social" modes determining the conformation of the personality of individuals. He locates, in principle, a "tension of social relations" of "artificial and economic" character that questions, according to his own words, the "feeling of personal synthesis" and calls into question a "psychological unity that gives the individual consciousness" (pp. 42–43). These ideas set the social relations of individuals outside an internalized psychological aura or isolated from unconscious and ethical processes.[1] Lacan (1932) makes a three-part exploration to study personality and thus proposes a "science of personality" that highlights the "machinery" of "concrete psychology" and even of "psychoanalysis" itself as the founding methods of a "properly human" science. According to Lacan, there are three "points of view" to clarify the distribution of the "personality phenomena" of individuals: "[T]he individual, the structural, and the social" (pp. 313–315).

Lacan referred to this as *pre-structural* thinking in the conception of personality. However, he is still far from the force the structure will have later in his teaching. In his social reading, Lacan (1932) proposes that "social tension" and its management give a "psychogenetic" character that "determines" the personality from the concreteness of the "intentional functions" framed in "human relations of social order" (p. 314).[2] In this stage,

DOI: 10.4324/9781032673837-2

personality for Lacan is a fundamentally external phenomenon; more precisely, it is a "tension" woven between individuals and the phenomenological intersection of concrete social facts and relations of comprehension.

In the same way, personality is defined by the "concrete tendencies" that delimit its genesis and the causation of the psyche due to a structural predominance of the social. All these social and structural personality phenomena are effectively "measurable," positing a science of personality treatable by measurement and classification. Therefore, the interpretative scopes of personality often read from psychiatry and, indeed, from normalizing practices avoid the concrete by focusing on the abstract formality of diagnosis.[3]

On the other hand, among these three elements mentioned, we want to examine the function of social tension suggested by Lacan (1932) when he carefully adds that "the first two attributes of the phenomenon—individual and structural of the personality—are engendered by the mental laws of participation" (p. 314). When describing "social tension," Lacan specifies a constitutive imaginary linkage between individuals. This link is where three factors essential to personality development are materialized: The individual, the structure, and the social as interindividual relation.

On an even more elementary level, Lacan gives a transcendental and theoretically relevant value to the social function within the phenomenon of psychosis as a "translation" of "forms proper to our civilization" centered on the "image" (p. 317). Amidst what happens externally, the personality occurs where the function of the image emerges as an imaginary link in the existence of the social individual and its singular structure. At this point, the social tension is a kind of personality catalyst at the social limits of "ideal" and "hate" (p. 318). In other words, this is Lacan's first passage to formalize the relation of alienation between the individual and the social milieu under the support of the image and the ideals. Thus, Lacan elaborates a cardinal inquiry into the outer surface of the personality, which is inseparable from the social images that abruptly intercept it and entirely removed from a biological origin. Consequently, personality arises and is caused concretely as a derivation of the tension produced amid imaginary social relations.

Lacan established a phenomenological science of personality and its relationship with paranoia without falling into a biologistic guideline as the ultimate explanation of behavior and delusional symptoms in psychosis.[4] The individual's personality is then organized under the auspices of a social and phenomenal ordering since it shares social functions divided and implanted in each individual through the Super-Ego. The formalization of a social relationship, as a determinant of personality and self-punishment fantasies, in Lacan's words, starts from an "intentional genesis" of an economic character since they are the product of "energetic tensions created by the social repression of organic drives that cannot be assimilated to group life." Indeed, the economy of drives, secondary narcissism, and repression are characteristics that Lacan directs to an economy of pleasures due to an "evolution" of the Ego-ideal as a "secondary identification of the Ego" (Lacan, 1932, p. 325).

The image and the economy of drives are part of the social tension produced through culture. As Lacan (1932) affirms, phenomenology is "the only science in which no experience of culture will be useless" (p. 315). This framing and its relation to phenomenology suggest the importance that Lacan will confer on culture and its avatars within the psychic conformation of the individual in the first writings of his teaching. Likewise, the above helps us to understand that the phenomenal appearance of culture will have solid and complex social implications for individuals within a social and group organization. Culture, anchored in repressions, has connotations of regulation, encounter, and transformation of the individual's experience at the crossroads of intentional interaction with their counterpart at the social level.

Lacan (1932) achieves the unification of a positive science of the personality, which he describes as "a double scientific hold" integrated on the one hand by a "communicable conceptual framework, in the phenomenal interactions," and on the other hand by "facts that have all the properties of the quantifiable." A science of personality phenomena caused by a social register and defined through "the relations of human comprehensibility" (p. 314). Therefore, personality is a social and intersubjective phenomenon that draws a phenomenological perception of individual exchange. From these first elements, social interaction produces imaginary identifications and supports the Ego. Lacan (1932) proposed a "genetic study" of the "intentional functions" in which "human relations of social order" are integrated from a phenomenological plane of the personality (p. 315). And he suggests that, at the bottom of this phenomenal manifestation of identifications, there is a "reincorporation" generated from the "Super-Ego" which has "a purely economic purpose, that is, entirely subjected to the pleasure principle" and, therefore, "the essential phenomenon is that of a libidinal introjection in the subject" (p. 321). Consequently, the Super-Ego takes a primordial place in the constitution of the human personality and distinguishes human societies from animal societies, as Lacan would state six years later (Lacan, 1938a).

As a result, from what has been reviewed in the previous paragraphs, it is fundamental to state that, in his doctoral thesis, two substantial elements converge around the phenomenological science of personality that enhance the place of social conditions in the human psyche: (a) Lacan locates personality in structural phenomena expressing concrete formations which include the relation between exteriority and introjection; and (b) the libidinal economy at play in personality determines, from this moment and beyond his conceptual approach to Freud, the exchange of pleasure and the regulated return of these in-personality phenomena due to the repressive intrusion of the Super-Ego. The concrete science of personality represents a consistent phenomenal approach to social circumstances. From our point of view, Lacan begins from this moment to centralize his perspective of psychism in the direction of a subtly anthropological character and, indeed, from the problematic manifestation of a repressive economy between exteriority and interiority amid the super-egoic expressions.

In *Beyond the Principle of Reality*, Lacan (1936) insists on the phenomenal foundation of personality within psychoanalytic work. He rightly notes the presence of a "social tension" in the interaction between the patient and their analyst. This tension, shaped by diverse intentions, such as a "demanding intention," a "punitive intention," a "propitiatory intention," a "demonstrative intention," or a "purely aggressive intention," discloses an elementary symbolic trait toward the consolidation of the strength of the structure through language and determines the scope of the comprehension.[5] According to Lacan, the "intention," at the moment it is "transmitted by language," is restricted in its "social function," which is "ambiguous" and reveals the "lie" of thought and of language itself (pp. 66–67). For this reason, the speaker's experience—adjusted to consciousness and thought—may well be a murky and deceitful account that, from social formations, leads to an unintelligible interposition of the relation between the conscious and the surrounding world (*Umwelt*).

In this first moment of his oeuvre, Lacan connects society with phenomenal and structural tensions, which have their substantial basis in the *imagos* as an imaginary and intersubjective referent, and language as the support of the ideals and artifices that it engenders and that become essential elements of the structural variation of a human nature. This approach is a decisive and radical break with respect to an essentialist natural biological condition since Lacan then begins to direct his gaze to the symbolic circumstances that push, cause, and intertwine the human psyche from the most pressing exteriority, even preceding the nascent biological body. The exterior, culture, social demands, and rational imprints begin to have a much more relevant place than the internalizing mental organization offered by the scientific discourse of psychiatry.

Lacan (1936) expands on the above, proposing in a suggestive mode, that "man has relations with nature that are specified, on the one hand, by the properties of identificatory thought, and on the other hand, by the use of instruments or artificial tools" (p. 70). In other words, identification—a key term for psychoanalysis—defines thought and, therefore, social life is sustained in its maw and the various instruments of artifice that reproduce the conditions of the identificatory relationship between the subject and external objects. As can be seen, from these inaugural years, the Lacanian reading of the social phenomena is fully influenced by the sociological and anthropological views that Freud proposed through identification and beyond imaginary identity.

For Lacan, the structure and the primordial relation of language and the social are conditions that undoubtedly have here a merely artificial background. In this sense, Lacan suggests linking man and his nature from the fictional advance of the structural interaction between individuals. Lacan (1936) states that the social group establishes an "emotional communication," which directly questions the existence of a biological nature of man and, as he describes: "[T]he 'nature' of man is its relationship to man"; whom he "exploits" and in whom he "recognizes himself" producing an "indelible psychic bond." To this, we should add that, through this relation of exploitation and identification, the social artifice, that is to say, the tools of communication and the objects of fictional support of existence, compose an indispensable relational bond in the social nature of the individual. When Lacan questions the mythological semblance of the harmonious nature of man, he also points to the "subversive hominization" of interhuman relations with the world (pp. 70–71). He also resizes the social disposition towards an anthropomorphic relational activity and planetary bonding of men that subverts the nature of the universe.[6]

Human nature is always already modified due to social relations between men, and from this perspective, there is a material and relational pre-existence of language. Individuals coexist and relate within a function of constant artificial interaction. The hindrance that biological nature keeps in its difference with society, within the relations between men, is of great importance in Lacan's thought since the pre-existence of language will cause, years later, a specificity in the Lacanian conception of antagonism of the natural and the cultural, as will be reviewed later. Likewise, exploring the hominization of nature will be a core Lacanian axis linking some of the central postulates of psychoanalysis—repression, ideals, complexes—with its social genesis under the inescapable shadow of cultural support.

In summary, the passage from psychiatry to the elaboration of the science of personality begins to have ties with the social and cultural processes that determine the condition of human nature. This relationship is far from concepts such as psychological associationism or psychophysical parallelism that reduce psychism to a mere internalization or, in their case, psychosis to a situation of personal or social deficit. Against the grain, Lacan begins, from his doctoral thesis, to reveal the links between *imagos*, ideals, identifications, and the super-egoic force of the structure. All this is sustained by Lacan's passage from the psychiatry of Gaëtan Gatian de Clérambault to Freudian psychoanalysis, which had as its hinge the phenomenological dimension of social tensions.

Second Turn: The Primitive Difference Between Nature and Culture

After revisiting the displacement from psychiatry to psychoanalysis, we will make a scale in one of the most relevant writings of the early years of Lacan's theoretical life: *Family Complexes in the Formation of the Individual.*

In this manuscript, published in 1938, Lacan suggests two elementary aspects inherent to the social institution of the family: a) The social production of complexes in the psychic life and b) the decline of the father from the parental family as a social condition —based mainly on the ideas of Émile Durkheim and his writing, in particular *La famille conjugale*. Durkheim's approaches were hegemonic within French sociology, contemporary to Jacques Lacan's early work, and made the Gallic sociologist a solid interlocutor of the psychoanalyst. The Durkheimian sociological system inaugurated and consented to the then preliminary Lacanian theoretical project regarding the distinction between nature and culture that was examined in his structuralist period. In an explicit sense, this sociological reference sustains, in *Family Complexes*, a cardinal turn of the screw in explaining the function of institutions and the social direction of the unconscious psyche.

In *Family Complexes*, Lacan (1938b) progressively evokes a peculiar social and economic turn that will mark a more ambitious theoretical breadth in relation to his younger manuscripts. This social and economic shift allowed him, sometime later, to anchor himself conclusively in a position close to post-war French structuralist thought. Lacan mentions that "the human race [*espèce*] is characterized by a quite particular development of social relations that is sustained by exceptional capacities for mental communication and, correlatively, by a paradoxical economy of instincts" (p. 23). These possibilities of communication outlined by Lacan testify here to the existence and power of language as a form of material and structural interaction between individuals which, without ambiguity, can be perceived beyond the formal biological reduction within the group organization of the family. It is fundamental that Lacan alludes to mental, relational, and communicative conditions framed in a social and cultural economy that determines, by laws of kinship, a causality of the psyche.

The participation of structural kinship relations and language as communication in the interaction of individuals is a trigger for cultural processes since, for the young Lacan, there are archaic cultural complexes in individuals that stipulate their social life and behavior within the family. The culturally contorted interactions among individuals are originated at the root of the complexes—of social background and repressed instincts—that cause the psyche within the institution of the family with its "interdictions" and "laws" (Lacan, 1938b, p. 24). In other words, without the family, without family complexes, and outside the laws of "social inheritance," psychic structuring is unsustainable. From this logic, the complexes enunciate a constant legalized economy in the social distribution of individuals in the culture.

The theoretical content of *Family Complexes* also scrutinizes psychic causality and social relations from imaginary and structural determinations. This approach is grounded in laws, family ideals, and the privileges historically provided by marriage. Lacan gives "protean" clues that sharpen the social influence of the family on the psyche. Like Freud, Lacan observed the economic-political transformation of the family that made the Oedipus complex emerge at the end of the 19th century. In doing so, Lacan identified the family as the first group to hold the cultural, political, and social organization conveniences that were the basis of human progress. Indeed, from a social perspective, it would be impossible to ignore the historical modalities by which the family elaborates, deploys, demands, and delimits several institutionalized dynamics, which will have a profound effect on the distribution of the structuring force that outlines the psychic life and the personality of the subject.

For the analysis of the social, cultural, and historical genesis of the psyche and family complexes, Lacan (1938b) points out that there coexist several "adaptive modes of behavior" whose destiny and "progress depend on their communication" because they "are, above all, collective works and constitute culture"; thus "a new dimension is introduced into social reality and psychic life" (p. 23). With the above, the family and its "adaptive" components trigger the emergence of culture itself, a transcendental cultural distribution in the dimension of the individual whose edification of a paranoid referent supports the psychological and imaginary communication of the Ego.

Adaptive communication—through "coercion" and "archaic moral formation"—is effective for the individual within the self-referential possibilities of the Ego and the process of social adjustment that represses instincts in the family. Consequently, in his family relations, each recreates the primitive evidence of the laws of culture, of the rituals of symbolic inscription and inheritance. Ultimately, he adapts himself to the various mythologies that are signified to him through a "psychic continuity" (Lacan, 1938b, p. 25). It is amid family relations that individuals' archaic reproductions assemble a reality through symbols and *imagos* constantly maintained in culture and its artifices. Up to this point, Lacan's proposal will be similar to what is put forward, partially and some years later, by symbolic anthropology.[7] Nevertheless, as we reviewed below, Lacan develops a different theoretical view of this way of understanding culture because he separates himself from the totalizing insistence on the culturalist context that is prey to reductionist or relativistic signification.

Lacan demarcates culture as a modular and substantial unity of human life through identification and the collective. In *Family Complexes*, the psychoanalyst claims the existence of a moral labor where the collective insistence of interests and their most primordial alienation reigns. The efficacy of the collective whole, partially delimited by culture in its most primitive form, clearly emphasizes the complexes or imaginary, alienating and totalizing adaptations that cover intersubjective relations.[8] Culture, with this, presents itself as a vast organizing whole and as an impregnable producer of desire based on the almost universal prohibition of incest. In this way, the collective is founded on a reproductive interest in the conditions of ordering the instincts and the moral and economic aspirations of a group of individuals in which "social progress" turns out to be the "decline that is especially noticeable in our days in the collectivities that suffer most from these effects: economic recession, political catastrophes" (Lacan, 1938b, p. 60).

We see, with the previous idea, that the cultural structure will always have indisputable identifying nuances which are determinant from the origins of the individual in the conformation and disposition of the family without this necessarily implying the primacy of an exclusive family model; in the opposite view, the problem resides in the tensions that the group produces through imaginary relationships. As a crucial digression, Lacan (1947), during a brief stay in the United Kingdom, noted in his analysis of *British Psychiatry and the War* that the complication of the relationship of identification consisted, in effect, of being trapped in the persistence of "homogeneity" which, within groups, is the "essential factor of their morality" (p. 105).[9] Moreover, from an analogous perspective, identification in families occurs due to an entangled primitive transformation of the different types of political logic and social organizations. We will elucidate this question later.

In the same vein, the adaptive social sense of the individual possesses, for Lacan, a cardinal determination, not only under a moral conditionality of family complexes but also due to the establishment of a social base that maintains imaginary feedback in intersubjectivity and supports the inclusion of the thirdness of the law;[10] this last point distributes the duality between individuals by introducing thirdness as a platform of "logical suspicion" and radical "difference" (Lacan, 1945, pp. 98–99). Thus, the antagonistic relation between the natural dependent on the existence of the individual as a biological body and the culture that introduces alienation and rational suspicion is delineated by logical structural support. In this way, social adaptation can only be achieved in the social practices of individuals by the inclusion of a third party; consequently, there is neither solely an instinct of self-preservation that ultimately determines the individual nor a stable or universally conforming relationship with otherness.

Lacan departs from the difference between nature and society in the conformation and inscription of the social order of complexes and the effects they produce in human interrelations. From his point of view, what Lacan (1938b) distinguishes in the antagonism between nature and society is the supremacy of the latter over the former since "the social instances dominate the natural ones" (p. 24); at this point, it is worth mentioning, the Lacanian distinction between culture and society is still not clear. On the other hand, the arrangement and disposition of the family give place to a social distribution so distant from an organic human nature that is homeostatic with the surrounding world. Lacan, in these years of his work, pointed out that what in the psyche becomes thought of as supposedly biological is nothing but a conclusive reference to an economic and social inscription if we observe the symbolic and practical creation of family socialization patterns. An individual wholly subdued by a natural psychism is a situation besides being insipid, laconic, and romantic. It lacks material sustenance if the psychic organization is not articulated within the language and possible social tension. However, it is also here where society is primarily what, through the family, shapes the *nomos* and the structure of signification that transfigure the psyche and human relations from political-institutional dynamics bound to the normative and hegemonic modes of reproduction.[11]

The social function of humanity's material modes of production quickly displaces the human's origin as an individual dependent on biological conditions. At this point, Lacan's wager could be defined in this way: Every matter relating to culture has a social significance beyond the intrinsic relations given in fact and by origin concerning culture and nature in their material dispositions. Lacan pursues to show how the cultural footprint, from the several forms of social structuring, causes repressive practices that dispose of the psychic dimension amid deprivation, separation, and competition or jealousy as economic and mental—conscious—distribution.

Lacan examines society and, in the background, already begins to speculate on the cultural foundation of a structure inherent to the social designs as a political administration of intimacy traced by social routes. The marked difference between nature and culture is due to a reference to the family as the nuclear center of the structural development of culture and normalized society where the institution and the psychic life converge antagonistically.[12] One of Lacan's fundamental theses concerning the family implies amplifying the limits of the Oedipus complex and, in effect, observing the family from a counter-natural point of view. The biological predisposition is relegated to the function of the mental instruments of communication and the mere social exchanges that operate against the fleeting bonds of consanguinity. In this way, material force is no longer a matter inherent to life but a matter of culture that transfigures the human state.

Lacan (1938b) affirms that from a "comparison" with ethnography, history, laws, and social statistics "coordinated by the sociological method," it can be demonstrated that "the human family is an institution" (p. 24). This proposition is not new; however, Lacan insinuates a symbolic, normative, and authoritarian formula for understanding the family from a structural and historical analysis based on filiation and marriage. Hence, the sociological character that explains the family phenomenon consists, ultimately, in a positive objectification that possesses a "complex structure." The family recreates a culture through kinship and legality framed in a specific historical and ethnological context and plays a role similar to any institution originating from hereditary distributions beyond the biological. The family group is thus recognized through society's forms of measurement in terms of customs, rights, and their corresponding social statistical disposition.

For Lacan, the family depends integrally on cultural inheritance and, as a social fact, the family organization exerts a political transformation inherent to the conditions of other parallel institutions such as the State, its laws, and even sociological science and its analytical instruments. From these apparatuses, from these socio-political facts, the family invests the coexistence of a cultural recognition of the individual and the affirmation of social rights as an arrangement dependent on the standards and ideals of the citizen, at least since the familial adjustments of the 19th century. Mainly, and with emphasis, the family is constituted from the social metamorphoses anchored within the imaginary identification of an oppressive and social dynamic of the conjugal form in the 19th-century individual, and this directs and regulates his subsequent paradoxical social progress. Likewise, and in retrospect, the conjugal distribution is the critical founding point of the Oedipus complex—although also the intrusion complex, with its "jealousy" and imaginary "sociality," and the weaning complex as a "metaphysical" and "totalitarian social utopia" form a "dark" and primitive "aspiration to death" in the states of integration of the family group (Lacan, 1938b, p. 36).[13]

From his encounter with the Durkheimian conjugal family, Lacan (1938b) tenuously questioned the Enlightened and Humanist vision of man since, in his words: "[I]n our time, it is more difficult than ever to understand the man of Western culture outside of the antinomies that constitute his relations with nature and with society" (p. 36). Thus, the progress of social antinomies in the particular life of individuals involves the interpretation of social constructions and archaic cultural mechanisms related to historical formations of culture and delves into how these institutions have been repressively perfected throughout the history of humanity. Such is the case, for example, of converting communal families to conjugal families and the existence of complexes originating from developing these new types of family arrangements. In the same way, these cultural relations modify to a great extent the nature—if there is one beyond the merely organic processes that may even depend on cultural conditions—of individuals as they are embedded in convoluted cultural relations.

Lacan suggests, from the social antinomies, that the relationship between family and culture is central and problematic for the conformation of social bonds. Society is defined as an alienating cleavage dependent on culture inhibited by contradictions. The family is the leading institutional bastion of the genesis of complexes because, in it, the social institution not only finds a place but insists on a social reproduction of the mechanisms of domination, regulation, and naturalization to specific modes of social organization in contradiction with the supposed natural purposes of human life. Analyzing the social dynamics of neurosis and its mythological drama, Lacan also delimits the role of the family as a producer of neurotic social affections and discomforts. These, according to Lacan (1938b), "are related to the double burden of the Oedipus complex: by its occasional incidence on narcissistic progress," which "affects the structural culmination of the ego; by the images it introduces into this structure," and which simultaneously "determine a certain affective animation of reality" (p. 73). His conjecture in relation to the structure indicates a formalization between the Ego and the Ego-ideal, as a representation of the individual with culture and its founding, repressive, and normalizing neurotic becoming. The imaginary Ego carries the first alienation and the subsequent structural passage of social functions. Subsequently, as Lacan mentions, there appears on the symbolic map the disposition of an insistent "regulation" of the "affects," which "concentrates in the complex as the formulas of social communion are rationalized in our culture." The "rationalization" fixes a "reciprocal" relationship which occurs at the moment of "humanizing the Ego-ideal" (p. 73). Beyond referring to an individual circumstance, this model stamps a dark sign of the culture in the imaginary conformation of the individual that deploys the stabilizing support of the self in the overwhelming definition of the canvas of the image.

Lacan (1938b) examines the meaning of the norm and its restrictions and states that "the disturbance of these effects appears due to the increasing demands imposed on the ego by this culture" (pp. 73–74). From his logic, these statements revolve about the regulatory mechanisms of the personality from the Ego-ideal under the cultural demands and the mechanical realization of the social. Cultural exigencies force the Ego to function under the ideals of neurotic orders in the midst of the conformation of society and its ideals. The latter, in fact, can already be inexorably traced back to Freud's *Civilization and its Discontents* and the well-known cultural *Zuiderzee*: Culture and its social enchainment gaining ground on the sea of drive uncertainty or capturing its direction under the super-egoic imperative.

In order to explain Lacan's distinction between the natural and the cultural, it is indispensable to remember that the Oedipus complex is not the only social complex in human psychic life. For Lacan, the weaning complex is integrated with the rest of the family complexes that found and elaborated the human psyche from the contact with culture beyond the situation of detachment from the cultural and not only biological mother's womb. Lacan (1938b) forcefully asserts that "in man, weaning is a cultural regulation that conditions abstinence" (pp. 40–41). This abstinence can be seen as a limitation of the individual in the face of the impossibility of total satisfaction of his drives, that is to say, a sort of beyond-the-pleasure principle and, from the latter, the weaning complex could be considered as a socially measurable demarcation of the individual. From this perspective, it is indisputable that for Lacan, the regulation, division, and measurement of existence as structural conditions of the complexes imply formal parameters that manifest an experience far removed from mere nourishment or purely biological dependence on the civilization. Lacan even suggests that weaning is the creator of several individual psychic traumas through the effect of ordinance. In such a way that the insertion of the complexes bends to a rigid formation of social behavior and, therefore, its inscription is the generator of what Lacan (1938b) designates as a "vital tension," which entirely distances itself from a trait proper to the animality and proves, inexpugnably, the feature of social channeling of the psychic by the effect of the cultural revolution and its changes.

On the other hand, Lacan (1938b) invites us to understand "objectification" as a "subversion" of the "instinctive" life through which the "unconscious representation" of the "*imago*" appears (pp. 28–29). In this way, the articulation of the complexes must be framed on the cultural plane rather than the biological perspective without completely discarding the latter as a "material basis." In parallel, these cultural—and social—complexes are induced by the modern transformation of the family constitution, which reinvented the primitive communal organization of families and changed the internalization of object relations. That is to say, in a new social division of the primitive family, communally engendered by the grandfather, the latter becomes part of a relegated lineage. What is being internalized are the repressions of the family in its heteronormative duality.[14] The above suggests a new conception of the family as a conjugal frame that Freud himself faced and which made possible, to a great extent, the emergence of the unconscious. This demand for a conjugal policy is located between the organic influence of the State and the constitution of a new form of partialized social cohabitation that unconsciously distributes the imago and the economy of instincts.

As a final point in this subsection, we will clarify the significant link between the relevance of culture amid that singular Lacanian social passage centered on complexes and the initial influence of Freudian psychoanalysis. For now, it is only possible to affirm that there are some general differences and particular encounters between Freud and the young Lacan; conditions that, perhaps, propitiated only a minor structural adjustment from the reading of the French thinker concerning Freudian theories, and probably this would be the prelude—or the necessary staging post—to the well-known return to Freud started by Lacan at the dawn of the 1950s.[15]

From a first approach, culture for Freud is relatively close to Lacan's conceptions and to what he elucidates in his first texts regarding the opposition between nature and culture. To approach this question, we turn to Freud (1927) when he mentions that culture

> includes, on the one hand, all the knowledge and capacity that men have acquired in order to control the forces of nature and extract its wealth for the satisfaction of human needs, and, on the other hand, all the regulations necessary in order to adjust the relations of men to one another and especially the distribution of the available wealth.
>
> (p. 6)

The interplay between nature and culture follows a line characterized by administration and antagonism, for it can be perceived as an effort of economic determination and a confrontation of human reality through knowledge and control but also as a resistance to the cruelties of the material circumstances of nature that are transformed to organize the economic and cultural life of men. Indeed, there is culture due to the distribution of force and the satisfaction of needs.

In the first place, individuals were confronted with the governance of the forces of nature and gradually learned to measure and manage them; they even dominated agriculture, which is the primary regulation and cause of life. We must inevitably mention that individuals needed a not entirely biological component as a mechanism that ordered and culturally sustained life. Since culture has already structured the natural existence of the individual, everything is destined to a cultural colonization of life through the governance of activity, of work. This approach relates Lacan to Freud from the point of view that culture has existed in order to subjugate the entirely natural and to organize and damage human life, not without first finding in it an intrinsic relationship with the *savoir-faire* of work and establishing an administrative means that sustains the cultural delimitation of existence. For Freud, the relationships of individuals are affected and besieged by exchanges driven by culture. It is there where the individual is inserted and depends absolutely on cultural requirements. Freud (1927) also sustained that "there are present in all men destructive, and therefore anti-social and anticultural, trends and that in a great number of people these are strong enough to determine their behavior in human society" (p. 7). This reveals that family complexes, including the Oedipus complex, have likewise an antinomic destiny for the cultural explanation of normalized society. The complexes are a positive adaptation of the cultural forms of relationship, and consequently, they also create resistance and disruptions in the social limits of the family.

In short, for Lacan and Freud, the construction and the scope of family complexes in individuals have a similar purpose. They are a socialized practice between life and death, between the normalization of the individual and unconscious repression, because of the barriers imposed on their psychic apparatus and the resistance to social mandates. However, for Lacan, at least at this theoretical moment, the fate of complexes is much more rooted in a social-cultural causation of the human psyche and not in a cultural dimension *per se*. From its social source, the complex has more a character of inescapable subjection designed to promote an adaptation to the repressed reality of subjective life.[16]

On the nature-culture tension, Freud (1927) wrote:

> But how ungrateful, how short-sighted after all, to strive for the abolition of civilization! What would then remain would be a state of nature, and that would be far harder to bear. It is true that nature would not demand any restrictions of instinct for us..."
>
> (p. 15)

Freud, in a persuasive approach, not only postulates that nature is different from culture, but also the helplessness of the subject before the natural force. Culture makes us "coexist" with the other. With this, the complexes come as agents of an adequate drive binding under the restrictions of the tyrant's administration of death. Lacan partially unifies here with Freud in pointing out that culture not only supplies organized social coexistence but also approves the first closures of interaction through the determination and support of family complexes and their unconscious *imagos*. Lacan links up with Freud (1927) in the fact that, for the latter, "the principal task of civilization [*kultur*], its actual *raison d'être* is to defend us against nature" (p. 15), and thus the complexes seem to safeguard the organized determination of a repressive culture of human nature and consequently of its concrete potency.

This theoretical tightness reveals that culture rescues, resists, and makes a difference from the management of the biological nature of individuals and sets the interactive progress of their life within culture. However, at the same moment, they also generate a socialization alibied and complexed by the primary group, the determinations of its power, and the abstraction of natural force. Lacan seems at times to move away from Freud when he insists on the relevance of the existence of a conjugal family and its interaction since it is there that the first abstraction of nature appears due to the hierarchical interaction through a declined father, as we will review later. With this, Lacan discovers the conjugal family as the fruit of a utilitarian mixture of historical and social modes that push the concrete natural human potency towards a controlled division of conscious pleasures that is perpetuated more by the social ideal than by human acts as such.

Our brief comparison on culture between Freud and Lacan reflects that, since the first Lacanian writings, the multifaceted—and sometimes even differential—relationship between the French thinker and the founder of psychoanalysis that will feed the first return to Freud in the imaginary explanation of a family bond aimed at the reproduction of the social adjustments that generally cause neurosis.[17] From this perspective, both his return to Freud and his departures from Freudian theory have a sharper and more subversive scope due to the exploration of the *imagos* and his Kojèvian reading of society, and not an attempt to facsimile Freud's postulates like some of the asocial and infertile trajectories of several post-Freudians. Lacan reads Freud in the cultural determination as structure and not in the apology of the psyche's individualistic, biological, material, and normative resolution. The political dimension between the domination of life through the power of the family in the symbolic-cultural and the path of the death drive and its irrecoverable affectation of existence becomes a remarkable distinction to glimpse the preeminence of the imaginary and symbolic reading of society elucidated by Lacan since his early theoretical years.

Third Turn: The Conjugal Family and the Astronomical Father's Decline

This third turn is less close to psychoanalysis, as it involves greater proximity to sociology and political theory. We want to show a peculiar parallel that Lacan noticed in the ideas of three singular and highly influential theorists in 20th century European thought. This circumstantial feature can be found in the social conformation of the conjugal family since, for Lacan, it is a crucial point to understand the vicissitudes of repression, domination, and cultural direction since the 19th century, its political advances and social organizations, within which could be briefly pointed out the reiteration of the heterosexuality of patriarchal character and, above all, the requirement of a commodified social work in the cultural exteriority regulated by industrial capitalism.

For Lacan, the core feature of the conjugal family is the declination of a paternal *imago*, which is close to the imaginary completeness and unity that supports the metaphorical function of the father. It is here that the precise trajectory of the word "declination" reveals, among other things, one of the most interesting theses: The existence of a cyclical degradation through the idyllic attributions of the father figure from periods before the time of conjugal families and in its adaptation to the structures of capitalism. In parallel, declination in astronomy—and here can be admitted an additional interpretation of paternal declination suggested by Lacan—alludes to the angle formed of an astronomical body with the celestial equator that weaves its centrality and its positive or negative ascension. Lacan interprets, from our viewpoint, the paternal declination in a way similar to this astronomical perspective and introduces the economic sphericity of bourgeois society and modern spherical psychology. At this point, the image of the declining father circulates in the same closed gravitational center, forming an angle that announces the father's agony, at least since Modernity.[18]

In Lacan's (1938b) words, the "structure" of modern man since the "sixteenth century" and its "economic revolution" reveals the emergence of "bourgeois society" and its "psychology"; these factors constitute the unassailable imperative of the structural and economic continuity of marriage and its "antinomy" with nature (p. 58). Some years later, and in line with the thesis on the declination of the father and the antinomic circularity of the world of language and culture, Lacan (1956–1957) will say that "the true father, the only father, the one and only father from before the dawn of history, has to be the dead father" as Freud mythically expressed it in *Totem and Taboo*. In fact, this implied "they forbade themselves [the homosexual clan of siblings] what it was a matter of stealing from him." Thus, "they killed him only to show that he cannot be killed" (06.03.56, p. 202). From this perspective, the death of the primordial father affirms that the eternal and impossible enjoyment of the totemic father as a celestial body gave rise to the enjoying hecatomb of the conjugal father finitely administrable in the cultural structure through repression. The father of the conjugal family exists in the central foundation of marriage as an administrative representation of sexual commerce in the closed and finite world. Consequently, the repression of the structure and not the real father dictates the jouissance of the psychological economy of the paternal function.

Furthermore, the father's *imago*, in its first antinomies and the improvement of the family institution, produces a new social and family conformation where the hard nucleus of the institution is a declined father who is no longer omnipresent and totalitarian but is closer to a symbolic redistributive function. The symbolic weight of the father is repeatedly ordered in a new conjugal family organization with a new father similar to the grandfather, although from a singular organization and not directly dependent on the previous family with the exception of the perpetuity of the name as a symbolic and juridical register. The father emerges as a transcendental entity due to the effect of the juridical conjugal ties in the symbolic system of culture, and this will allow it to deploy his agonizing jouissance around the phallic organization in bourgeois society. This situation will be underlined with relative frequency by Lacan (1967a), since it establishes, from modernity onwards, a conspiracy between the State and science which, due to the "Oedipal ideology," enhances the "value of the petit-bourgeois family in civilization," that is to say, in "the society conveyed by science" (p. 256). In parallel, it constitutes "systematic exploitation," which "takes ethical form in the bourgeoisification it seals on a planetary scale" and sharpens "managerial exploitation" by "psychology" (Lacan, 1966a, pp. 206–208).

The father's decline is always already centered on loss and decentering. From these effects, the totalitarian father's *imago* can be understood from a sense of fragmentation and, subsequently, from the structural attempts to reestablish a phallic power very often carried out by culture in the direction of capitalism. In effect, an antinomy is generated that starts from the conflict between the logic of the omnipotent father in terms of his jouissance and the bourgeois social law deployed by the new mercantile position of the father in the conjugal family. In the latter, Lacan sets a "conjugal anomie" through which the symbolic law distributes the exchange of bodies and their force from the marital dynamic. This change transforms the authoritarian force of the father and generates the effects of individualism and rivalry among family members.[19]

The conjugal law that allows the emergence of the Oedipus complex—and the unconscious—is a dominant agent of the decline of the father figure, which produces a distribution of pleasures and the social alignment of a psyche limited to the impossibility of enough satisfaction. All this goes hand in hand with culture and its specialization in the bourgeois family through which one can only access a partiality to an object that fulfills the impossible lost. Likewise, the father's decline is a substantial component in elaborating the concept of the Oedipus complex and the metaphorical condition inscribed in a dialectic. In these moments of his work, Lacan (1938b) gives several theoretical shifts around the neuroses, and it is in them where he sees primarily drawn the figure "lacking, absent, humiliated, divided or artificial of the father"; these vicissitudes will have as a consequence impotence and inhibition, from the social links, in the psychic life of the individual (p. 61). It is not only the father's decline but also the social design of alienation produced by the symbolic inheritance and the fragmented image. These adjustments will support a partialized overcoming of castration and, consequently, a perpetual effect of individual uneasiness in the new conventions of object relations.

Suppose there were still doubts about the cultural background of the Oedipus complex as the original, non-universal, and ontogenetic social point of cultural uneasiness in societies. In that case, Lacan (1938b) even further recognizes—before his well-known structuralist moment—that "the Oedipus complex is relative to a social structure" (p. 56). It is not any structure but that of the bourgeois social modes of production. It is not only culture but also the social ordering of culture that gives support—and direction—to the keys of discomfort and desire.[20] The neurotics, as a result, do not invent his unease but suffer it from the demand and disposition of the social structure that grants them a place for the limited exploitation of their pleasures. Lacan (1938b) affirms that what causes the Oedipus complex is a "social dialectic" and not a dependence on the mother or a paternal subjection internalized by the individual. On the contrary, the individual inherits the sufferings that a society engenders through its mechanisms of political-economic organization (p. 56). In its conjugal form, this dialectic is the first unequivocal expression of a historical family whose social bond underlies the struggle between the Master and the Slave. In the same way, this dialectic confers a divided and utilitarian interaction of a necessary social nature between men and the family in the logic of industrial capitalist adaptation in the 19th century. Consequently, the capitalist conjugal organization remains in the shadow of its own complexes that are produced by a new management of cultural canons per se. This administration institutes, therefore, the social forms that determine kinship laws due to the emphasis on recognition.[21]

There is in this *first* Lacan (1946) a retroactive reading of Freud about the origin of society, starting from a broad approach built by the French thinker in his *écrit Presentation on Psychical Causality*:

> I think that the Oedipus complex did not appear with the origin of man [...], but at the threshold of history, of "historical" history, at the limit of "ethnographic" cultures. It can obviously appear only in the patriarchal form of the family as an institution, but it nevertheless has an indisputably liminary value. I am convinced that its function had to be served by initiatory experiences in cultures that excluded it, as ethnology allows

> us to see even today. And its value in bringing a psychical cycle to a close stems from the fact that it represents the family situation, insofar as the latter, by its institution, marks the intersection of the biological and the social in the cultural.
>
> (p. 150)

In this direction of culture, the father has been declined by the instruction of democratic societies. If, for Freud, the totemic father facilitates the mythical origin of society through his murder at the hands of the clan of siblings, for Lacan, the father has lost, in the new social conformation of the modern family, his capacity for domination to become only a symbolic functionary of repression. The father figure today has been captured in a name that is subjected to the designs of the social machine because of the neurotic repression of drives. Let us recall that for Freud (1913): "The neuroses are asocial structures" which "endeavor to achieve by private means what is effected in society by collective effort" and the "social instincts [drives]" are generated on "the combination of egoistic and erotic elements" (pp. 73–74). As a result, the structure of capital governs, through paternal repression, the drives leading them towards a profitable and reproducible vicissitude. The problem here, of course, is not the social organization as such but the asocial and egoistic destiny propelled by the neuroses in the capitalist structure.

We must keep in mind that the figure of the father is described as a decline caused by culture in a logical and symbolic measure. Like the mercantile regulation of labor and commerce, there are external ruptures and antinomies in the organizational distribution of his figure within the productive and repressive relations of the family. Lacan (1938b) mentions, following the latter, that in "the father's *imago*" we find the "spring" that grounds "the function of repression." The effect of castration sustains this and is part of "the social determination of the paternalistic family" (p. 56). The rules and regulations are the positivity which determines the channel of the structural politics of the family. Lacan draws a figure of the father and his oedipal function focusing on the repressive effects originating from the economy of the homosexual clan of siblings since he presents it as an ulterior social form that eludes the universal effects of the *imago*. Repression, from a paternal *imago*, achieves nothing else but to become a kind of nodal, sequential, and structuring mirage of the social regulation of the family. From all this, repression would have a strict social and, in parallel, political sense since it determines the administration of access to pleasures and the subsequent weak governance of the Ego.

In *Totem and Taboo*, Freud reminds us that prohibitions are essential to all societies and are intertwined with hatred, punishment, and guilt.[22] As a digression, the theoretical adjustment made by Lacan restores the political astuteness of the strength of the clan concerning the omnipotent figure of the totemic father.[23] Lacan explains how the declination of the father is a restrictive dam in the masculine governance of pleasures. And in effect, it suggests a politics of opposition to the clan's directives of domination of the father. For Lacan (1938b), the "meaning of the totem" is equivalent to the function of the "Ego-ideal" (p. 73). This equivalence prescribes the usefulness of the totem and its oppositional effect on the part of the clan of siblings. It is there, in the midst of the primitive family struggle, that the symbolic force becomes the antagonism of the act. In a second moment, the "primitive conflict" implants "the oedipal identification" through "which the subject transcends the aggressiveness constitutive of the first subjective individuation" (Lacan, 1948a, p. 95). Therefore, the conflict originates the management of the subversive opposition and watches over—from the uniformity of love and hate—the earthly economy of the drive force.

Some years after the publication of *Totem and Taboo*, Freud (1924a) wrote that the "threat of castration" takes a "deferred effect"—a kind of retroactive sequel (p. 176).[24] This successive and retroactive moment not only accounts for a subjective position in the Oedipus complex but also socially triggers an economy of the Ego-ideal under the designs of the Super-Ego and its emplacements at the social level. The reorganization of identificatory ambivalence determines the social and synchronic trajectory of repression. Consequently, Lacan's later idea of the paternal metaphor can express, in terms of value, what is introduced by the effects of retroaction as the spatial and temporal determination of force in terms of synchronic and diachronic systems of exchange.[25] As Freud (1913) suggested: "Society was now based on complicity in the common crime" (p. 146). The collective crime introduces the regulatory social norm and its sanction. It institutes the cultural effect of an economy of guilt as a subjective position before the law of the dead father—although also communal resistance.[26] The mythical father of the horde has two fundamental particularities. On the one hand, he is the presence of a dominating father, a father who controls sexual commerce. On the other, he is the basis of a social organization that finds a regime of repressed access to pleasure and drive and its insufficient satisfaction. The control of the totemic father over the brothers retroactively explains the procession of a new social ordering dependent on the annihilated father, who is now unconscious and condemned to eternal enjoyment.

In his Seminar on the *Wolf Man*, Lacan (1952a) points out that "the subject will have to situate himself in relation to the father" and it is in this manner that "Freud makes the facts of totemism intervene" from the "drama of Oedipus" to the "drama of the murder of the father."[27] "Sublimation," as vicissitude, is the "socialization of instincts" and, in this way, "the Oedipus" has "a normativizing function," a conscious measure that "excludes" relational animality for the establishment of a "sphere of amnesia" according to the social requirements that will depend on the entry into the conjugal father's function—and of its rites, taboos, and relationships (p. 13).[28] As a result, the Oedipus complex entails a social antinomy that is structured at a time after existence and is dependent on a total and unattainable image.

From these times, Lacan begins to speak of a subject and not of an individual, and it is because he has oriented the father in a symbolic position (that he will later delimit, by way of a structuring metaphor). The latter defines two cardinal moments in Lacan's social description of the mother-father bond in the constitution of the subject. At first, the alienation from the mother will sustain a presumably complete individual, and later, depending on the social conditions of the family institution, the father will appear as fundamentally supported by the symbolic structure that has been socially and historically determined.[29] Due to its origins and imaginary and symbolic effects, the father's figure moves towards an inscription that stabilizes the repression of meaning. This situation would not have been possible without the distribution of the contemporary family device and the places and social mechanisms by which the mother and the father account for the child from a third party on the scene. Lacan does not entirely deny the social function of the Oedipus complex in structuring the subjects' psyche. On the contrary, Oedipus has a structuring weight associated with the demands and the cuts and turns of pleasure and displeasure.[30]

Regarding family changes in the 19th century and from a specific sociological influence, Lacan took the conceptions of the French sociologist Émile Durkheim as an anchor. Lacan (1938b) accepts Durkheim's (and Paul Fauconnet's) appreciation of the value of the concentric bond of "kinship," "family names," and "inheritance law" (p. 26),[31] assuming thus—from the family dynamics and the "sublimation" of the paternal *imago*—the relational mode through which "new relations" are "introduced" in the "social group" (Lacan, 1938b, p. 35). The anachronistic bond with the mother not only sets up the alienating and primary insistence of culture but a forward cut in the organization of the complexes, and this displaces in a particular form the insistence for the organic and biological instinct that would sustain all human practice in the first years of life.

The father figure within the conformation of the normative family relations is as indispensable as the delimiting *imago* of the family political reality in which a drive anomie emerges that singularizes the children and their jouissance. This new hereditary family bond, on which Lacan supports his thesis of the complexes, has scopes that oppose a particular deterministic judgment of Freud on the father of the primitive horde. From all this, it is necessary to review the impasses of the communal relationship due to the effect of segregation and oppression of conjugal families. To amplify these approaches, we will review some aspects pointed out by Durkheim about them.

Durkheim (1892) specifies that

> the conjugal family results from a contraction of the paternal family, the latter comprising the father, the mother and all the generations arising from them, except the daughters and their descendants. The conjugal

> family comprises only the husband, his wife, and their minor and unmarried children.
>
> (p. 36)

This organization generates a total detachment from the dependence on a totalitarian and leading father. In other words, it breaks with the idea of the ancestral and dominant father and proposes the configuration of a new reduced family as a social fact. It is in it where there is a division and rupture with the ancestor fathers and alludes to the foundation of a new family assembled by a recent variation framed in the legalized marriage—the afflicted joviality of the bond resides there in the fracture and reconfiguration. All this suggests a crucial alteration with respect to the totemic father, where Lacan (1938b), thanks to Durkheim's proposal, affirms that "filiation is demonstrated by marriage," and this rule-contract-constraint becomes so only because of social regulations (p. 26). Thus, the distribution of links depends on a fragile father exalted by the centrality of the law.

The above quotation suggests an argument that points to the institution and perpetuity of a legal contract that the State develops as a juridical and, above all, cultural and symbolic form. This circumstance harbors the repressive ideology of a family sustained by a legalized father who attempts to oppose the mythical Freudian totemic father and who, in his marital condition, accesses a specific enjoyment of sex commerce. With Lacan, this parental situation is differentiated from the Freudian horde since the genesis of a new family positions the conjugal father independently from his absolute predecessor because of a legal redistribution. Likewise, this manumission also removes him from a place of complete control and direct domination because the repression falls into the organization of legal forms of social supremacy. This social cut does not focus on forgetting the primordial myth but on looking at it from the unconscious effect of the social determination of life and the sexual commerce of males.[32] It is for all this that appears, with the imposition of the law of symbolic castration on the homosexual clan of brothers, the formation of an unconscious oriented to the secularization of pleasures. The above has a purely cultural extract since society itself designates the importance of marriage as a persistent phenomenon of symbolic forms.

Lacan (1938b) defined "the modern family" not "as a simplification" but as "a contraction of the familial institution" (p. 27). The family constitution now falls on a cultural figure delimited by the social prism and situated within the symbolic framework that subjects it to social and legal codes. Society regulates parental exchange through a contract that supposes the essential terrestrial angle of paternal decline. For Lacan, this family arrangement does not only obey the inner psychic constitution of the subjects. On the contrary, it expresses the economic direction of a loss in which production and goods change their destination and order. Besides, in the structuring designated by the marriage laws—where the symbolic implants the exchange and use circulation—the society systematized by marriage invested in new economic dynamics centered on a temporal conjuncture reorganizing the economic cycles.[33] A contraction, in economics, does not necessarily entail a recession but an adjustment of production times. And this is precisely a retroaction at the level of synchrony—a metaphor. Consequently, the configuration of a distinct social order because of the conjugal family follows the impotent primacy of a damaged father who sustains a profitable economic exchange of social life and its malaise during practically the whole of the 20th century.

The morbid crisis of modern society, situated exactly in the destruction of the paternal totalitarianism that preceded the declining father, harbored the hope of an autonomous society. However, it gave rise to a social project that focuses—in an individualistic and liberal position—on the exploitation of the family and the subjects that make it up. The social structure captured the relative symbolic weight of the father to presuppose the vitality of the male fantasy of power and coercive volition. All this is the prelude to what Lacan proposed years later as the father's name and the primordial metaphor's formation in the subjects. Beyond this, for us, there is an economic reading of the family that points to the social fragmentation by fixing measurable and manageable angles within the symbolic system of culture.

Lacan's critique of the totemic father suggested that the Freudian "hypothetical primitive family [...] imagines a drama of the murder of the father by the children" that can be harshly questioned if it analyzes the "foundations" of "culture" within the "matriarchal structure of the family." It is there, Lacan points out, that "the order of the human family has foundations that are subtracted from the force of the male" (Lacan, 1938b, p. 49). The history of capitalism, at least during the three centuries of its conformation and technification, testifies to the importance of the regulation of structural elements that could not be tamed by patriarchal logic. Above all, the mode of containing and arranging the dykes of sexual life by regulating certain sexual practices and disposing the permissibility of many others. Thus, the function of limiting sexual life was entirely linked to a political factor of perpetuating the economic interests of the already highly articulated industrial capitalism during the 19th century and the whole of the 20th century.[34]

Lacan (1938b) clarifies the reduction of the "tyranny of the chief of the horde" to an "increasingly uncertain phantasy [*fântome*]" (p. 59). Where lies the power of the fantasy of a tyrannical father? This question reestablishes the status of the imago and the law, but not from the omnipresent figure of the father—as Freud posed—but from the displacement of the relation of thirdness of the father and the primordial group to give way to the alienation of the "moral and cultural" idea of the neighbor through the instauration of the law. Hence, the social fantasy attempts to make amends for the damaged life of a supposedly omniscient father. Likewise, the configuration of this paternal fantasy becomes profitable when, socially, political figures emerge who hold the disposition and shepherding—as pastoral power—of the fellow man, guaranteeing an imminent illusion.[35]

For our French psychoanalyst, the patriarchal law and modern man are inseparable parts that reveal the persistent fragmentation of culture on the part of society. Before continuing, and in function of the temporality of Lacan's oeuvre, it is indispensable to examine Lacan's perspective on modern man from the emergence of the conjugal family. We insist here that at the same time as the bourgeois revolution of the State, which authorized the development of conjugal families, the political-economic relation founds the modern relations of men and implants for their adaptation to normalizing psychology, far from the concrete, which Lacan differentiated in the family complexes. This reductionism was continuously modifying and forming new forms of understanding and psychological repression of the subject and in the references of the family as the first form of measurement of society. It was in the 19th century that a scientific zenith of individual psychology was finally designed as the science of modern man's centralized and earthly behavior and the evolution of the family. Subsequently, both principles developed a pillar of psychology's inaugural scopes for determining functionality parameters.[36]

The ambiguous analogy of modern man and social regulation through the psyche and its complexes, elucidated by Lacan, exhibits psychology as an ideology that has served from its beginnings to delimit social dynamics in a servile mode and clarifies the conspiracy of psychology with nation-states and science. Between psychologism, science, and social practices, a spherical and earthly limitation has been prevailing that excludes the infinitude of the openly contingent real. Lacan, in his way and with a constant critique of psychology, in a latent and manifest point of view, uses some psychoanalytical insights to interpret the evolution of the family structure beyond the pragmatic reductionisms of the behaviorist psychology of his context in 1938. Cultural formations are thus exalted by Lacan precisely because they have a substantial weight on the surface on which the causation of the psyche is mobilized in the individual and not only as a reflection of an individual and internalized behavior.

The alliance between psychology, behavioral measurement, and doctrinal variants of the mind directed by the State and its political alignments reflects a normalizing reiteration in the pragmatic conception of families and the effects of conjugal political organization of the family. In connection with the above, Durkheim (1892) wrote that "the most distinctive feature" of conjugal families is "the increasing intervention of the state in the inner life of the family" (p. 40). It is the State and its institutional forms, under the connivance of science, that delimit a new family form that insists on a more specific control of the members, and it is there that interior conduct becomes a modulable and repressive register.[37] Likewise, psychology interprets social practices by encircling their parameters from the regulations of modern man, generating new scientific links of individual political distribution at the social level. For Lacan (1953a), "psychology does not cover the field of human existence" but is only "particularization." It is there where "the function of the ego [*moi*]" is determined by the "social, technological and dialectical conjunctures with which the cultural Gestalt was visibly constituted at the beginning of the 17th century" (p. 142). In the 19th century, it even went so far as to confront, mediate, and analyze directly the manifestations of the masses, the cerebral measurements, and the individual differences proper to liberalism and the requirements of excitation.[38]

Family subjection imposes the regulation on all members of the conjugal family and thereby guarantees a certain perpetuity of assimilation and internalized control of social practices. In Durkheim's (1892) words, it is "the State which, in the person of the magistrate, presides over the family councils [...] who pronounces and sometimes demands the prohibition of the adult" (p. 40). In this way, the State determines that the continuity of the social order has been assigned to the father. Lacan (1938b) adds that it is precisely in "the demands of marriage" that the paternal "decline" occurs—as "social decline"—which is "intimately linked to the dialectic of the conjugal family." The figure of a third actor, the State—which establishes the laws of constriction of the family—articulates a biological integration with a social structuring of the psychic sufferings reigning in the conjugal family. It makes the "collectivities" suffer the effects of "progress," such as "economic concentration" and "political catastrophes" (p. 60).

We can see here again an explanation of paternal centrality in decline—the function of a law—dependent singularity within the sphere of the political world. However, the father's role, as a supposed totality, has been mediated because of the institutionally framed incidences of the State. Family politics constructs a new adequacy to reproduce the psychological and coercive family conditions under the understanding of men's rights and civil obligations. These circumstances are typical of an advent of cultural regulation delimited in society under a scientific-biological basis that also serves as a misleading background and support for normative social determinations.[39] Indeed, Lacan encourages the question about the direct bond with the biological father based on the social grouping that conforms to cultural and political impositions that admit the state malleability of families. Biology—which sustains a heteronormative *nature* of the union between man and woman, father and mother—is extremely limiting in comparison with the alleged cultural progress of contemporary societies and yet remains constantly unquestioned to this day.

According to Lacan (1938b), "the decline of the paternal *imago*" is a "decline conditioned by the return to the individual of extreme effects of social progress" (p. 60). His perspective is a pointed critique of the intentionality of the progress of capital under the shelter of the conjugal family. At first glance, the Lacanian approach may seem provocative and decontextualized, but are we not dealing here with a social relation closer to the political economy than to the reductionism of solipsistic behavior determination? From the latter, the confrontation of paternal declination and its political function alludes to a social disposition of a political regime of the State and its economy rather than to a natural relationship between individuals and between a consanguineous kinship. The latter confirms, after all that has been reviewed, the nodal influence of Durkheim on Lacan and his exploration of a collectivity framed by economic and political conflicts, which, ultimately, are an indispensable part of the social degradation that disfigures the cultural acts of the human race.

On the other hand, Lacan revisited, with a particular provocation, the social transfiguration emanating from the different political and economic disjunctures as axes that transpose the social to the individual and the conjunctural spheres of the political system as social management. The "religious ideals and their social equivalents," Lacan (1938b) asserts, are "vehicles" of "psychological oppression" delimited "to signify the demands of name and race" (p. 80). These appreciations are elementary to raise the contemporary position of families and their relations with oppressive organization through the repressive effect aimed at the forms of social ideals and the care of individuals.[40] It is the conjugal family, under the auspices and direction of the State, which sustains and perpetuates the repressive social structure and in which the scope of a normalized and derived psyche can be located through State institutions and no longer only through the cultural actions of the individual.[41]

Lacan refers to Hegel when the German philosopher indicates that "the individual who does not struggle to be recognized outside the family group never attains personality before death" (Lacan, 1938b, p. 36). Does this idea not evoke the struggle for mere prestige between master and slave within the family and in the group tensions outside? In other words, Lacan's quote hints at a form of detachment from the father to found a worldly and, paradoxically, transcendental battle amid social relations—this itself is an accurate critique of Freud's universalist Oedipalism. The social demand for recognition-identification makes the father dependent on the State's laws and traditions. Or, in Lacan's (1938b) words, complexes break all "metaphysical mirage of universal harmony," that "mystical abyss of affective fusion, the social utopia of a totalitarian tutelage, all arising from the obsession for the lost paradise before birth and from the darkest aspiration to death" (p. 36).

The constant seeking of filial recognition in the individual is due to an identification with the similar other—as a figure of traditional authority. An other that not only could be located in the father but also in the siblings and particularly in the mother as a result of her first contact with the child. Lacan argues, from this perspective, that incorporating an individual into the singular family group responds to the repetitive directive of the symbolic space. Imaginary identification grants a first brittle social sustenance to an individual who passes through the legal fiction of the State. Imaginary identification alienates and directs toward the illusion of an autonomous personality of the individual. However, to speak of the subject, the situation of the image is traversed by the demands of the structural and social conditions that enslave the drive life of the subject.[42]

From Freud's (1913) viewpoint, "parricide" and "social fraternal feelings" have exercised "a profound influence on the development of society" (p. 146). This reminds us that there is a social bonding supported by acts external to the individual, the social force of the external man. Is it not Oedipus who idealizes his becoming in Theban society by leading the people? Is it not Oedipus who is rebuked by the chorus in the tragedy? Oedipus does not idealize his living father but the social legacy that persists after his death. Oedipus submits to the society of Thebes in which he governs and abhors, seeing that which, in the voice of blind Tiresias, reminds him of the parricidal act that finds his social position and governance. It is amid the parricidal act and its legality on the surface of knowledge that precedes the possibility of Oedipus becoming King of Thebes. From this reading of the tragedy, Lacan's shift catapults the father's position into the legal dimension of economic and social progress and its regulatory moral power.

Before Oedipus and his inner misery, indeed, there is the social structure of Thebes and its external moral machinery. Perhaps Lacan—who knew Bonald's oeuvre—would recall in those years that "the union of the inner man and the outer man, of the soul and the body, constitutes the social or political man" (Bonald, 1796, p. 121).[43] Maybe, we also find here a primary nucleus of Cartesianism or Aristotelianism: "man alone of the animals possesses speech." Man, according to Aristotle (1932) in his *Politics*, "has [the] perception of good and bad and right and wrong and the other moral qualities, and it is partnership in these things that makes a household and a city-State" (p. 11). These two points are the knot between the politics of the first community (the house, its economy, the *Oikos*) and the second (the city-State and its management), between the inner and the outer.[44]

The transition from the clan to the conjugal family reveals that private property began establishing itself as a guiding axis of the family and social order. That is to say, a father takes property no longer for the very fact of being a father but because a law decrees his spherical possibility of sexual and family control. The paternal figure finds himself captured within a transcendental legal crossroads for the further development of the culture and its traditions. Lacan's (1938b) proposal warns of a social fall of the father or, more specifically, a weakening of his representation and power within the new conjugal family in which a "domestic tyranny" takes place whose "eminent expression," is "at once symbolic, moral and material, in the satisfaction of 'managing the economy of the house'" (p. 83).[45]

Lacan's reading of family complexes assumed the form of a critique of the family and the social organization of neurotics due to two singular interlocutors in his youth. First was his controversial fascination with Charles Maurras, with whose ideas Lacan consistently demonstrated a very close relationship and, likewise, with Frederick Engels, whom he does not mention directly; nevertheless, we can find echoes of the work of Marx's close colleague in Lacan's thought.[46] From the speculation on an unconfessed appropriation by Lacan, as it was since then his style, Frederick Engels is helpful to approach an interpretation of the family and its social function. In addition to his writing on *The Origin of the Family*, there are also essential revelations in the construction of ideas critical of society in the *Anti-Dühring* and his *Dialectics of Nature* that serve as a mute dialogue with Lacan's ideas.

In seeking to argue this insinuation, Engels (1884) states that the "bounds imposed by official society" have a "traditional conception" that "knows monogamy only" (p. 47). Such an affirmation evokes an intrinsic relation with the configuration of conjugal families in which Lacan takes sides and where he locates cultural progress and moral tradition. In other words, monogamy, as a partialized form of human relationship proper to modern society, is a crucial part of the contractual conception of the conjugal family and, going a little further, this now allows us to understand that the idea of such a family is closely related to the power of possessing only one woman. This notion is close to the deprivation of the Freudian totemic family, thanks to the culture that can be administered in capital and the repressive conventionalism of patriarchy.[47] At the same moment, we can find a fundamental hinge in the ideas of Alfred Espinas (1878) to understand that both Lacan and Engels distinguish the "antagonistic" phenomenon between the horde and the family (Engels, 1884, p. 49) because "the order of the human family has foundations that are subtracted from the force of the male" (Lacan, 1938b, p. 49). Nevertheless, the guarantee of possession of a woman and a family does not originate, according to Engels (1884), exclusively in the conjugal family as such, but in "monogamy" that

> arose out of the concentration of considerable wealth in the hands of one person—and that a man—and out of the desire to bequeath this wealth to this man's children and to no one else's. For this purpose, monogamy was essential on the woman's part, but not on the man's; so that this monogamy of the woman in no way hindered the overt or covert polygamy of the man.
>
> (p. 81)

Here, there is a tiny digressive emphasis on the desire to transmit the law, in this case, economic. The desire is fixed beyond the weakened paternal figure as it follows the key to the efficacy—patriarchal and repressive—of an economy that is also symbolic. This transfer regulates one's own property, a condition that not only can be the basis for a particular heir's wealth but also recalls an acceptance of the law of the father and the permissibility of benefiting economically from a woman, a situation categorically forbidden in Freud's totemic father. Bourgeois monogamy implants the regular measure of the possession and value of a woman, at least since the end of the 19th century and throughout the 20th century, in order to reproduce the forms of social exploitation capitalism and the direction of human passions.[48]

Another enthralling match between the economic politics of the family in Lacan and Engels (1884) appears, from our perspective, when the latter writes—quoting Lewis Morgan—that the family "is the creation of the social system, and will reflect its culture" and "fail to answer the requirements of society" (p. 87); in the former, the family had been understood from "the original order of reality that social relations" designate (Lacan, 1938b, p. 27). Therefore, the approach to the relationship between society and the family is understood as a social product and, in turn, as a reflection of morality, which designates the foundation of psychism and the impossibility of satisfaction of the passions in civilization. Lacan, let us remark, opts for culture as a structure rather than civilization or biological statute.[49] Moreover, Engels (1876) criticizes, in his tone, the fact that "the swift advance of civilization was ascribed to the mind, to the development and activity of the brain" and "men became accustomed to explain their actions from their thoughts instead of from their needs (which in any case are reflected and come to consciousness in the mind)" (p. 16).

From this logic, Lacan's family complexes could reflect the social needs of reproduction and failed satisfaction of a given social order in the identification figures and their consciousness. Sexual activity suffers from the restrictive methods in which the psychic life of individuals in a civilization resides. Sexual politics is, consequently, the frontier of sexuality in its economic character, always already irresolvable, differentiable, and non-commensurable. The fantasy of bourgeois social equality, in the dimension of monogamic sexuality, is subsumed in the parameters of the men who head the families, and as Engels (1878) critically pointed out, when "women are not considered, it further proves that they are subordinate" (p. 90).

On the other hand, the social progress of families cannot be comprehended only from our contemporaneity—hence the need to examine the social origin from diverse historical conditions, from the transformation of the ape into man, through the relations of the Greek *polis* and in particular the Roman *civitas*. This singular familiar progress becomes, from the 19th century, a new social structure that has been forged from diverse points of ordinance, among which we find the cultural order as support, the economic as a failed interaction, and the political as an antinomic sequence. These three surfaces stimulate social progress in the dialectical reason marked in the economic and libidinal exchange of sexual monogamy. On this last point, if "the paternal imago projects the original force of repression onto the very sublimations that must overcome it" since it is "invested by repression" and "knotted" by the Oedipus complex in that "antinomy" (Lacan, 1938b, p. 57), then, in the same mode, "social production" is "subject to the interplay of unintended effects from uncontrolled forces and achieves its desired end only by way of exception, but much more frequently the exact opposite" (Engels, 1886, p. 331).

There is no choice *without* duality and *without* a borderline stance: Not without Engels, not without Maurras. Amid a primordial anti-philosophical style, these two thinkers —profoundly opposed—are confronted and extra-ctivized in *Les complexes familiaux* even though both authors are not directly quoted. It is worth remembering that the French writer and politician Charles Maurras was intimately related to Lacan's youthful ideas and belonged to the *L'Action Française* movement.[50] Maurras was an undisputed forerunner of Gallic nationalist sentiment, as well as having a marked influence on the post-1920s fascist movements in Europe. As a curious enigma, Lacan could not completely separate himself from a particular right-wing political position. However, this did not prevent Lacan's later Marxist approach from being captured by reactionary positions.

From Maurras' perspective (1937)—and contrary to Rousseau's ideas—"Society, civilization was born of inequality" where the individual, "exploited" through a "capital that he created," is "driven by interest [...] by filial love or the recognition of finding this exploitation pleasant, useful or, at least, tolerable" (p. 43). In other words, Maurras invests, from his review of societies, a utilitarian background propelled within filiation and recognition in usufruct. The family, in its modern boundary, is a group dependent on usufruct and antagonism regulated by paternal recognition. Maurras' work interprets—similarly to Lacan in 1938— the family as the most primitive bond of society and the *ab initio* condition of all social conformation. On this basis, Maurras (1937) proposes that "society is not a great animal of which individuals are only subordinate cells. But neither is it one of those 'groupings' of wills that we call, in law, associations. Society is not a voluntary association: it is a natural aggregate." Society is not brought about by a determination of aggregates but as an imposition, or in the words of Maurras himself, "our native society is imposed upon us. Human society is part of the necessities of our nature" (p. 80).

Also, for Maurras (1937),

> industry in the broad meaning of the word, that is to say, the transformation of nature, that is to say, man's work, that is to say, his life, does not have the sole result of changing the world, it changes man himself.
> (p. 64)

The above suggests, of course, the idea of an individual whose work, alienated to an industry, transforms him and of someone who finds himself faced with the irresolvable modification of his social and mental life caused by industry. Its existence not only underlies the work itself but, in a parallel way, a whole social foundation of industry and the social means of production. This last idea parallels Lacan on a crucial point: The industrial and mercantile *anti-nature* of the human state. The social nature of man cannot be understood as the natural man *per se*, but as the man traversed by the culture of alienated industrial labor and, in turn, culture is a transforming force of man and his creations.

Maurras (1937) furthermore mentions that "tradition is not absent because there is no point in society without tradition nor of men without society" (p. 65). Tradition is present in society as an ancestor; it cannot exist as an isolated or singular element but as a repetitive effect. For this reason, tradition and its social exchange grants, for both Maurras and Lacan, a familiar and economic distinction of psychic and social oppression in the conformation of all ritual organization of societies. In such a way, society, for both Lacan and Maurras, has bourgeois overtones that account for the hierarchy of alienation and the link between capitalism and tradition. In this sense, for Lacan, this alienation can be shown in the light of a degraded cultural background from the disposition of family integration and progress of identification.[51]

In conclusion, the so-called youthful readings of Lacan had a decisive influence on the revision of Freud's approaches. These influences made possible, in his approaches to Freudian theory, an epistemological diversity to understand the social framework under the brightness of a primordial closeness to political economy and the critique of the degradation of progress and societies. With the above, and by way of closing the chapter, Lacan's turn, in its dubitative aspect, detected the social anomie and the contingencies of the family from the dynamics of law, tradition, and the avatars that these elements present in the social organization of a paternal *imago* that, thought from a geocentric centrality, defined the usury of the complexes as a spherical manifestation of order, psychologism, normality, and the unequivocal uneasiness of progress under the inner shadow of marriage.

Notes

1 From these first manuscripts, Lacan will deeply doubt the psychological positions and reductions to understand human acts. This will be the basis of his constant criticisms of psychology.

2 On this point, Lacan is very close to Politzer's (1972) concrete psychology, which explains the life of the "concrete individual" from its "acts," calling into question abstraction as a formal illusion (p. 69).

3 According to Baños Orellana (2013), "Lacan" attacked "the relativistic continuums between normality and pathology that make us lose sight of 'the non-psychogenic basis of all these states' [of paranoid character]" (p. 269).

4 This theoretical position and the inclusion of psychoanalysis were strongly criticized in Lacan's thesis, especially by the Swiss psychiatrist Hans Steck. See Sierra Rubio (2021, pp. 24–25).

5 At this point in his work, and at later times, the figure of Karl Jaspers is central to Lacan's thought and critique of the phenomenological comprehension of the psyche. For further exploration of Lacan's position on Jaspers, see Holmes (2021).

6 This exploration also reveals Lacan's liminal critique of Galilean and Cartesian physics or, in Koyré's (1966) terms, the partial failure to move from the "Cosmos—a closed unity in hierarchical order—" to the notion of "Universe—an open whole bound by the unity of its laws—" if the basis is the anthropomorphic knowledge (p. 165).

7 See Geertz (1973; 1983).

8 In Barzilai's (1999) words, "identification leads" also to "fusion or desire for fusion; love, to alienation" (p. 39).

9 It is exciting to review that, from his early writings, Lacan maintained a robust intellectual exchange with English thought beyond psychoanalysis and how this had effects on his links to thinkers of the caliber of Bentham, Joyce, and others. See the careful reading on this subject done by Jean-Pierre Cléro (2017).

10 To further explore the role of thirdness in specular family relationships, see Hadar (2013), specifically Chapter 4. Likewise, as Bion (1961) observed, similar to Lacan and the thirdness, "The minimum size of the group is three. Two members have personal relationships; with three or more there is a change of quality (interpersonal relationship)" (p. 26). Indeed, an interpersonal relationship can only be produced from the number three.

11 In his critical interpretation of Lacan's *Family Complexes*, Jacques-Alain Miller (2005) notices that "even with the animals there is a social element that is not strictly natural, but with humans, however, the social takes the form of culture" (p. 35).

12 For a more specific review of the historical and social distribution of the family since the 17th century, see Badinter (2010).

13 This "philosophical" reading, as Lacan himself calls it, of the complexes, seems to us to be closely linked to Kojève's Hegelian understanding of the family and the antique master. In Kojève's (1947) words from his 1935–1936 course, the family consists of a "particularization" where death establishes a "totality" that "transcends" the "instinct" and the "natural" and has its origins in the "tyranny" (p. 109). Let us not forget that Kojève's influence is decisive for the Lacanian conception of the social aspects of psychic experience. Roudinesco (2003) points out at least three Hegelian-Kojèvian ideas present in Lacan: "[T]he I as subject of desire; desire as a revelation of the truth of being; and the ego as site of illusion and source of error"; and "these concepts would also be present, mixed in with the two theories on the origin of madness and the essence of the family, in all the texts Lacan published between 1936 and 1949" (p. 28). See also about the relationship between Kojève and Lacan in Luchelli (2017).

14 Jules Falquet (2006), from a lesbian-materialist perspective, proposed that "conjugality" also forces "towards a model of couple hood that is quite conservative and not very compatible with participation in collective struggles for social transformation" (p. 76).

15 From Ellie Ragland's (1995) perspective, "Lacan's Freud is [also] dynamic and dialectical, then, and the topological unconscious from which one draws a sense of being an ego or 'self' is symbolic and relational" (p. 19).

16 In Ian Parker's (2011) words, the "normality" in the "symbolic" components of the family, which transform natural laws, questioned in *The Family Complexes*, makes a serious "description" of the "patriarchal society" in the West that has the effect of a consistent analysis of the social forms of imaginary organization of the phallus (p. 58).

17 As Daniel Tutt (2022) mentions: "Neuroses are formed based on family complexes, and these complexes are structured by the social conditions of the given time" (p. 55). On the relational construction of neurosis, its adaptation, and renunciation, see Otto Gross's (2018) critical proposal on the communist conception of the symbolism of paradise.

18 This thesis can be contrasted in the epistemological proximity of Lacan with the proposal of Alexandre Koyré (1957) who mentions that "the earth is not in the centre of the Universe; it is central only to our surrounding space" (p. 42). Thus, our planet and its symbolic *Umwelt* become an adjustment and measure for the celestial bodies as figures that have at least one feature that is impossible to measure.

19 Markos Zafiropoulos (2002) mentions that "Lacan prefers to emphasize the law of familial contraction, valid to explain the conjugal anomie that he posits as the social condition of Oedipalism and the most modern morbidity." And, due to the structural effect of culture, "the murder of the father, a collective and social act, modifies these [incestuous] desires of humanity by producing the unconscious" (pp. 88–89).

20 Wapeemukwa (2022) further observes that "Lacan's analysis ends before he considers what it means to be castrated not by the language of your father but your colonizer," an issue that highlights the oppressive direction of culture in the social modes of production (p. 84).

21 Hegel (1807) has an excellent perspective about it: "[T]he relationship of husband and wife is in the first place the one in which one consciousness immediately recognizes itself in another, and in which there is knowledge of this mutual recognition. Because this self-recognition is a natural and not an ethical one, it is only a representation, an image of Spirit, not actually Spirit itself" (p. 273).

22 Stephen Frosh (1999) mentions, along these lines, that in order "to prevent a repetition of the primal situation, the brothers, under the shadow of the totem, imposed certain rules on themselves to regulate their relations and restrain their passions" (p. 43). Hence, it is inferred that the Ego-ideal is the first form of economic management of the passions.

23 Galiussi & Godoy (2013) locate, in Lacan's *Seminar VIII*, two "slopes" where the totalitarian decline of the father is "refracted." The first one pointed out as an "impotent bureaucracy" centered on the "dimension of the symbolic emptied that does not allow for any exception," and the second aspect focused on "obscenity" where what mobilizes is "pure ambition."

24 The specific German term used by Freud is *Nachträglich*.

25 To explore synchrony's value, timing, and position in economic systems, see Kōjin Karatani (2020).

26 Let us not forget that for Freud, this social imposture also engenders the exaltation of destruction and hatred which, towards the end of his life, he associated with anti-Semitism and the reactionary politics of oppression over communities and minorities. See Freud (1939).

27 The drama, beyond the Politzerian critique, demonstrates that the "individual" is essentially an "abstraction" in which there is invariably a "relation" of "socio-economic determinants." Ultimately, these elements support the relational conflict between the *imagos* (Deleule, 1972, p. 31).

28 For Radcliffe-Brown's (1952) anthropology, "the relation of ritual and ritual values" is essential to "the constitution of human society" and, in these terms, "while in animal societies social coaptation depends on instinct, in human societies it depends upon the efficacy of symbols of many different kinds" (p. 150).

29 Due to this, Zafiropoulos (2002) states that according to Lacan, "the Oedipus would not be universal, it would be socially determined and the neurotic forms would vary according to the history of the family institution" (p. 78).

30 By the way, Zafiropoulos (2002) also proposes that Lacan "re-examines the Oedipus complex, to make it a variable of the social, whereas in Freud it is universal" (p. 90).

31 According to Fauconnet (1928), "Filiation is a social bond that generally fulfills the functions of a physiological bond and, in the communication of hereditary responsibility, contact and kinship merge" (p. 168).

32 This elemental short circuit in subject life produces an inevitable "castration anxiety" that, as Žižek (1993) mentions, is "the moment at which the very possibility of castration, its mere threat, produces actual effects in our psychic economy" (p. 159).

33 Zafiropoulos (2002) notes in this regard that, for Lacan, "the family and its law of contraction, in particular, makes marriage the ultimate symbolic operator of the production of family bonds" (p. 70).

34 Silvia Federici (2004) refers, for example, to "divisive sexual politics," at least since the 14th century, that responded to regulating workers' force and organization (p. 49).

35 Do not several schools and enterprising societies of psychoanalysis work this way nowadays? Is it not the phantasmatic *imago* of the father that orders them and identifies them from the ways of doing reactionary politics with psychoanalysis? Some current psychoanalytic societies—and in some way political ones as well—end up becoming confraternities that claim political correctness and the capitalizable elements of psychoanalysis. In short, the poison of psychoanalysis is isolated to turn it into a docile explanatory practice or a hermeneutic without consequences from the association and not from the community. Against the current, Jorge Alemán proposes to drill universalisms from the cause and effect of psychoanalysis as a political contingency. See Alemán (2006).

36 See Ian Parker (2007) on "certain interlinked conditions for 'psychology' to become possible" (pp. 11–12). See also about this historical context Merani (1976), particularly the chapter on "The Man of the Bourgeoisie and His Ideals."

37 As Yamamoto (1987) argues, from a critical and Marxist perspective, "liberal ideology" attempts to "objectify" the "liberal reality" through "modern right" from its "rational and formal" character and as a "bourgeois form" of the "citizen" (p. 28).

38 See Laurent de Sutter (2018), in particular the chapter entitled "The Politics of Overexcitement."

39 In this regard, Marie-Jean Sauret (2000) proposes a severe critique of the delimitation of the passage "from the symbolic to the real," which is carried out by psychology through the "biological reduction of the drive served by a misuse of the letter" (p. 100).

40 Foucault (2001) also noted these political reasons for the care and pastoral channeling of the subject in the State order, taking it from the religious dynamics.

41 This same management of the psyche, at least since the mid-twentieth century, has been related to psychological science in the search for "the security of the citizen, the welfare of the employee, integration of all actors in production in a joint partnership for productivity, management of the human relations of the enterprise in the name of happiness and productivity" (Rose, 1999, p. 79). Likewise, on this point, Lacan seems to be very close to Auguste Comte (1875) because for the positivist philosopher: "…a society therefore can no more be decomposed into individuals, than a *geometric surface* can be resolved into lines, or a line into points. The simplest association, that is the family sometimes reduced to its original couple, constitutes the true unit of society" (p. 153). The italics, on the geometric shape of society are ours and explain, to a large extent, the spherical centrality of the father in societies.

42 Joan Copjec (2002) mentions, in this regard, that due to the drive force, "one can no longer expect to find the subject among the sedimentations of imaginary identifications, that is to say, in the evidence of personality" (p. 62).
43 It is fascinating that for Bonald (1826): "There are vicissitudes and revolutions only in the material of society, just as there are changes of figures and forms only in matter. The morale of society must no longer change than the morale of man" (p. 354). This statement could be confronted with Lacan's doubts about materialism and revolutions. Also, for Bonald (1830): "[the] language [*parole*]" is the "first means of all conservation, of all perfection, of all sociability" (p. 48).
44 Bertrand Ogilvie (1987) makes a detailed analysis of the influence of Aristotle, Spinoza, and Maurras on the early Lacanian perspective on family and society. In his words: "The idea retained by Lacan: the individual is several things at once and in particular a network of social relations that condition his existence, presence, and duration," beyond the "society as an organism" devised by Aristotle (p. 58).
45 To explain the circumstances of the clan economy and its differences in the primitive social organization reviewed by Lacan, see Lowie (1936).
46 Of course, there are many more authors involved in Lacan's manuscript. See Bétourné (2002) for a detailed review of the references in *Family Complexes*.
47 See Pavón-Cuéllar (2021) about Engels, Freud, and primitive communism.
48 Franco Moretti (2014) has shown, in this context, that the figure of the bourgeois as "abstract hero" does not present a "narrative of imbalance." On the contrary, the bourgeois logic is "regularity," and in the case of the family, possession, and inheritance, what is transmitted is, from our point of view, a regularity or constancy of desire administered in objects-bodies as commodities. On the other hand, let us not forget that for Charles Fourier (1822), all "social theory" is a "geometry of passion," a "calculation which we understand by instinct," which "women understand very well going beyond everything applied to science". Every "woman," according to Fourier, "will understand the theory of neutral agreements or overcome antipathies, the links between inappropriate classes, such as rich and poor, masters and slaves, young and barbarous" (p. 162).
49 About the debate between Edouard Pichon and Lacan around *The Family Complexes*, Roudinesco (1997) mentions that the "diatribe concerned the difference between 'culture' and 'civilization'" as Lacan suggested. In the historian's own words, "Lacan rejected out of hand any claim that French civilization was better than all others. In so doing he was dismissing Maurras' teaching, based on a belief in the universal superiority of France's eternal, monarchical, rational civilization over all other cultures" (p. 148). These tensions between Lacan and Maurras will be reviewed later.
50 On the theoretical passions of the young Lacan, see Roudinesco (1986). See also the remarkable biography of Maurras written by Stéphane Giocanti (2008).
51 It is undoubtedly dizzying to think of Lacan's relationship with the French right and with anti-Semitism and all the implications that this entails. See Nathalie Jaudel's (2011) critique of Roudinesco's biography of Lacan. It is equally interesting to note the criticism of Edouard Pichon (1939), who insistently reproaches Lacan for his detachment from the French tradition of psychoanalysis, attacking him as a Hegelian and a Marxist. Perhaps this last adjective was a premonition.

Chapter 2

Between the Imaginary and the Symbolic Approaches to Society

Beyond the Ego (*moi*) and the I (*je*): Identification as the Core of the Society

For the Chilean writer Roberto Bolaño, in his novel *2666*, "culture [is] a chain composed of links of heroic art and superstitious interpretations" (p. 853). From this literary insight, it would be worth asking: What is it that inscribes and deploys culture? Is it a piece of knowledge about death and life? Is it possible to free oneself from irremediable destiny through superstitious chains of knowledge? What can *I* do in the face of the misfortune of knowing myself to be so weakened by the force of nature and culture? From the vicissitudes and accidents of cultural determination to the enigmatic links that the signifiers bear, there are structurally superstitious dimensions and impressions intertwined in the mythologies that decree, from a knowledge and a representation, the disfigured predictive destiny of death.

The 1950s were the vindicatory road of the French as a philosophical response to the uncertainty of the post-war period. In this panorama, the vicissitudes of the reading of Hegel were elementary. From Jean Hypolitte, through his effects on Alexandre Koyré and his disciple Kojève, Hegel had an irremediable impact on Lacan's work. There was a constant retroactive propitiated by structuralism that became the best excuse to rescue the *Hegelian hysteria* and to diagram and insist on the dialectical perspective on and from psychoanalysis. In a more detailed way, if one accepts the expression, the Lacanian structural period is impossible to conceive without the influence of Kojève's courses around the Hegelian work. It is there that the singularity of a first return to Freud through the Hegelian path is registered, mounted on the vast, persuasive, and fast theoretical machinery of the dialectic of the Master and the Slave lent to Lacan by Kojève, and in whose supposed misunderstandings of translation the Lacanian subversion to the German idealist's proposal is embodied.[1]

The period of Lacan's well-known first return to Freud propelled a breath of novelty and profound changes within French psychoanalysis and, at the same time, elucidated a remarkable—and unavoidable—rupture with the

DOI: 10.4324/9781032673837-3

institutional and political sphere of the most conservative psychoanalysis. In 1953, Lacan gave his lecture, *The Symbolic, the Imaginary and the Real* at the French Society of Psychoanalysis, the predecessor of the famous *Rome Discourse*. As is well known, this was the immediate precedent of *Function and Field of Speech and Language in Psychoanalysis*, writing that catapults Lacan's theory towards a structuralist orientation and positions the understanding of psychoanalysis on the route of language and speech as a demanding force and not as a merely communicative context or position.[2]

It is from these encounters we see that Lacan's theoretical manufacture had, at that time, a strong tendency towards the understanding of the subject through language as structure. Lacan began his journey along the lines of Claude Lévi-Strauss' structural anthropology, and his approaches to Ferdinand de Saussure and Roman Jakobson were decisive. Lacan extracted his linguistic radicalism from these three thinkers to produce a logical-formal reading of the unconscious, often taking them to their ultimate consequences. He knew how to find the originality and the surplus of Lévi-Strauss' symbolic effectiveness, the Saussurean situation of mutability and immutability of the linguistic sign in its inversion towards the signifier, and the condition of metonymy and metaphor as a rereading of Freudian displacement and condensation that underlie the work of the dream in psychoanalysis thanks to the influence of Jakobson. Lacan makes use of the linguistic sign by emphasizing the complexity of the signifier and the functions it weaves through the action of the structure in the layouts of the subject's life. Thanks to these scopes, the theoretical constitution of the subject begins to emerge with great force and gradually displaces the notion of the individual.

The emphasis Lacan deposits on language and the power of the signifier is vast and, to a certain extent, *sui generis*. It is impossible to appreciate his theoretical position without the relevance of the linguists that he studied, and it is fundamental to point out that it was not a standard reading since Saussure was read by practically all his intellectual contemporaries. Lacan's Saussurean interpretation is intensely seditious for two reasons: It allows him to rotate the situation of the unconscious towards the modes that sustain it structurally concerning the subject and to reorder the crude, solipsistic, naïve and pragmatic process that placed the Ego as the central element of psychoanalysis.[3] From the Lacanian review of the *Course on General Linguistics*, the well-known bend of the linguistic sign towards the power of the signifier reveals the amount of time and movement in the synchronic and diachronic trajectories in the structure and the turn of the screw of the subject complexified by the signifying order.[4]

Let us go firstly to *The Mirror Stage*, where Lacan confronts the individual with the experience of the specular other, with the feedback that prescribes the imaginary surface of the most insipid and primordial servitude of any social bond. Before being seized by the symbolic father's function, the individual has to deal immediately with the totalitarian maternal *imago*—the first constitutive alienation. The imaginary capture is an original social process whose scopic supremacy returns to the infant an inverted message before being impregnated, disturbed, implicated, and affected by the metaphor.[5] According to Lacan (1949a), the imaginary experience of the infant is expressed "as an identification, in the full sense analysis gives to the term: namely, the transformation that takes place in the subject when he assumes [*assume*] an image." The image in which the infant is pinpointed is lodged in the imaginary space and referred to within a social spectrum bound by resemblance, the intentional idea of completeness, and imprecise totality. The other is already part of the *social whole* of the infant and is the one who places the "social determination in a fictional direction that will forever remain irreducible for any single individual" (p. 76).

The presence of the other as similar is totalizing due to the alienating specter of the image. It leads to the very first framing of a social relation of alienation sustained in the register of the imaginary, a field that is certainly ideological. In effect, there is a fantasmatic insertion of the positive social being in the framing of the Other that represents only an early moment of the subsequent constitution of the subject. Lacan proposes, in effect, the imaginary register as the inauguration of the itinerary of the first social and totalizing contact of the individual with his narcissism encapsulated in the alienated image of social determination.[6] The primordial alienation of the image lays the ground for a second alienating-structuring inscription of the subject at the symbolic level. In Lacan's (1950a) words, in addition to a "social organization," the first constitution of the individual requires "a painful alienation of the individual from his fellow man and finds its passages in the twists of aggressiveness"; a route that makes the presence of the other essential (p. 122).

The ratio of the imaginary register with the bodily dimension is, for Lacan, the precedent in which the symbolic register is slid as a necessary sequel and from which a highly problematic object relation is formed since the other, beyond representing a figure of love, is also a threat that takes on conditions opposite to the infant. The connection with the other is predicted to be complex since it will not cease to point towards a constant impediment; the hope for completeness begins to point out itself as a social imperative of bonding with that which crystallizes from the other as the completeness of the ego.[7] From here, the subjective plot is intersected between a body alienated from the image and, subsequently, structured by the Other in a dialectical, triadic, and operational experience. That is why, we assume, Lacan (1949b) is explicit in mentioning that what "psychoanalysis can contribute to sociology [...] is an adequate apparatus for engaging [*attaquer*] the subject ('I never say the individual') at the level of subjective experience" (p. 319). Above all, from this moment in Lacan's oeuvre, there is a torsional apparatus, not a toolbox, to pierce the subject; there are elements and functions and not one analytical sociology of the subject in society.

The psyche depends, in the beginning, on slavery to the image. However, as Lacan perseveres in this, the narcissistic and social identification is adequate, deformed, and exploited by the symbolic breeding ground. Thus, "the Ego, syndic of the most mobile functions by which man adapts himself to reality, reveals itself to us as a power of illusion, even of lie: it is a superstructure involved in social alienation" (Lacan, 1950b, p. 129). Incorporating a traversed intersubjectivity depends profoundly on the imaginary as a functional fallacy. If in the mirror there is an image, and therefore an alienated social and subjective relation, then in the symbolic, the orientation of the surplus not contained in the image of the infant emerges, as seen below.[8] In other words, subject and intersubjectivity are characterized as two separate and differentiable moments founded on the exchange of registers and their effects at the level of the social bond.

At the core of the imaginary and alienated identification with the other, the first thing to be taken into account is that the image of completeness specified by the ego [*moi*] is a gestalt incapable of rendering an individual or decontextualized support. The subject can only come into being as a deformity of the individual that escapes the *imago* of the other and its imaginary performances. If we understand that the social alienation of the image of the other is a fundamental and enslaving moment of the infant—an illusion momentarily fixed to the social logics of solipsistic feedback; then this mirage reflects "to imply the emergence of a new type of man: *Homo psychologicus*, the product of our industrial age," in whose subsequent dispersion, "the relations between this *Homo psychologicus* and the machines he uses" will turn out to be almost indistinguishable (Lacan, 1951, p. 17). That is to say, the machine of the signifier will articulate itself very well in the traumatic splitting of castration and the fragile identity of the ego.[9] It is truly extraordinary, too, that Lacan (1951) warned us, from then on, that: "This relationship between man and machine will come to be regulated by both psychological and psychotechnical means; the necessity for this will become increasingly urgent in the organization of society" (p. 17). Consequently, the register of the imaginary is responsible for the polarization of the social subject because it identifies it with a psychological idea that is supposedly biological and imaginary, which embodies a first false recognition of the social world: An alienation from themselves.[10] Only Ego obfuscation and functionalist ignorance can appear in this spectrum of the psychologically socialized and totalizing image of the Ego [*moi*].

The subject who comes through the effect of the signifier starts from a first imaginary identification. The subject's estrangement alters the body, force, and the world to admit identification relations within a secondary symbolic alienation [*Entfremdung*]. The first alienation [*Entäusserung*] was similar to that observed by Marx (1844) in which "objectification as loss of the object and object-bondage; appropriation as estrangement" occurred (p. 71).[11] It clearly shows that language pre-exists the subject since the infant's mother is already inserted in the signifier and is the subject of desire; the image and the signifier have already alienated her. Lacan's idea of the subject and its first alienating bonds refers to the presence and absence of objects, that is, to an intermittent imaginary and symbolic foundation that subsequently accompanies the existence of subjects and codifies loss as an essential element of subjectivity. This is the reason why the raw truth of "alienation" is a "deceptive power" that "situates," in two times, "desire in the Other's field" (Lacan, 1966b, p. 56).

For the theoretical moment of the *Mirror Stage*, the formalization of social relations is presented in the Rimbaudian duality: *Je est un autre*, as a condition precedent, alienating, normalizing, and inconclusive from a specular register towards the insertion of the signifier within the infant. Regardless, it is at this moment of his work where society is inscribed from another totally due to a specular shift that becomes a social totality of hallucinatory character, what Lacan (1949a) affirms as "paranoiac alienation." The figure of the weaning complex, previously reviewed in *Family Complexes*, is enhanced by the adequacy of the alienating register of the image. This symbiotic relationship consolidates, in the first moment of Lacan's teaching, a solid referent for understanding social reality as a delusional and self-referential device in the passage from the "specular I [*je*] [...] into the social I [*je*]" (p. 79).[12] As Lacan (1953b) said in his lecture *The Symbolic, the Imaginary and the Real*, from the imaginary function of the subject, "alienated from himself," it can be understood that "the Ego is something in which the subject cannot recognize himself at first except by alienating himself" (p. 24). This alienation from the other invests an upside-down subject's self-image, dependent on a specific modality of a totality that confronts the symbolic system.

The alienated individual in society is cut off, normalized, and exploited by the symbolic register, which, for Lacan, becomes an axial principle of culture and its relation to the subject, social bonds, and neurosis. In this reading, there is a Lacanian bet in favor of the signifier, the paternal metaphor, and the symbolic castration. The *imago* of the ego [*moi*] as an alienating social moment is structured from the symbolic function deposited in the Ego-ideal (s). The recognition of the social, from this imaginary condition of the ego, supports the conformation of human societies through the symbolic bonds that erect laws and positions both as repressive and perverse.[13] The imaginary, from the above, is the obligatory step by which Lacan commences to turn towards culture and begins to check the presence of the social by delimiting, at least at this moment, society as a practical illusion sustained in identifications.[14] Lacanian exploration shifts towards the symbolic, although he does not lose, even until his last years, the reference to the imaginary-symbolic alienation that he articulated in the '60s to the forced choice within the symbolic system of culture.

Towards the end of the 1940s, Lacan (1948a) discusses the contrast between the ego as a purely imaginary function and the ego-ideal as a cultural key. Both are "connected" through a "libidinal normativeness and a cultural normativeness, bound up since the dawn of history with the *imago* of the father." Also, in this writing, Lacan recaptures a derivation of the father's image from *Totem and Taboo*, where "Oedipal identification is thus the identification by which the subject transcends the aggressiveness constitutive of the first subjective individuation" (p. 95). This position later echoes Lacan's interest in the symbolic figure of the father and the insertion of the law within culture. As an inference, Lacan found in the opposition between the ego and the ego-ideal the unveiling of a specific libidinal bond instituted by cultural law framed via ideals and an imaginary ego that propagates and sanctions the demarcations of social requirements.

Through his reading of the imaginary Ego, Lacan (1948a) questioned what is proper to "the anti-dialectical mentality of a culture which, dominated as it is by objectifying ends, tends to reduce all subjective activity to the ego's being" or even autonomous activity to the being of the ego (p. 96). Again, the gaze is at the center of the subjective dimension of the individual and is imaginatively reflected in the other, so it is dialectically unimaginable to reduce psychism to an individual or ontological consciousness per se. Indeed, there is a socialized other from which the individual gets his first subjective and dialectical confirmation.

The imaginary status of otherness, framed as a simulated mode of autonomy, will sooner or later be traumatized by culture and its structural changes. The latter puts on hold the extravagant capacity of transformative autonomy in social practices, as is often read in the instituting and instituted imaginaries of Cornelius Castoriadis.[15] This approach is called into question because it obeys an imaginary and naïve identification that gives rise to a self-referential circuit in which an understanding of the other is only admitted within the limits of the image. An imagined subject that is in frank opposition to the autonomous chaining of signifiers produces, among other matters, a problematic but fundamental aspect of the subject: The desire. The instituted and the instituting, at the level of social practices, ultimately lead to the absurd reign of a solipsistic imaginary conceived only in appearance as a supposed autonomous and creative radicality of the subject.

Lacan, after this, expressed the need to leave behind the argumentative reduction of the individual to give way to a detailed, if you will, primordial description of the subject of the unconscious in an attempt to obliterate the infamy of sociology around the dialectical circumstances of subjectivity. Lacan's intention was not to do psychoanalytic sociology but for psychoanalysis to force and elucidate the forcing of society in the regulation and deformation of relations, its enjoyment, and the domination of social practices from the fetid waters of the symbolic system of culture.[16]

Lacan (1952a) also detailed the borders through which "the whole difficulty for the human being, before properly genital sexuality, is to be an Ego which recognizes itself and alienates itself to the other" (p. 14). This identity recognition, consequently, is of a similarity assimilated compulsorily. Here, alienation does not require an idea of difference in the image but a social reproduction of resemblance. In this sense, a *society where we are all equal*, or *where we all have the same opportunities*, or *where a world where all worlds fit* and other *mainstream* phrases would only have a place in the register of the imaginary since the insertion of the economy of the signifier will unleash a multitude of indissoluble positionings and antagonisms in this imaginary totality, indeed inhibiting social metamorphosis.

Lacan ventures down an exact route to arrive at another component destined to fracture that idyllic, totalitarian, and autonomous image of the Ego. Precisely in the fracture, in the trauma as that which makes a gap, lies the importance of the symbolic law inserted by the function of the metaphor of the father's name. Lacan does not rush; he seems to be shaping the implication of the Other in the subject; he provides time and space to the first imaginary identification of the subject, given that the alienated individual reveals a position of singular helplessness: The vacuous force of ego. The factual background will be woven into the invention of the subject, which can only happen through the symbolic register. That is, in the way out of the Oedipus complex through the retroactive metaphor inscribed by law and ideals.

The dual identification instituted under alienation is not enough for Lacan (1953b) when he points out that any relationship of "two subjects require *mediation*" to acquire a "symbolic value," needs "the *mediation* of a third personage" (pp. 27–28).[17] The triadic relationship, beginning with the Oedipus complex, cannot be thought of only in the imaginary world. It is there that the symbolic figure of the father and the structure of the language that sustains him come into play. In addition, this third character goes beyond, on a symbolic level, emerging from the order of desire and its effects: Guilt, shame, symptoms and anxiety; and in this sense, all this evolves a contingent cultural and social effect of the law of prohibition of incest. As was elucidated by Freud, and despite the criticisms of his "method," "what was essential was his recognition that man began with law and crime" and his socialized inhibition (Lacan, 1950c, p. 106).

Lacan reaffirms the hierarchy of the cultural condition and its laws as an indispensable remnant in social construction. However, suppose the first social bond with a similar one is imaginary. In that case, it is appropriate to examine in-depth, *hic et nunc*, the second identificatory position that Lacan addresses, that is, the position of the figure of the father as representative of the symbolic order. The father, in his abstract formalization, has in his name the castrating and inaugural function of meaning. This formula is nothing other than the insertion of the infant into the symbolic universe with a signifier and the regulation of the life of pleasure in the disposition of civilizing conventions. The symbolic frames the identification sustained by language in a new form of bond and social repression of the subject's action. The insertion of the law as a metaphor, at the level of structure, is a fictional reduction sustained in organized civilization. Consequently, it has a measurable and standardizable extension by the relation between signifying elements. In this respect, the tyranny of identification begins indispensably in the power of language, its values, and the use of temporality.[18]

The symbolic father's function dwells, of course, in the despotic registration of a signifier; as Lacan (1952b) describes:

> The assumption of the father's function presupposes a single symbolic relation in which the symbolic and the real would fully coincide. The father would have to be not only the *name-of-the-father*, but also the representative, in all its fullness, of the symbolic value crystallized in his function. Now, it is clear that this coincidence of the symbolic and the real is totally elusive. At least in a social structure like ours, the father is always in one way or another in disharmony with regard to his function, a deficient father, a humiliated father, as Claudel would say. There is always an extremely obvious discrepancy between the symbolic function and what is perceived by the subject in the sphere of experience. In this divergence lies the source of the effects of the Oedipus complex which are not at all normalizing, but rather most often pathogenic.
>
> (p. 423)

Although extensive, this quote is pertinent since it encompasses the approach to the father's function from a fragmentation of the hegemonic totality and adjusts his humiliated social condition. If the father is a function, it can only express the impossibility of the real covered by the signifier. The father, sustained by the cultural environment, is in a position of misfortune, given that he is not the omnipresent father but is charged with carrying on his back a place destined as symbolic law. The father holds the force of the symbolic system of culture and its subsequent social developments—a mark that through the "ideals" in the "democratic" world tends to "isolate" the "individual" from the "social communions," delivering him to the "pathogenic virulence" of the "formidable narcissistic subjection of the tyranny" (Lacan, 1948b, p. 176).[19]

In contrast, the Freudian father of the primitive horde is now only an ancestral cleavage of the culture in which the subject finds the dictatorial function of his ideal of the self. Or, in Lacan's (1953c) words, the father is the one who sustains the "function of symbolic identification allowing [the] primitive man to believe he is the reincarnation of an ancestor with the same name, and even determining an alternating recurrence of characteristics in modern man" (p. 230). Additionally, the function of the father, framed in the symbolic, offers the subject a chain of signifying domination. The position of the symbolic father does not depend on an organ but on a structure that expresses a father abruptly stripped of his force since he is also subject to the symbolic castration of language. The system of signifiers and structure supports and drives this symbolic castration on the subject's action.

The death of the primordial father, represented by Freud as a mythical inquiry taken up here by Lacan (1953c), implies two questions in its broad sense. On the one hand, the prohibition of incest, inherent in every social and cultural formation, "reveals" the "primordial law" as "identical to a language order" (p. 229). And on the other hand, the opening and setting in motion of the subject's desire through the uncomfortable forcing of culture. The value of the Oedipus complex lies in the insertion of the mythical idea of Oedipus and his knowledge, as it reforms the categorical functions of symbolic reality and converges with the predominant morality in societies.[20]

The myth—understood as the minimum set of symbolic values in diachrony that are structured and chained to each other—admits here a reading of the strength of the structure to symbolically border the real and structured social life with a common archaic referent, essential, and of sociological effect. As Lacan (1953c, p. 236) suggested, "myths" thread "the synchrony of mythemes," and, indeed, it is the myth, in that unity of general reduction proposed by Claude Lévi-Strauss (1964), that deploys the functional synchrony of the social laws of the signifier because, as the French anthropologist observed, "the total body of myth belonging to a given community is comparable to its speech" (p. 7). Myth, in its cultural function, designates a systemic representation that contains and unfolds the possibilities of the emplacement of knowledge. Let us not forget that "the tragedy of Oedipus lies in the fact that 'he did not know' he had killed his father and was sleeping with his mother" (Lacan, 1960–1961, 11.01.61, p. 100). Starting from this appreciation, the myth that emerges from Oedipus reveals that what remains inserted in the neurotic's culture is a socialized law that depends on the mythical adequacy of the structure, of a system that gives a millimetric alliance to the significance and that will provoke disastrous impressions such as the obscene kiss of the Other's demand towards the subject.[21]

If the Oedipus complex fixes the symbolic law, via castration in Freud, and leads to the emergence of desire according to Lacan, then it is through the signifier that a mytheme represents a retroactive adequation—a "gross constituent unit" that ultimately defines collective practices, their rites, and their cosmovision (Lévi-Strauss, 1955, p. 431). It is not only the introduction of a desire but the formation of a mythical dialectic whose effects succumb to the modalities of the *ethos* and the domination of freedom over the subject.[22] This dialectic, hooked in the mode of myth, presupposes a closed direction of the death drive that will be reduced to the maniacal impressions of the Ego at the social level. Lacan, instead of becoming insensitive to the mirage of the autonomy of the Ego and its identity—as fragile and evanescent as a figure in the mirror—found the individualized mythology of the subject. Thus, Lacan reveals how archaic knowledge is reduced to the ideological, social bond initially positioned from the reflection. Moreover, due to the dialectic of desire, Lacan augurs the regulated horizon of a fight for pure prestige where death is the pivot that must be ordered via the knowledge that adapted the mythical to functionality and its profitability.[23]

In Lacan's (1952b) terms, "after all, for this dialectic of the death struggle, the struggle for pure power, to be initiated, death must not be actualized, since the dialectical movement would cease for lack of combatants; death must be imagined" (p. 425). In this logic, for the function of the father to be installed, there must be a cultural law and a restrictive social framework that delimits and dissuades a passage to the real of murder; the social and singular neurotic mythology repressively sustained amid a deadly dialectic: The struggle for pure prestige between the master and the slave. Concerning this dialectic, Lacan (1953–1954) also regarded that "Hegel gives an account of the interhuman bond" and that this "has to account not only for society but for history"; it is "struggle and labor" that organize societies (02.06.54, p. 223). The dialectic of the master and the slave is, at the same time, a critical element that ratifies the historical insertion of socio-political antagonism and, of course, the insistence of negativity clarified by death.[24]

Lacan recurrently appeals to the hospitality of Hegel, *the most sublime hysteric*, as he came to anoint him, not directly, but by the hand of Alexandre Kojève (1947)—as we mentioned above—who, in his reading of the dialectic of the master and the slave argues:

> if human reality is a social reality, society is human as a set of desires that mutually desire each other as desires. The human desire, or better, anthropogenic, constitutes a free and historical individual conscious of his individuality, his freedom, his history and, finally, his historicity.
>
> (p. 5)

From this point of view, the subject is a desiring being; however, desire cannot be inscribed independently and is far removed from the blissful individual psychological illusions that proliferate in the precarious limits of the Ego and very close to the domination of the signifying structure.[25]

In the core of the subjective experience prevails a primitive and contingent ground that penetrates, via the signifiers, the consistency of the body to focus its subsistence towards a cause. The big Other, that treasure trove of signifiers where Lacan locates the smooth surface of language, merchandises from the social mode in which desire wanders. In other words, Lacan's Other is a regulative reservoir of economy and structure, an insistent archive, a signifying heaviness that allows the mapping of desire. The Lacanian maxim repeated *ad nauseam*, Desire is the desire of the Other, has been a political cornerstone as it consists in the tercerized dimension of the subject's existence as flesh that depends on language and on the social mode of productive organization of desire and not only on its disposition in the natural world.[26]

As Kojève (1947) pointed out, "human desire must overcome the desire for conservation" (p. 5). In other words, man does not "consider himself" human if he does not "risk his (animal) life in function of his human desire" and the fluctuations of his condemnation to antagonism. Kojève emphasizes the founding dimension of desire that will be embedded in the dialectic of Master and Slave, and it is here that the desire of the slave chained to the desire of his master is at work. This previous theoretical platform is where Lacan will knot much of his theory on culture, the dialectic of desire, and later, the social demand of jouissance. The consequences of his entire Kojèvian reading of desire are powerful for Lacan since this interpretation is an operation of philosophical extraction, not of elucidation, which bases his elaboration on the bond permanently anchored on antagonism and the overcoming of opposites.

Desire, for its part, also evokes the unconscious, more precisely, the unconscious of sexuality in its drive and cultural meaning, where it is possible to recognize Lacan's close relationship with Freud (1908) in specifying the founding ambivalence of the subject sexualized by culture. For Lacan, there is a dimension of the "object" as "other people [*l'autrui*]," in which the sexual "exchange" turns out to be the "root of the social contract" (Lacan 1958–1959, 17.12.58, p. 107). Just in this class of his seminar, for the first time—it is essential not to forget this—Lacan made the first explicit reference to Marx, and it is on the issue of the exchange of commodities under the shade of "social utilitarianism" and the subjection to the shared ideal of regulation of desire for the more or less stable reproduction of society. In other words, the utility of desire for controlling the social spectrum and the utilitarian management of pleasure and women.

Lacan (1955) indicates, in parallel, that it is in the "sexual relations," amid order and "regulating them according to the law of preferential marriage alliances and forbidden relations," that the place on which "the first combinatory for exchanges of women between family lines relies, developing the fundamental commerce and concrete discourse on which human societies are based in an exchange of gratuitous goods and magic words" (p. 359). In that, the exchange of symbolic values of the unconscious instituted by the law gives rise from the signifier register and its vicissitudes to the sexualized and commodified exchanges of society by adapting desire. Nevertheless, this question is even more intricate if a rigorous line of logical understanding of the above passage is set up, namely, that all desire exchange is always already symbolic and that desire can only be mobilized in the broad coordinates of the treasury of signifiers as a currency whose value is supported in the structure.

In effect, values, their movement, and the commodification of identification in language integrate the surface where the commercial sexuation comes into play from the setting up of the law of the father and the subsequent idyllic exchanges of the subjects. Therein lies a fundamental theoretical reason for the *economic return* to Freud. The Lacanian lesson is a reading of the value of the signifier in the structural field as the producer of the logic of psychic conflicts due to the determination of the signifier in the utilitarian laws of society, which are stagnant in profit. It is from these social exchanges of sexual dynamism that a delimited association of the symbolic identification of the subjects in a patriarchal and bourgeois society can be installed. Undoubtedly, identification, concerning desire, is socially adequate for the subjects. In Lacan's (1958–1959) perspective, "what presents itself in society as culture" admits "stable conditions," administered, and "latent constants," which in the social framework "determine the circuits of exchanges within the flock." It is there where Lacan perceives the implantation of a circular and compulsive "movement" to a utilitarian repetition of the enjoyment and the politics of the Other. The traumatic gash and the alienating passage from *Ego* to *I* "establishes a movement or dialectic in society that leaves open there the same gap as the one in which we situate the function of desire" (01.07.59, p. 483).

Lacan *avec* Lévi-Strauss: Society *Speaks* Through the Measure of Structure

A few pages ago, we partially presented the link between Lacan and the structuralist ethnologist Claude Lévi-Strauss, focusing on the function of myth and its subjective consequences. It could be said, *stricto sensu*, that the latter's influence on the former around several notions taken essentially from *Structural Anthropology* and *The Elementary Structures of Kinship* was decisive in his structuralist period. Lacan (1959–1960) went so far as to say that it was thanks to Lévi-Strauss that "the primordial character of the Law as such, namely, the introduction of the signifier and its *combinatoire* into human nature through the intermediary of the marriage laws, which are regulated by a system of exchanges that he defines as elementary structures" could be confirmed and with it much of his structural position on society was formally framed due to the prohibition and its link to the emergence and reproduction of modern societies (16.12.59, p. 67).

In his paper, *Theoretical Introduction to the Functions of Psychoanalysis in Criminology*, a communication previous to the famous Rome conference of 1953, Lacan discusses the relationship between society and the criminal *behavior* of subjects. The discussion in question is relevant since Lacan (1950c), drawing on the ideas of Marcel Mauss, demarcates that "the structures of society are symbolic" (p. 108). This idea points out a structure of society that originated within the antipode of the symbolic and the natural. In other words, the origin of society is to be found in the elaborations coming from language, culture, and their adaptations and not from a mere animal condition. The structure gives society the support to mediate human nature with desire and structures through the signifier and the law, the circulation of bonds with the other.

Lacan examines structure in Mauss' terms close to the symbolic function and group contraction that accounts for psychopathology. Lacan proposes that this function is decisive because it allows us to understand structuration in the dimension of sceneries and exclusion. This position germinates from the reading that Lévi-Strauss gave as an introduction to the work of Marcel Mauss in his book *Sociology and Anthropology.* There, the social function is a formalization of symbolic ordering that dimensions the exchange within the limits of language as a system. Lévi-Strauss (1987) writes in the well-known prologue: "Mauss still thinks it possible to develop a sociological theory of symbolism, whereas it is obvious that what is needed is a symbolic origin of society" and, in the same way, to understand that "social reality" is, in an exact sense, a "symbolic system" (p. 21–22). Why the origin? On what basis is society becoming organized? From this logic, the threshold of society must be pursued based on the symbolic networks woven in exchange, bodily techniques, time, and mobilization, which support and engage the wanderings of the subject in society.[27]

In a parallel way, the function of the Gift lies in order, time, and movement, and the social control of these points condescends and arranges the continuity of a social structure, even if it is fully entropic.[28] In this sense, the exchange produced through the "potlatch" accounts for how the man "retreat[s] from goods, a retreat which enabled him to link the maintenance and discipline of his desire" (Lacan, 1959–1960, 18.05.60, p. 235). It is there where, due to the mobilization of the symbolic function of value, the subjects in society animate their actions. In other words, the symbolic function of exchange responds to the same modes of functioning of the economic logic of the distribution and mobilization of wealth. There is no longer an invisible hand but a temporal administration and a mobile economic-political exploitation of desire. For Lacan (1956–1957),

> Within this symbolic aspect of the Gift, all sorts of things can be given in exchange. Indeed, it is because so many things can be given in exchange that ultimately, we find so many equivalents of the phallus in what effectively occurs in symptoms.
>
> (16.01.57, p. 116)[29]

Many years later, Lacan (1971–1972) gave "potlatch" a status close to the "real" by delimiting that it "supports the impossible" in his "geometry of the tetrad" as a topology of the social bond and its algebraic notation: The object *a* (09.02.72, p. 75).

Furthermore, there is an ineluctable symbolic effectiveness in the symbolic system and its functions, which leads us to ask ourselves, what does Lévi-Strauss propose concerning it? His theoretical proposal initially suggests a relationship between the psychoanalytic cure and the shamanistic cure. However, what is interesting in Lévi-Strauss' ideas lies in the role of language as an original cultural function, which would be a kind of background located not only in the origin of the myth but also in the construction of the cultural laws of exchange that it designates. As Lévi-Strauss (1963) himself remarks, "the effectiveness of symbols would consist precisely in this 'inductive property,' by which formally homologous structures, built out of different materials at different levels of life—organic processes, unconscious mind, rational thought—are related to one another" (p. 201).

Symbolic effectiveness unfolds on the margins of the sorcerers' practices, which refer to a symbolic depth traversed on the plane of the real of the bodies knotted to the other two registers (symbolic and imaginary)—menstrual blood and childbirth attest to this. In other words, the existence of the myths and the value of the signifiers that structured the practices of the witches have a socialized value in the reproduction of the symbolic system of the subjects who require a bodily contingency. The idea is taken to the psychoanalytic interpretation by the way that what emerges in the practices of the sorcerers is precisely the value of the symbolic order beyond the cure. Language is the enunciation of the word that reproduces and mobilizes itself in the untimely universe of the real to tame it, adapt it, and try to guide it.

In his analogy with psychoanalysis, Lévi-Strauss (1963) has remarked that

> the unconscious ceases to be the ultimate haven of individual peculiarities—the repository which makes each of us an irreplaceable being. It is reducible to a function—the symbolic function, which no doubt is specifically human, and which is carried out according to the same laws among all men, and corresponds to the aggregate of these laws.
> (pp. 202–203)

This comment by Lévi-Strauss is a landmark of the ideas around what Lacan initially bases as his original interpretation of society and symbolic orchestration. Although he does not universally trace that myth as the univocal founder of a society, language, through its laws of exchange, is the operator that underlies the shadows of other structures that would form a social framework and feed the unconscious with a symbolic support.[30] Lévi-Strauss (1963) reminds us that sometimes "the notion of structure is to permit the introduction of measurement in social anthropology" (pp. 282–283). If this is so, the structure of society is delimited in the measure of a structure that speaks in and beyond its mathematical-geometric function focused on the values of the signifier. There is no collective unconscious, but measures of the collective through the structure of unconscious values are positively reduced to significance. Or, in Lacan's (1975–1976) words, "There is no collective unconscious; there are only particular unconsciouses, to the extent that every single one of us, from one instant to the next, gives a little nudge to the tongue we speak" (11.04.76, p. 131).

On the other hand, Lacan (1954–1955) comments:

> Lévi-Strauss demonstrates that there is a correct classification of what the elementary structures of kinship make available to us. This

> presupposes that the symbolic agencies function in the society from the start, from the moment it takes on a human appearance. But this is nothing more nor less than what is presupposed by the unconscious such as we discover and manipulate it in analysis.
>
> (01.12.54, p. 30)

Lacan's approach, for Lévi-Strauss, then deepens the distinction between nature and culture, now already in the dimension of the values that culture and the subject produce. From his perspective, in the primitive forms of social alliance can be foreseen that societies depend on the progress of the symbol as the first regulator of life. In this sense, there is no historicity of the unconscious but symbolic relations that have their particular organizational background located in the repetition of the regular modes of the signifier.

As a reader of *The Elementary Structures of Kinship*, Lacan amplifies a nodal and original paradigm of psychoanalysis: The study of the subjective position attached more to an anti-natural state than to nature itself. Lévi-Strauss gave an account of the distinctions between nature and culture, the same differences that Lacan takes advantage of to relate the radical Freudian proposal in *Civilization and Its Discontents* to the defense of culture and its resistant returns on a symbolic interpretation of societies. According to Lacan (1954–1955), "we are obliged to concede to Levi-Strauss that numerical elements have a role in the constitution of a collectivity" and "it would be wrong not to take in Buffon's extremely apt remarks on the role played by statistical elements in a group, in a society." There is no "soul" of "society" but "practical" management of space: "[H]exagons" with causality and not with "finality" since "bees," unlike social subjects, do not "know geometry" despite living in one of its examples (the hexagon) (01.12.54, p. 28). In terms of Lévi-Strauss (1956), "the societies of the demographer are thus artificially homogeneous groups, ignoring the most fundamental features of their structure; [...] the real behavior of the population conforms very little to the abstract models of demographers" (p. 530).[31]

Lacan is more than a mere interpreter of Lévi-Strauss. On the contrary, the ethnologist further substantiates and stylizes Lacan's early structuralist postulates to make the signifier a symbolic pillar that sustains an anthropologically contingent and causal function of society. While societies enclose and distribute the geometrical forms of inhabiting, existing, and being measured in society, Lacan (1954–1955) asserts that "in the symbolic order the totality is called a universe" and, in its complexity, "everything is ordered in accordance with the symbols which have emerged, in accordance with the symbols once they have appeared"; it is in this way that "everything which is human has to be ordained within a universe constituted by the symbolic function." Lacan mentions from this logic that "it is not for nothing that Levi-Strauss calls his structures *elementary*, he does not say primitive. Elementary is the opposite of *complex*" (01.12.54, p. 29). The elementary is in the open forms of organization and the indeterminate distribution of subjects; on the contrary, the complexes obey a demand for social order that the enjoyment of the structure has directed. The structure, as Lacan mentions, supported from the perspective of Lévi-Strauss, is not "limited by any *natural* hierarchy," and its "minimal limitation"—due to the encounter between signifiers—is "geometrical" (1960b, p. 544).

Lévi-Strauss (1969), for his part, pointed out that "everything universal in man relates to the natural order, and is characterized by spontaneity, and that everything subject to a norm is cultural and is both relative and particular" (p. 9). The social nature of humans entails that natural conditions are framed in existing symbolic contents, which remain open to the causal modification of the symbol. The ethnologist is well aware that there are relative and particular attributes that qualify, in opposition, the universal terrain of language, and this allows us to suppose that the supremacy of culture will have to deal seriously with the modes of knotting of human reality as opposed to nature through beliefs, rituals, and exchanges.

The relational and symbolic particularity of the human processes normalized and found within culture has a regulatory boundary, and the latter situation is subordinate to the social processes related to structuring its systems of norms, legal laws, and cultural appropriations proper to the place where they are replicated. It is also a matter of partitions of language that can be outlined in proverbs, gossip, and, of course, in-jokes that make particularity a contingent sign of language. That is to say, language functions by framing reality and disposing of the subject to the structural confrontation that ties the social sense of reality and the opposites to the law. Reality ordered by employing norms and measures constitutes the *rational soul* of a social reality sutured by the effect of the chaining of signifiers.[32]

As we have seen, the symbolic law, its mystical presence, its utilitarian suppleness, and its cutting repressive avatars reference the subjects' ulteriorly ordered culture. The allusion to the mystical disposition of the law is a structure-giving function within the subjects and their social codes and not a universal totality of the subjects' acting, psyche, and social behaviors. The law labors in the capacity and extension it has to demand from culture modalities of action profoundly adjusted to the formation of partial requirements on pleasure or, at least, one could speak of an attempt to inspect, commercialize, and insist on such regulation from the juridical norms whose effect is morality as the political adequacy of men.[33]

For Lacan (1966a), let us recall, "the object of psychoanalysis is not man" but "what he lacks, not absolute lack, but lack of an object" and that lack "is not the scarce bread, it is the cake [*brioche*] to which a queen referred her people in times of famine" (p. 211). This reading of lack does not distance Lacan from anthropology; on the contrary, it adjusts accounts and reveals the relevance of structure to explain human action amid the habitat of the surplus, the *brioche* beyond the conquest of bread.[34] Because of this, the imperative and categorical regulation founded by the social system explains the forcing of culture delimited in moral values as the formative and limiting way of the subjects in society.

Lacan appreciated that Freud's theory could not elucidate the subject in a totalitarian way since he finds, in Lévi-Strauss' interpretation of culture, the most precise manner of describing the symbolic law and that which escapes from the cultural register. What will later be located as castration as the inaugural element of the signifying path to suture the insertion of the metaphor of the father's name and position of the lack of being. Due to the forcing of the law, castration is "the altogether new mainspring Freud introduced into desire, giving desire's lack the meaning that remained enigmatic" (Lacan, 1964a, p. 723).

Freud (1930) explained that

> the word civilization [*Kultur*] describes the whole sum of the achievements and the regulations which distinguish our lives from those of our animal ancestors and which serve two purposes, namely to protect men against nature and to adjust their mutual relations.
>
> (p. 89)

In this regard, Freud's idea about the cultural nature of the subjects poses a different feature to the social interface. It also highlights that society expresses and designates, and the normalized subject acts in reciprocal consequence. Even for Freud, although culture is the entity in which individuals' social function is mobilized, some attributes of a primitive-symbolic nature are in the subjects that return immeasurably.[35] In this place, Freud (1930) lodges requirements "untamed" by culture, where things of the drive level of the subjects, called by him "original personality," are deposited (p. 96).

It is for this reason that the totemic myth can be read not only in the key of the father's supremacy but also in the retroactive social function that falls on the primitive cultural scenario whose ordering it divides and establishes as an adaptive and utilitarian knowledge that accommodates the formulation of signification. Is this not one of the prominent abilities of the unconscious, a product of secondary repression?[36] Lacan says, "Man thus speaks, but it is because the symbol has made him a man. Even if, in fact, overabundant gifts welcome a stranger who has made himself known to a group, the life of natural groups that constitute a community is subject to the rules of matrimonial alliance—determining the direction in which the exchange of women takes place—and to the mutual services determined by marriage." At the same time, "marriage [*alliance*] ties are governed by an order of preference whose law concerning kinship names is, like language, imperative for the group in its forms, but unconscious in its structure" (Lacan, 1953c, p. 229).

On the other hand, the role of incest within culture for Lévi-Strauss is a cultural state, perhaps the only universal found in culture. Lévi-Strauss

(1969) observed, concerning the prohibition of incest, a "theoretical contradiction" given that it is a rule of the social order and yet possesses a quintessence of "universality" (p. 10). Lacan seriously took up this renewal of the prohibition of incest as a universal law. Nevertheless, Lacan specifies it in the limits of deprivation and efficacy in and from desire as a critical point for the conformation of the subject—an articulating zero signifier. The situation that poses an oedipal reproduction in subjects that can perhaps be inserted universally is the echo of social organization through paternal law. However, this is not the case for Lacan, given that Oedipus comes to articulate the neutered and blind social law, which must be questioned or put in abeyance through tricky identifications.[37] The psychologized story of the desire for the father and the mother is no longer a trivial matter because, in Lacan, the form that the law takes, thanks to desire and social regulation, designates the parameters of cultural existence permeated by unattainable and repeatable objects. This regulation makes the law a fictional entity that produces an "attraction of utility" for "people damning themselves for the pleasure of giving their [modern] conveniences to other people who, they have got it into their heads, cannot live without their help," a matter that is "one of the most curious phenomena of human sociability" (Lacan, 1960a, p. 20).

In short, what is truly remarkable in this brief tour is to highlight that the law of incest is a prohibitive statute and generator, in parallel, of regulated and inciting subjective permissiveness, as it has been known since Freud. For this reason, the functionality of Oedipus in Lacan will fall on the deployment of the disposition of a law that admits the insertion of the symbolic field in the subject from the place of the signifier, subsequently adequate by institutional and phallic signification.[38] For Lacan, the prohibition of incest is situated in a more complex place by the implication of signifiers, in that exterior territory of the Other that demands a subject beyond his love-hate-separation affections with his first object relations.[39] Moreover, this exigency is already an earthly configuration of the order of signification produced by the repressive and social castration sequence. The law castrates and centralizes in the logic of phallic signification the repressive power of social structures.[40] According to Lacan (1959–1960), that is why Moses is the "rationalist," the "Great Man," the "legislator," and also the "politician" who dictates the guidelines of socialized comportment under the Tablets of the Law (16.03.60, p. 173).

Lévi-Strauss (1969) also highlighted that "the prohibition of incest has the universality of bent and instinct, and the coercive character of law and institution" (p. 10). This confirms the requirement of the universality of the prohibition of incest and its cultural entanglement—it is a complex mixture of elements. In Lacan's reading, all this takes greater relevance from the viability of a reduced psyche as a product of the prohibition. One is not a subject by existing in the body but by the symbolic rule that measures the concrete of human life, which is spoken by the structure and its constraints. This assembles, from Lacan's exploration, an intricate revision of the Oedipus complex in the light of the structures that foresee that the universal is not the Oedipus but the law, its functions, and its norms of social regulation. In his *Seminar V*, Lacan (1957–1958) commented: "The very existence of the Oedipus complex cannot be justified socially—I mean, cannot be founded on any social teleology" (29.01.58, p. 181). What reproduces is the insistence of the law and not only as an ultimate goal of the aspirations of social progress or as a step of human development.

As Lévi-Strauss (1969) wrote, based on an incisive reflection on incest, "Society expressly forbids only that which society brings about" (p. 18).[41] Lacan (1957–1958) smartly mentions that "as soon as man arrives somewhere, he builds a prison and a brothel—that is, the places where desire truly is—and he waits for something, a better world, a future world" (15.01.58, p. 161). Social morality is nothing more than a loophole that allows the subject's enjoyment in spaces where desire is strictly forbidden and encouraged in the social, urban, and ordinary world, systematized within the parameters of social impositions. These fundamental issues will be developed in the following chapter.

Besides, society judges the very fact of incestuous relations. However, culture rescues gaps through which these prohibitions can be reproduced, reworked, or sublimated. It seems paradoxical that, as the function of conjugal endogamy is inserted in modern families, on the one hand, problematic desires of incest made possible by marriage and reconfigured by culture can exist and, on the other hand, be highly contested by societies. Nevertheless, the regulating work of cultural law persists and constantly occurs as Moses undid the cult of the golden calf, which moves from the identification of the image to the joyful identification with the law. Or, as "Freud demonstrated in repression [...] the sort of discordance between the signified and the signifier that is brought on by all censorship of social origin" (Lacan, 1954, p. 310).

In *Seminar XI*, Lacan (1964b) returns to the notion of the totem as follows:

> Before any experience, before any individual deduction, even before those collective experiences that may be related only to social needs are inscribed in it, something organizes this field, inscribes its initial lines of force. This is the function that Claude Levi-Strauss shows us to be the truth of the totemic function and which reduces its appearance—the primary classificatory function. Before strictly human relations are established, certain relations have already been determined.
>
> (22.01.64, p. 20)

At this point, the worth of the symbolic register disposed of in the subjects from a primitive scenario is essential for ideating neurotic mythology. The relevance of Lévi-Strauss is fundamental because, in Lacan, the totem is invested with mythical significance in which the subject's acts in his society are performed. Lacan gives a distinction of his own to his understanding of the relationship between signifiers to take a step beyond identity and anchor the structural support in the identification function.

In addition to modifying the place and value of the signifier in the inversion of the linguistic sign, he even goes so far as to detach himself from the notion of significance to recall that what is indispensable in the language is the signifier and not the lure of sense but the three, four, five senses, which obey a particular mode of signification. Lacan sharpens, insistently, the anthropological theory of Lévi-Strauss by entrusting the emphasis on the entire psychic experience of the subject amid relations between signifiers and their structuring function. Those mentioned above clearly indicate a precision underpinning an unassailable symbolic matrix for Lacan with the proliferation of signifying relations within the social development of the subject after the insertion of language. At this crossroads of language, appears that "truth without which there is no way of distinguishing the face from the mask, and apart from which there seems to be no other monster than the labyrinth itself" in Lacan's (1955, p. 338) own words.

It is in the framework of the symbolic system's demand that an unavoidable social destiny is fixed for the subject, and it is there that the politicized unconscious is fabricated, the *little chessboard* with no *beyond*. For Lacan (1964b), remember, "the unconscious is manifested to us as something that holds itself in suspense in the area, I would say, of the *unborn*" (22.01.64, p. 23). At the outset, this poses a symbolic charge waiting to take normative root in the subject that has not yet "appeared" in life, a subject affected by the signifier. If we put this in quotation marks, it is precisely because, in a prior manner, the subject is already disposed in language, in the desire for someone else and its unnatural relations by the alienating effect of *your money or your life!* Lacan uses precisely this example to elucidate the pre-existing symbolic charge in the alienated subjects. That charge escapes the biological condition of the child within the mother's body. From the above, the subject emerges through biology affected by the most unrestricted symbolic sense.

The successive temporal demarcation transmitted by the paternal figure fixes the diaphanous form of the primordial signifier, which is configured from a metaphor-place that causes the essential game of the signifying chaining, permeating the desire of the subjects and the utilitarian fictions of the sense to contribute to the social order and its supposed perpetuity. The father is the principal linguistic metaphor because of the symbolic measure given through the structure and not because of his imaginary or biological position. Thus, the position of the primordial signifier grants, in Lacan's point of view, the institution of language in the form of an indomitable and material, inextinguishable nucleus of desire uncovered in the dimensions of the field of the signifier. However, it also makes the father a concept located in the reign of the Other and not only within the strict family function. It is in the midst of this maelstrom that, again drawing on Lévi-Strauss, Lacan (1956–1957) remembers that "the political power is androcentric, even in matriarchal societies, it is represented by men and by male lineages." Moreover, because of a series of "anomalies" in the "exchange," the "order of power" at the political level, and "the order of the signifier" copulate: it is there where "scepter and phallus merge into one" (27.02.57, p. 184).

As a clear example, Oedipus, the unaware traveler of Thebes and the blind *clochard* of Colonus, tragically suffered the dysfunctionality of his family, as it could be said today in a psychologized way. Nevertheless, he did not avoid for a single second the constant demand of the Other and the unavoidable price of not knowing that he murdered his father and coupled with his mother. In effect, in the Oedipus complex, "the imaginary and symbolized phallus takes on the economic importance" which "transcends individual development" (Lacan, 1956–1957, 27.02.57, p. 184). Likewise, Lacan (1955–1956) explains: "If Freud insisted on the Oedipus complex to the extent of constructing a sociology of totems and taboos, it is obviously because for him the Law is there *ab origine*." It is the law that exiles Oedipus to Colonus. Of course, Lacan points out,

> The law is there precisely from the beginning; it has always been there, and human sexuality must realize itself through it and by means of it. This fundamental law is simply a law of symbolization. This is what the Oedipus complex means.
>
> (11.01.56, p. 83)

For Lacan, the Oedipus complex is symbolic within the conscious psychical processes dependent on social determinism and framing. Similarly, at the level of the unconscious, since it appears in an untimely or primitive way within the structuring of the subjects, it is the founding support of a non-knowledge and a legalized regulation, that part of the singular *where the Id was*....[42] Indeed, the dialectic inscription of the void by castration is disputed between the negative of desire and the positive of the law that destines the advent to the same, to the eternal return of the enjoyment practices. It is a forced choice by which Oedipus, like any citizen in today's *civitas*, can walk meditatively and blindly towards his inextinguishable Colonus. What is configured there, in the Oedipal tragedy, "is not the absence of the real father, for this absence is more than compatible with the presence of the signifier, but the lack of the signifier itself" (Lacan, 1956, p. 465).

In concurrence with the dialectic of the law, there is the chance of the confabulation of the myth as a track between the imaginary and the law of the signifier and its ordering chaining to desire. Thus, together with the prohibitive conception of incest thrown by the mythologized idea of Oedipus, its invocation, reproduction, and recognition within society (and of many psychologizing readings) leads to the exchange of signifiers and their representations as an allegorical manifestation of the social within the *intersubjective* world. In Lacan, the function of myth re-emerges as the regulatory parameter of the social function of the signified as a normative element of the subjects. In other words, the function of the signifier in its social adequacy is an insistence on the perpetuity of sense [*significance*] that has a motive that guarantees its chaotic continuity and perpetuity in the dialectic of the law. From this point of view, the idea of Lévi-Strauss (1962) concerning wild [savage] thought [thinking] is relevant, since in

> all societies and all civilizations, terms never have an intrinsic meaning [*signification*]; their meaning [*signification*] is "positional," a function of history and cultural context, on the one hand, and, on the other, of the structure of the system in which they are called on to figure.
>
> (p. 63)

As positioned speaking, the function is configured amid a parameter of legal totality, which it intends to maintain in its social reproduction within its prescriptive limits.

Lacan considers the law as the foundation of the culture of the subjects, which accompanies the origin of the mythological and fictional plot of existence in the function of the material absence of a signifier. Thus, culture has appeared where law exists and set an organizational precedent. The counternatural condition where Lacan gravitates a clear distinction between his psychoanalysis and the interpretations of some of Freud's followers will also flourish. Lacan chooses *Beyond the Pleasure Principle*, in which the subject is becoming in the frenzy of the death drive instead of being content with the absolutization of corporeality centered solely on the life drive. In such a way, incorporating the subject into culture introduces a *Cartesian*—and material—*body* different from its biological condition. It chains it to the treasure of signifiers via Freud's irreducible and borderline invention: The drive.[43]

The structure emphasizes, speaks, and measures similarities between biology and science, so society blurs its modes of control and standardization of desire through phallic signification. Consequently, society is spoken and measured by the prevailing social structure to demand from the subject a quantitative and functional measure for the system that supports the economic-political structure. It is a question not of "the thinking of savages but, as one might say, the savage state of thinking," that is to say, "thinking in so far as it functions well, effectively, with all the characteristics of thought, without having taken on the form of scientific thought, of modern scientific thought with its status" (Lacan, 1961–1962, 06.06.62). The elementary structures suggested by Lévi-Strauss allow Lacan to consider the signifier's effects and function. Nonetheless, it is precisely castration and the void, in addition to symbolic materiality, that produces a *beyond*-structural anthropology.

It could even be affirmed that Lacan found in the death drive the grip of the whole culture. The traumatic inscription of the signifier attempts to regulate the abject presence of the drive by guaranteeing social disciplining using the substance of *jouissance*. This entails that Lacan radically transmutes the perspective of culture. The social nature of the subjects, in this way, is the mythological accumulation of images regulated with the caution of the signifier as a computer and organizer of the power of the proletarian drive unconscious.[44] The dialectic of the law, the producer of desiring subjects, is not only satisfied with the struggle for mere prestige between master and slave but also distributes the denaturalization of the subjects' symbolic material nature for the perpetuity of the enjoyment. The signifying machine, which will be analyzed in the following chapter, tries to render the libidinal conditions an automaton apparatus. Nevertheless, it is inevitably confronted with the indissoluble circumstance of the non-sexual relation.

Society As a Signifier and As a Signifying Structure

It is well known that in Lacan's oeuvre, the place of the signifier is sui generis. Beyond his inversion of the Saussurian linguistic sign and the peculiar disuse of the signified, Lacan discovers a way to extend the subject's status to its ultimate symbolic and real consequences in language and signifying materiality. Freud, from Lacan's (1958a) perspective, was the first to formulate the enigma "of the relations that link [*liant*] the subject to the signifier" (p. 185). "Language," we must emphasize, "with its structure, exists prior to each subject's entry into it at a certain moment in his mental development" and transfers the imperative force of the power of chaining that confers a tricky consistency to the symbolic world (Lacan, 1957a, p. 413).

Amid the scope of language in the everyday life of subjects, Lacan (1957a) affirms that

> the subject, while he may appear to be the slave of language, is still more the slave of a discourse in the universal movement of which his place is already inscribed at his birth, if only in the form of his proper name.
> (p. 414)

The subject alienated—via images and also the master signifier—is an ideologized servant and, at the exact moment, proceeds from the signifier because he is already condemned to its virulent stalking from before his birth: Language is the primordial master that has affected nature. Subsequently, the subject will partially share a place among many signifiers that will give them identification (and identity), uneasiness, desire, and traumatic relations with other signifiers.

Lacan (1961) is close to the notion of servitude since that which constitutes "subjection" in language is precisely the enslavement to a signifier. This signifier not only "nominates" but directs its "materiality" towards a "gesture," which "is not even enough to designate what is named in the indicated object" (p. 181). Due to the untimely situation of language, the subject is subordinated to an oppressive signification, anchored to a quasi-one-dimensional signification centered on managing the servitude of each historical moment.[45] In parallel and with categorical force, submitting to the desire of the Other and the hegemonic function of the latter as the symbolic system of culture entails a political and moral linkage. Lacan saw in language the capacity for structuring and dominating the subject, as did Étienne de La Boétie (1574), who was already aware of the scope of "tyranny" and "habit" since they have more "power than nature" (p. 22). When the relation of the signifier is introduced with the master's insistence and his symbolic ordering of the subject's life, the subject is an animal constrained by the chains and gears of the signifier from which he cannot escape and cannot go beyond it.[46]

According to Lacan, the subject is a servant of language, which has captured, divided, and alienated him. He is prey to a suspected universal discourse closed and calculated in the master's exploitative articulation. In such a way that "reference to the experience of the community as the substance of this discourse resolves nothing. For this experience takes on its essential dimension in the tradition established by this discourse." It is in "this tradition, long before the drama of history is inscribed in it," where the "elementary structures of culture" are founded. In fact, "these very structures display an ordering of exchanges which, even if unconscious, is inconceivable apart from the permutations authorized by language" (Lacan, 1957a, p. 414). The structures, despite the unashamed claim of the students of 1968, not only go down to the street but allow the signifier to fuse with a mode of existence that makes the signifier the unrecognizable and inciting master. From economics and politics, the "master-slave duality," Lacan (1955–1956) says, "is generalized within each participant in our society" (08.02.56, p. 132).

The existence of language as a mode before nature, recognized from Mauss' and Lévi-Strauss' ideas, can be prescribed from a dual function of culture and, at its core, is a reproductive opposition of the repetitive history of the master's discourse. Culture, as the unshakable basis of the Umwelt, can only be diluted among the diverse spectra of signification that the signifier allows. With the above, it is worth asking, against the grain, what does the instance of the letter reveal to us? What is its call? Lacan recognizes, through the letter and the summoning structure, an "ethnographic duality of nature and culture" which "is giving way to a ternary conception of the human condition—nature, society, and culture—the last term of which may well be reduced to language, that is, to what essentially distinguishes human society from natural societies" (Lacan, 1957a, p. 414).

This latter confirms the opposition between nature and culture and the tertiary management blurred in the cut of society through the signifier. Language is that uncomfortable bug, making it conceivable to discuss managed human societies and not natural animal societies. The problem of structure persists in a differential mode, even in "the leaf," which "has the structural features of the plant from which it has been detached" (Lacan, 1958b, p. 519). Despite the language, life is an intricacy of the offshoot—of the rest and reproduction. That question is inherent to the *zoon* and the *logos* before the *zoon politikon.* [47] Basically, behind language, there is the life of the drive, that of the "plant" that "enjoys" (Lacan, 1974a, p. 22). The same emerges there in a similar way as *l'hommelette* [*Manlet*], "the egg" that becomes "Man," or the group of eggs, as a "lamella" whose body sustains libidinal energy and that can be opposed, in a mythical figure, to castration as the clan of homosexual siblings as will be seen at the end of the volume (Lacan, 1960c, pp. 717–718).[48]

To conclude this distinction partially, Lacan (1957a) throws an accurate dart at the singular and vitalist illusion of the speaker-being [*parlêtre*]: "I shall neither take sides here nor take this as a point of departure, leaving to their obscurity the original relations between the signifier and labor" (p. 414). Indeed, the signifier is a dead labor (not work), a structured modality of human activity conveyed in the transformation of nature. It will be, in parallel, a necessary condition for that signifier to move, to fly, and be stolen. The structure of the signifier has the omnipotent characteristic of being indestructible as long as it presents itself in the flattest conditions and transmutes, with its commodified work, into other signifiers. However, this will be reviewed later around this little *clin d'oeil* of Marxian blow that will focus on the mobilization-circulation of labor in knowledge whose function can only be thought of from the phenomenon of the machinery of the signifier that finds the social order.

One of the most exceptional arguments for our study of society in Lacan is the following:

> What distinguishes a society grounded in language from an animal society, which even the ethnological standpoint allows us to see—namely, the fact that the exchange that characterizes such a society has other foundations than needs (even if it satisfies them), specifically, what has been called the gift "as total social fact"—can then be taken much further, so far as to constitute an objection to defining this society as a collection of individuals, since the immixing of subjects makes it a group with a very different structure.
>
> (Lacan, 1955, p. 346)

That is to say, the basis of society arises in exchange for the perversion and redirection of need as an incentive to desire. The mechanical, incisive, and demanding operative structure is not content with simple exchange; on the contrary, it is based on a beyond, a surplus of which it is possible to be already aware because the subject works for the surplus of knowledge that takes the form of exchange in a signification based on the fictitious dispersion of the useful. The fatuous and the necessary are differentials where the excess of pleasure increases, from the limits of society as an efficient signifier, a specific commercial glitter, to the opaque master signifier imprisoned in its mercantile little world. An immixtion that seated the "*tempo*" of "progress" in "our world" due to "science in the modern sense" (Lacan, 1966c, p. 726). While science dictates a "unifying unity" amid the *méconnaissence* of significance and relational intersubjectivity, Lacan insists on a "countable unity" in whose "repetition" the movement inscribes in a new way the "one" not without the "three" included in the immixtion itself (Lacan, 1966d, p. 190).

Lacan discussed the disparity between animal society and human society from the fading imposed by language and, more specifically, as one signifier among many others that serve the discourse of the master signifier. Regardless, he later offers a definition of society beyond the signifier, focusing on its structuring form. It is the signifier society that intrudes into culture and not vice versa. Society, like any signifier, is invariably susceptible to enchainment and circumscription. Following Saussure (1916), "the signifier" in its relation to "the signified" is "arbitrary." The imposture of the signifier society and its intertwining in the symbolic universe exhibits strongly that arbitrariness, as Saussure taught, is not a free "choice" of the "speaker" (pp. 68–69).

There is, of course, a singular and nebulous liaison of the signifier with the signified for the world of the subject. However, for Lacan, the articulatory capacity and the reach of the signifier involve the whole process of imaginary signification. That is to say, from his perspective, the signifier has a substantial and binding value when it is joined to another signifier since, in his words, "experience proves it: the more the signifier signifies nothing, the more indestructible it is" (Lacan, 1955–1956, 11.04.56, p. 185). So, a signifier as volatile, wily, elusive, and yet effective as the signifier society would, by its symbolic disposition, be indestructible, positive, lucrative, and standardizing.[49] As Lacan (1955–1956) announced: "There is indeed a relationship between meaning and the signifier; it is what the structure of discourse supplies," and there materializes a "signifying temporal chain" (15.02.56, p. 155).

This leads us to the essential need to reflect on the transcendence of language and its signifiers in a substantial way, its ordering effects, and its indestructible selfhood and character as a gear of signification. In other words, it is to take to its ultimate consequences the representation of a signifier for another signifier and not to think of it as one more allegory among many. In the interior of the signifier society, there is a disposition of articulation of the representation in the social horizon of the subject, not the subject as such, since the latter is, in the last instance, a partially indeterminate and caused association.[50]

To discuss the essence of the signifier for Lacan emerges *hic et nunc* as a possibility of referring to society as a cardinal signifier for existence. This reveals its weight and potency from its relation of representation with other signifiers, such as the already classic Lacanian expression verses. In parallel with the exploration of the signifier logic, Lacan (1955–1966) pointed out:

> It is, of course, easy to criticize what may be arbitrary or fleeting in the use of a notion like that of society. [...] It is not so very long ago that this word was invented, and it is amusing to see what dead ends result in the real from the notion that the society is responsible for what happens to the individual—a notion the requirement for which was ultimately expressed in socialist constructions.
>
> (11.04.56, p. 186)

From a critique of the idea of nation, Lacan argues that the signifier deploys a social requirement at the symbolic level that gives supremacy to the signifier to order the phenomena in society, to alienate them to a functional and utilitarian reality. Speculating about the signifier society as the forced structural unity of the subject in its *Umwelt* and its relations, positions from the outset, an order of hierarchization, a rule and the status of language itself, of life, subjected to a sense.[51]

Society as a signifier for Lacan first appears as a resonance of the intersignifying nexus, a trajectory along which this signifier is paraded with so many others. In other words, a primordial signifier entwined with yet another signifier within the treasury of signifiers bestowed and supported by the symbolic order of the big Other. The chained singularity of the signifier thus introduces an elemental negativity. This relation, so evident and therefore indestructible, supposes the introduction of society into a world of signifiers, which is organized in a primitive way by the transmutation of the driving force by a small death caused by the signifier. Society, as a signifier, is omnipotent, and its firmness is consolidated in a particular stabilizing impediment to escape from it, to dissociate it from its appellative function in the organization and political administration of nations and in the (un)confessed love that modernity and the Nation State have given to the support of a socialized reality.

Lacan (1955–1956) also says that "there is in effect something radically arbitrary in the emergence of the notion of society—I am not saying of the city." Its capricious character lies in the assumption that "the nation," the founding "goddess of population," whose lap "presides over births," is nothing more than a signifier that does not follow the Greek horizontality of the *Polis* but the verticality of the Roman juridical *Civitas*; in more exact words, "the modern idea of the nation is not even on the horizon of classical thought, and it is not merely the fortunes of a word that demonstrate this to us" (11.04.56, p. 186).

What does Lacan propose with all this? First, to ubicate that in the society positioned as a signifier, there is not something implicit or natural that is found in the order of the real; the latter is something that seeks to exclude the signifying machinery. The chained signifier hierarchizes and fixes the directionality of the succession of elements; it nourishes the signifier by its capacity to signify what is not there —a lack. Ultimately, the order of the signifiers, giving a specific imaginary solidity, states that society means *always-already* one of the most polished degrees of alienation by the historical-social conditions assigned in a given society in its structure by way of the signifiers. In other words, if society appears as just another signifier, it is also constituted in an alienated mode within each subject and in the modes of political organization of its reality. However, it represents nothing more than the organizational determination of subjects to the order of signification. Society is a signifier that traces the management of death by representing the drive.

Lacan (1955–1956) describes the "subjective" as that which is embedded in the "real" because it allows the subject to "deceive" themself and thus create a meaning, alienation of the ideals of representation (11.04.56, p. 186). Therein lies the deceptive potentiality of the signifier that is circumscribed to a general understanding of something, which is nothing but a conscious enunciated, instituted, and fictionalized. The *res publica* has knelt before the *res cogitans* of individual signification because of a common end realizable in civil society.[52] Lacan determines in this a founding idyll of the whole psychologizing dogmatism by which the subject and his psyche can only be servants of an ideology, of the common good exploited and realized by the master, under the rainbow (or auspices) of human rights in modern societies. These elements condense, as a general rule, the quilting points [*point de capiton*] where the "signifying unity" produces a "circle [*boucle bouclée*]" constituted by various signifying "elements" (06.06.56, p. 263).

Lacan (1955–1956) is decisive when he observes,

> One is free to conclude from this that doubt can be cast on the notion of society. But it is precisely insofar as we are able to cast doubt upon it that it is a signifier. It is also for this reason that it has entered our social reality like the prow of a ship, like a ploughshare.
>
> (11.04.56, p. 186)

By doubting society, Lacan reveals that it is only a signifier, an element sordidly represented in the world and its political categories. The metaphor used by Lacan qualifies the introduction of the real, its overwhelming and destabilizing force, subjected to the condition of pretended universality that incites the symbolic to make its mark on the real, like the plow on the earth. In this sense, it would not be adventurous to state that society exists because it is erected by a furrow of mechanical signification in the real world. We need only refer to the idea that the signifier will always keep something unknown as a whole in its chain, but this is enough to affect the uneasiness of the subject's cultural existence and its socially organized political disposition.

If society is one more powerful and almost indestructible signifier, it is valuable to ask: What is instituted and reproduced there? With petulant eyes and at the drop of a hat, one can invoke effective communication, the social and repetitive illusions of communicative significance that come from it and require a point of union between subjects.[53] In this way, it is possible to understand a unifying concept of society, its relations, and its bonds, which are more or less in conformity with particular sociological perspectives. Nevertheless, if society is defined in this way, with this *totalitarian* and *immovable* link coming from signification, society would be observed, from Lacan's theory, with a particular myopia. Because as Lacan (1955–1966) himself describes, "I sustain him, but there remains something completely uncertain and problematic in this fundamental communication, which is the announcement, not to say the annunciation. The *I* is fleeting in nature and never entirely sustains the *thou*" (20.06.56, p. 287).

It is precisely there, in the relational uncertainty, where we find an *impasse* in the communicative and social exchange that reminds us precisely of the random content of the signifier. As Lacan (1955–1956) reaffirms, "experience proves it—the more the signifier signifies nothing, the more indestructible it is" (11.04.56, p. 185). In other words, the structure on which the intersubjective signification of society is supported is a mirage of human communication that is pretentiously effective and limpid. From this, the rationalization of a particular possibility of forming a link with the other, when the similar and the self are not able to distinguish the strong chains that subject them to social signification, makes the subjects blindly believe in a *genuine* intersubjective relationship through the significance and adequacy of a mirror's reality.

Therefore, following Lacan (1955–1956), "there is no other scientific definition of subjectivity than one that proceeds from the possibility of handling the signifier for purely signifying, not significant ends, that is, expressing no direct relation" (11.04.56, p. 189). The above intensely questions the widespread idea by which society is compelled as a univocal, universal, or merely relational signification. That is, as a determinate rapport between subjects. However, in Lacan's thought, the relation is functional and fictional since it is the signifiers and not the related subjects.[54] The structure arranges the social relations and not the perverse beliefs by which it is pretended to know, tame, channel, domesticate, subdue, deceive, and settle the founding lack of the link with the other.[55]

Let us clarify the idea of structure and the reason for its enunciation here. As is generally known, structure refers in its ontogenetic sense to a question close to architecture and assembly, to a retroactive and suturing effect. History, however, recalls that it was Saussure and, sometime later, Jakobson who began to develop a fundamental theoretical turn by giving primordial importance to language and its designs. Lacan, sometimes unacknowledged heir of structuralism, took structure to its limits and opportunely distanced himself from the structural charm that would have deeply curtailed his topological theorizing. From his well-known phrase: The unconscious is structured like a language to his anti-philosophical reading of Hegel, and Lacan took advantage of a *sui-generis* structuralism thanks to Marx's influence, as he acknowledges in his *Seminar VI* on desire. With the above and as reviewed, the structural anthropology traced by Claude Lévi-Strauss was also of utmost importance within Lacan's thought, but it was not his only transcendental reference to structuralism. Indeed, the strength of structuralism in Lacan is undeniable as it allowed him to nest in language and broaden the spectrum of unconscious phenomena and psychoanalysis.

Structure can only be oriented and erected in terms of inter-significant relations.[56] In other words, the structure orders, stages, and sets up the parameters and values of existence in the medium of the articulated linguistic sign. Articulating signifying elements designates the structural support and is a summons, a demand. In Lacan's (1956–1957) words, it is a demand by which "the structure of speech implies in the Other that the subject receives his message in an inverted form" (06.02.57, p. 174). Moreover, a structure *speaks* by the relations and circulation of its elements in the language (signifier-signified); therefore, structurally combined elements result in axes of direction for the social organization of sense. Consequently, society speaks and creates a retroactive message that directs sense repetition in socialized human practices.

What is defined in terms of articulation of elements of language and their combinatorics alludes to Lacan's idea about the inversion of the signifier over the signified, adding a logical possibility in its relation and its ensemble. As Lacan (1960b) explains,

> I accept the category 'set' with which he introduces it, insofar as it avoids the implications of totality or purifies them. But this does not mean that its elements are neither isolated nor summable [...] —at least, if we are looking, in the notion of set, for some guarantee of the rigor it has in mathematical theory.
>
> (pp. 543–544)

In its synchrony and determination of linear significance, "the signifying structure" is a "metaphor" in whose "return" it takes "value" (Lacan, 1970a, p. 398).

There is a possibility of exchange between the components in the structure, but such combinatorics will have to deal with the conjuncture of the formation of sets. It could be thought that these relations are handled randomly as if they posed a form of encounter.[57] The subject and his desire are, consequently, amalgamated into that structural dimension, which, although it seems closed, is contingent at the same time. In its logical sense, the subject is "in intersubjective relationships," and "this dimension, which is that of desire, is found in a relation of interaction and exchange with everything that crystallizes on that basis in social structure" from his desire and the compulsion to repetition (Lacan, 1958–1959, 01.07.59, p. 483). Consequently, the "social structure" will always highlight the "exchange" and the circulation of subjects in the function of the reproduction of an alienated position of their existence in the world through the "inter-signifying relation" (Lacan, 1964–1965, 06.01.65). Furthermore, this circulation and its *logos* begin "in our era" around "what sort of gap it represents and at what distance it is situated for a certain social *inertia*" (Lacan, 1958–1959, 01.07.59, p. 483).

Language, at the level of structure, is treated by Lacan as a materialistic and aleatory event. Regardless, it can be directed across the demands of the structure and its founding void partially filled with objects. At this point, the structure cannot be separated from randomness and from the encounter at the moment of being concretized in a historical condition.[58] Lacan detaches himself from the notion of totality and the univocal sense of the social. Thus, the structure can be read from the deadlock of signification and tends towards an open universe. Society is first a signifier and then a signifying structure since it is related to other active signifiers and forms an articulation supported by discourse and its ordering. Society as a signifying structure is a consistent and multiple signifier machine whose symbolic gearing sets the signifying circulation and convenes discourses in motion.[59] The vicissitudes of this overdetermined machine, of course, will always be conditioned to the unexpected but effective fate of its linkage, which cannot emerge autonomously but is guided by the enjoying insistence of signification and of the Other.

Lacan tried to redesign the Freudian idea of sexuality from the keys of pure contingency. To do so, he uses the relations between the signifiers that appear within the interactions of individuals in a jouissance machine and their overdetermination. As observed, according to Lacan's gaze at this historical moment, the insertion of the Oedipus complex allows the insertion of a signifier, an empty signifier that ends up structuring desire and lack in the subjects. The Oedipus complex inserts the signifier structure of society into the subjects' interior. Lacan (1956–1957) goes further and comments:

> The deep complexity of men's relationships with women emanates precisely from what we could call in our coarse language the resistance of male subjects effectively to admitting that female subjects are truly not endowed with something, and all the more so given that they are endowed with something else. [...] It is literally on this level that a

> misrecognition takes root which is often maintained with a tenacity that influences the subject's entire world-conception and especially his conception of social relationships.
>
> (03.04.57, p. 265)

Lacan argues that the first relational sequel of the subject is a chained signifier. Properly speaking, an unknown signifier and master by which not only the woman but the man also find themselves reduced to an alienating void and retroactively borne in a signifying structure. It is the lack, the lack of being, that condescends to an attempt to complete with a phallic object, not reducible only to the penis, the ontological impossibility of being.[60] In its unmeasurable inquiry, destiny is none other than the incitement of the enjoying apparatus to function structurally in the signifying circuit of that same partialized object.

Two matters can be inferred from the above. The first one is that sexuality is not limited or extended to a merely corporeal concept but is cut within the symbolic order of culture. Thus, sexuality is partially handed over to the autonomy of the signifier that has remained hidden in the unconscious. In this way, men and women are subject to and exposed to the dialectical conditions of the unconscious and its transindividual signifiers.[61] This constitutes an effort at the universal formalization of their inscription in the machinery of the signifier and its contingent aspects. The second one reveals the signifier society as the master signifier that affirms the internalized signifying structure of the already abstract relations of sexual exchange. That is to say, the master signifier provides a symbolic base in which the social relations of the sexed subjects can be implanted.

Lacan (1957–1958) notes this circumstance in the following way:

> What we observe, effectively, in the dialectic of the child's entry into the system of signifiers is in some ways the other side of the woman's passage as signifying object into what we can call the "social dialectic," in quotation marks, for the entire accent has to be placed here on the dependence of the social with respect to the signifying and combinatory structure.
>
> (12.03.58, p. 268)

The dialectical sense is the insertion of the signifier into the subjects' inner (*res cogitans*), placing the notion of society on the side of one more structuring function for the subject within his social world of signifierized signifiers. On the side of the big Other, the significance and the imprint of the values and vicissitudes of the social relation are deposited, depending on the profile the signifiers take via signification within the structure. As we have pointed out, this is a fact that is never fixed and refers to the structure's arbitrariness and flexibility.

The alignment of the social structure is a contingent signifying dimension responding to the distinction made by each subject singularly before the demand of the Other. In this respect, language is a system open to the structuring emergence of the culture in the subject that is not entirely global and has reminiscences in the subject's trans-individuality. Society should be understood as an open, changing, contingent structure, despite the efforts of the big Other to determine it, in clear words, as a partially organized and covariant set.[62] As a signifying structure, society is not an isolated state but an arbitrary and fictitious gear through which each subject's signification and repressive sense are forced to contain their desire.

Lacan (1957–1958), advancing in these stages, indicates:

> The signifier plays a part since we encounter this signifier every step of the way. We have encountered it from the outset since man would not enter into culture—or rather into society if we distinguish between culture and society, but it is the same thing—if the relationship to the signifier were not there at the origin.
>
> (26.03.58, p. 298)

From this point of view, it is only viable to understand a subject within the scope and origin of the signifier. For this reason, social relations, intersected by the signifier, will be modulated through a signifier connected to other signifiers. The fact is that being represented by a signifier, a subject does not respond univocally to an individual body but also to a social body, to a collective, or a group, as Lacan (1957–1958) describes it around the original group par excellence:

> What makes it possible for the subject to become aware of this Other, the locus of speech, as itself symbolized. [...] the system of the familial Oedipal triangle comprises something more radical than anything that this social experiment of the family gives us [...] the dead father, the father as the vehicle of a signifier.
>
> (18.06.58, pp. 437–438)

Lacan also traces here the archaic insertion of the Other as a field, which allows the subject to be symbolized but simultaneously feeds for the efficacy and oppression of the social structure. If something can exist within the social framework for Lacan, it is precisely the socialized position of the Oedipus complex, which designates the insertion of a structuring social signifier from the place of the organization of the Other. It is here where the family appears already in the exploitative demand of the Other as a degraded cultural system in its designations and ordering social distribution. This brings us back to the notion of signifying structure, from the family and society as such also become the signifying, structuring, social, and organizational mode capable of articulating the subject in the dialectic of the Other's desire. Because of this primitive demand, the family, as the first social gear, is responsible for building and stabilizing complexes with a profoundly social and regulating pleasure consistency.

The position of the signifier and its structure is essential to society in its structuring function as it delimits the dispositions of the enjoyment machine of the cultural system in its redundantly mechanical and repetitive parts. The restrictive structuring via the signifier society always refers to the Other, who demands the repression of pleasure, removing it entirely from a conscious position and giving way to the mechanics of imperative enjoyment. In conclusion, what is frankly transcendent of the signifier and its articulation is the possibility of the Other to insert itself within the subject and mobilize his desire through the partiality of objects. For this reason, society will be shaped as a utilitarian and signifying representative of the Other, which will mold the subject's activity inserted within a culture degraded by the action of the social structure in which the subject is inserted.

Notes

1 Five letters—unknown until then—from Lacan to Kojève have recently been published. Their contents recover several singularities of their relationship, which, undoubtedly, were decisive in the trajectory Lacan took in his teaching. See Luchelli (2016).

2 As Marini (1992) mentions: "Lacan returned to Freud but this return was a re-reading in relation with contemporary philosophy, linguistics, ethnology, cybernetics, and topology" (p. 122).

3 It is curious that "Saussure used the term 'structure' only three times in his *Course on General Linguistics*. Later, the Prague school (Trubetzkoy and Jakobson) generalized the use of the terms 'structure' and 'structuralism'" (Dosse, 1997, p. xxii).

4 For Flower McCanell (1986), there are "destabilizing forces [...] for example, diachrony, or temporal existence, which [have] variable force in different kinds of societies" (p. 122). As a consequence, we can infer that a synchronic and metaphorical form of the signifier directs the normative world

5 In fact, for Chiara Bottici (2014), the imaginary becomes the first "structure" of social life because the individual is "captivated" by the imaginary (p. 37). Obviously, the trouble is that the imaginary is *always already* an illusory fragmentation.

6 Frosh (2013) has suggested that in this "alienation," the "'subject' is turned into an "'object'" such that "gaze ensures that nothing that happens can be reduced to the status of an ordinary relationship" (p. 71).

7 This first alienation confers the keys to "the taboo of personal isolation," which Freud (1918)—inspired by Crawley—proposed as the ground of the "narcissism of minor differences," where the first elements of "hostility" against the "fellowship" would be founded and where the totalized image of the object points towards a singular possibility of intersubjective linkages (p. 199).

8 Alemán (2021) notes that it is elementary "to see who or what figure of the Other symbolically sanctions that image, which tells the child: Yes, you are that"—complexing the subject's ideological determination (p. 51).

9 According to Stavrakakis (1999) "If the imaginary representation of ourselves, the mirror image, is incapable of providing us with a stable identity, the only option left for acquiring one seems to be the field of linguistic representation, the symbolic register" (p. 17). However, both identifications are destined to fail.
10 Neil (2018) argues that in the imaginary register, there is a "misrecognition [*méconnaissance*]" of some "external model" and this whole false scenario can only be confronted retroactively (p. 72).
11 To amplify the difference between alienation [*Entfremdung*] and alienation as a subjective division [*Entäusserung*] crucial for the homology between Marx and psychoanalysis, see Pavón-Cuéllar (2019, p. 278).
12 In Pavón-Cuéllar's (2010) opinion, "it seems that the thirties are the time when society has the greatest importance in Lacan's thought. From that moment on, thought focuses on the individual outside of society" (§ 2).
13 On alienation and perversion, see Masud Khan (1987).
14 Copjec (2004) even remarks that "the imaginary relation produces the subject as master of the image" (p. 21). From our perspective, this would mean that he tries to define her/his narcissistic coordinates isolated from collective life.
15 *Cfr*. Castoriadis (1975; 1986).
16 Lacan (1975a) said eloquently that culture [*Civilisation*] is the "cloaca maxima" (p. 60).
17 The emphasis is ours due to the Lacanian insistence on the measure and regularity introduced by thirdness, as we reviewed in the first chapter.
18 Language is itself the oppressive catalyst of the subject. According to Pavón-Cuéllar (2017), "Lacan knows that nothing real is at stake in History and that no historical event can end the symbolic tyranny of language" (p. 75).
19 In Mladen Dolar's (1993) opinion, "the subject can only be liberated from its natural bonds by being tied to the chains of the signifier" (p. 82). In such a way, his entire existence hangs on that which delimits and enunciates him as a subject, not as an individual, due to the force of the signifier over nature.
20 Andreja Zevnik (2016a) argues in this sense that "the barrier the subject experiences at the entry into the society [is] one of desire[s] (what to desire?) translated into the prohibition in the form of law" (p. 223).
21 Roland Barthes (1957) has illustrated that "myth is a type of speech, everything can be a myth provided it is conveyed by a discourse" (p. 107). For this reason, the myth is a "system," so it cannot be detached from the structure. In fact, in "bourgeois society: Myth is depoliticized speech" (p. 142).
22 As Plato (2000) writes in Book VIII of *The Republic*: "the chances are that democracy is the ideal place to find the origin of tyranny, the harshest and most complete slavery arising, I guess, from the most extreme freedom" (p. 277, 564a). We ought to point out that Lacan had read this chapter of *The Republic*.
23 Louis Althusser (1993) pointed out, in concordance with Lacan, that the imaginary "is marked and structured in its dialectic by the very dialectic of the Symbolic Order" (p. 26). In other words, the symbolic dimension is a condition of the historical antagonistic struggle to regulate the mobilizations of desire in society.
24 For Bou Ali (2018), "negativity" operates "in the social order"; in fact, "capitalism" as a historical condition "works precisely by foreclosing this negativity" (p. 31).
25 Horkheimer and Adorno (1987) noted that "language itself endowed what it expressed, the conditions of domination, with the universality it had acquired as the means of intercourse in civil society" (p. 16).
26 As Jean Allouch (2013) remarks, "Lacan," in 1968, "distinguishes man's desire from the desire of the Other," and that is why "the subject leaves an analysis when

he no longer needs the demand of the Other (his demand) to sustain his own desire" (pp. 85–86); a situation that does not free him from the structure but relinquishes his liberty and drive force at the level of social practices.

27 See on technique and labor, Mauss (1924). Likewise, with Marx it was already possible to understand, from his inaugural structuralism, that "social time is different from uniformly flowing natural time; it has different essential characteristics in different phases of history" and, consequently, managed time is one of the keys to the economic functioning of the structure (Wujin, 2006, p. 119).

28 Mauss (1954) states that "societies have progressed in so far as they themselves, their subgroups, and lastly, the individuals in them, have succeeded in stabilizing relationships, giving, receiving, and finally, giving in return" amid the dynamics of "exchange" (pp. 105–106). Stabilizing is here synonymous with regulating the time of giving and mobilizing the given. On the other hand, for Derrida (1992), "time" is essential to understand the "*a priori* synthesis" in the exchange from the Gift. Exchange would consist in "the animation of a neutral and homogeneous time by the desire of the gift and the restitution" (p. 40).

29 Carina Basualdo (2011a) suggests a Lacanian linkage of the Maussian Gift concept with the symbol. More scathingly, she also proposes a differential revaluation of the failed relationship between Lacan and Lévi-Strauss by placing the Maussian Gift as a fundamental element for psychoanalysis (Basualdo, 2011b).

30 For Edith Kurzweil (1996), "Lévi-Strauss correctly connects unconscious components of language with the exchange of women between tribes. And he showed how Lacan, for whom desire itself is said to be a system of signification—a process that binds the signifier and the signified in a sign whose floating relationship (at certain anchorage points) represents the repression of the signified—differs from Saussure" (p. 181).

31 See Lavoie (2012) on Lévi-Strauss' mathematics, society, and human sciences.

32 Miller (1966) poses the term "suture" as a "supplying element" that sets up the "relation of the subject to the chain of its discourse" (p. 39). This means that reality is "sutured" by a liminal element that makes up for the absence left by the signifying articulation.

33 Derrida (2005) thoroughly explores these topics from the mystical dimensions of authority and its impasses on the state and civil law.

34 However, as Kropotkin (1892, p. 50) affirmed, "Bread, it is bread that the Revolution needs!"

35 To Zafiropoulos (2010), Lacan "thanks to Lévi-Strauss, can isolate the existence of a signifier that is in the place of an exception" and from "Freud's theory of the symbolic father—the totem—and Lévi Strauss' theory of the zero symbol, he can see that the totem is the foundation of the 'completely unconscious systems' that constitute the subjective fates of individuals and make them part of a group" (pp. 145–146).

36 Likewise, according to Zafiropoulos (2016), "Lacan, '*l'ancien*,' of 1970, sees in the totemic myth a structuring myth of neurosis, at least in male subjects" (p. 21).

37 Derek Hook (2011) rightly argues that "practices of identification," at a social, political, and cultural level, by their own problematic "inner/outer distinction" revolve around "failure" and "irresolvable" (p. 113)

38 According to Zevnik (2016b): "The problem of institutional law for psychoanalysis is in its origins—the foundations of paternal law are instituted upon the authority of the Freudian myth of the dead father, as are the foundations of institutional law" and "they both derive from traumatic violence—murder—the presence of which cannot be made absent from the field of the social, and indeed the law" (p. 35). See also Zafiropoulos (2017), specifically Chapter I on "The phallus as a crossroads signifier" and "The phallus as signifier last."

39 In the words of Oscar Masotta (1976): "[T]he prohibition of incest" introduces the "forbidden object," which is later "valued by the group" because "the love of the mother has previously valued it, or the father or the others" (p. 38).
40 Samo Tomšič (2016) portentously suggests, with a decisive influence of Koyré, that "the space of linguistic production is curved, decentralized, the structure is disclosed." Consequently, the "material" structure of language is "infinite," but on the same surface, there is a chink of repressive closure of geometrical signification (p. 133).
41 Indelible and essential here are the opening words of Ignatius J. Reilly in *A Confederacy of Dunces* when he reproaches the policeman who stops him: "Is it part of the police department to harass me when this city is a flagrant vice capital of the civilized world? [...] This city is famous for its gamblers, prostitutes, exhibitionists, antichrists, alcoholics, sodomites, drug addicts, fetishists, onanists, pornographers, frauds, jades, litterbugs, and lesbians, all of whom are only too well protected by graft" (Toole, 1980, p. 6).
42 As Colette Soler (2014) mentioned: "[T]he real unconscious of *lalangue* as unknown knowledge, the knowledge acquired is the knowledge of an end to the aspiration to knowledge: the synonym for castration" (p. 77).
43 See in Freud's (1920) manuscript, his comment on the analogy of the society "vital" of "cells," which, in its "multicellular character," constitutes a means for the prolongation of its life and where the "sacrifice" has partly "neutralized" the "death instincts [drives]" of other cells (p. 50). In the same text, Freud recalls that society is "merely hypocritical" in the face of the sexual drive (p. 51). Hypocrisy is one of the most complex repressive effects of a civilization whose shame is on the way to extinction.
44 Adrian Johnston (2006) mentions, in this respect, that "the reason why human nature is (from an analytic perspective) invariably denaturalized is that individuals are submerged in a world of images and signifiers from their earliest beginnings onwards" (p. 34).
45 As Marcuse (1964) noted, the ethical aspect and freedom of the subject in "one-dimensional societies" have been transformed by technique and industrialization, there "merges a pattern of one-dimensional thought and behavior in which ideas, aspirations, and objectives that, by their content, transcend the established universe of discourse and action" (p. 14).
46 On the question of language and its limits in psychoanalysis and Wittgenstein's analytic philosophy, see Dolar (2014) and Hadot (2004).
47 The question of the plant's *jouissance*, from an Aristotelian and Lacanian perspective, is extensively studied by Barbara Cassin (2020); in her words: "Language is an 'offshoot' [*rejet*] of life, and what testifies to this is the relation between *lalangue* and language" (p. 69).
48 To explore more about this neologism, see Pélissier et al. (2002, p. 49).
49 Maurice Merleau-Ponty (1964), Lacan's dear and close friend, has noted since Saussure that "signs do not signify anything, and that each one of them does not so much express a meaning as mark a divergence of meaning between itself and other signs." There, "the unity" of signs in the language "is a unity of coexistence" (p. 39).
50 Pietro Bianchi (2012) comments in parallel, "in the classical Lacan," that "the subject—an unsubstantial void lacking any positive determination—is destined to never find a single signifier able to successfully represent it: the latter being precisely defined by not being something or in other terms, a pure negative difference in respect to another signifier" (p. 115).
51 In order to enlarge an approach to the *Umwelt*, it is appropriate to recall Jakob Von Uexküll's (1934) remarks on it. The *surrounding worlds* [*Umwelt*] refer to a

"perception world" and an "effect world" in which perceptions and acting come into play and where, in the "magical environments [*Umwelt*]," magical thinking can also be confused with experience (p. 42 & p. 119). This idea would explain, to a large extent, the inclination of the first Lacan to give a fundamental status to the *Umwelt* as a function of the encounter of signification with the mythological and then rejected after the "cretinous" feeling that "behaviorism" gave it by reducing it to the ideology of the environment (Lacan, 1971a, p. 18).

52 Samo Tomšič (2019) goes further and even claims that life as *Bios* is nothing but *Zoe* "colonized and transformed by the signifier" (p. 43). For Thomas Hobbes (1651), in this logic, "the law is the public conscience, by which he hath already undertaken to be guided," and every act done "against" that "conscience" is "repugnant to civil society" (p. 214).

53 In this context, for Parker & Pavón-Cuéllar (2021) "People repeat with their words the same things they have been repeating over and over again in their lives [...] Such is how they try to make sense of the way that material and ideological conditions of life are embedded in the unconscious" (p. 75).

54 According to Frederic Jameson (2002) and his Lacanian regard, "the symbolic order has most often science-fictional overtones; language then becomes a strange property inflected by a race of extraterrestrial travellers on the unhappy human animals" (p. 174).

55 Let us not forget that the "signifying chain," in Miller's (1966) words, a "*structure of the structure*," which is "circular and non-reciprocal" (p. 49). Likewise, the "human 'dissatisfaction' (such is Lockean *uneasiness*)" explains the "transparency of interhuman relations" because "the subject-support, element, of the structuring, which only appears as a subject in the real by miscognizing itself in the imaginary as an element in the structuring" (Miller, 1964, p. 99).

56 For Lucien Sebag (1964), "the intelligibility of human facts" is discovered through the structure (p. 12). Also, for Louis Hjelmslev (1957), the "structure" is an "autonomous entity with independent dependencies." It is "used" to "designate, as opposed to a simple combination of elements, a whole formed of interrelated phenomena, such that each one depends on the others and can only be what it is in and through its relationship with them" (p. 100).

57 Here, we understand the "encounter" like the last Althusser's (1978) materialist perspective: "[A]gglomeration of atoms induced, in a chain reaction, by the initial swerve and encounter" (p. 169).

58 See Stalin (1950) about language as a historical and social structure.

59 According to Pavón-Cuéllar (2006), the Lacanian "signifying structure" has a "double promotion." On the one hand, it is "the real set of the structure understood, in the manner of the Prague Circle, as a 'dynamic set' and on the other as a symbolic dynamism of active, relative, multiple and overdetermined signifiers" (p. 27). In effect, from a Lacanian perspective, there is no "social structure" but a "signifying structure" (Pavón-Cuéllar, 2010, p. 5).

60 See Joan Copjec (2016) on the sex as "not a property or predicate of the subject, it ex-propriates the subject from herself, de-sequesters her interiority by linking it to the common" (p. 110).

61 For Gilbert Simondon (1989), "the transindividual does not localize individuals: it makes them coincide; it makes individuals communicate through meanings" (p. 192). See also Guchet (2010) on society and its need for automaticity and inability to generate homeostatic regulation from Simondon's transindividual perspective.

62 As Stavrakakis (2007) explains, Lacan mentions "structure" as a form far removed from "totality" because he thinks of a "set" that escapes any possibility of closure (p. 39).

Chapter 3

Society and Enjoyment

The Stupid Machine

Society as the Hades of Enjoyment

The Lusitanian poet Fernando Pessoa (2010) once wrote that "the impossibility of existing" can be "abdicated by living" (p. 33). These words could be immediately applied to the untimely articulation of language and culture in the subject's trajectory through the world and its possible working through [*Durcharbeiten*]. Language is that contagious virus from which it is inconceivable to escape once inside. A symbolic bug attached to the body and to existence whose permanence is perpetual and overlaps even death. At the same time, language, as a support of culture, begets ways of identification and oppression through the closure and partial annihilation of concrete existence. In this way, language—with its politics of speech—represses, adapts, and standardizes the outer and inner subjective life.[1]

The structure is the fabricant of adequacy, social adaptation, and enjoyment. As a hinge, this last condition is undoubtedly singular and portentous, since it goes beyond the chain of signifiers and is arranged in the insistent and repetitive form of enjoyment of the subjects. Amid this structural disposition of the subjects, one can discover how the threads are woven and the gears of the social structure are lubricated with the oil of the *jouissance* substance.

Amid illusion and fantasy knotted in the meaning, Lacan (1957–1958) draws a remarkable clarification around Jean Genet's theatrical work *The Balcony*, in which, according to his words,

> Genet presents us with what, at the level of perversion, gets its name from there, namely what, in explicit language, we can at times of great disorder refer to as the brothel in which we live. Effectively, society cannot be defined in any other way than as a more or less advanced state of degradation of culture.
>
> (05.03.58, p. 248)

Lacan explains a relation that engages the subject with his word and its structure. At first glimpse, the enunciation is an encounter, a symbolized

DOI: 10.4324/9781032673837-4

stumble whose support is now framed in perversion; or, defining it more clearly, think of the social brothel as the abode of the socialized being. Or, in economic-libidinal terms, a managerial *Inferno* of lust. A place where the alloying of a "coin [*monnaie*]" emerges as a "perverted symbol" and manages to "adulterate" through a "fraud" the "natural values" and their "relations" due to the bite of "*Maître* Adam." Its effects, in the "public affaire [*chose publique*]," manage to "swell" with "wealth" the "prince" of the "social body" in order to subsume the rest of the "community" (Lacan, 1965–1966, 19.01.66).

There is an enigmatic aspect to perversion at the level of the social framework. Perversion, as an inversion of the fantasy and with its share of enjoyment, consists a transgression of the law with a slight excess of regulated pleasure. From its singular, mystical, and operative sense, a law is essentially the function and formal arming of a demand, symbolized by the names (surnames) of the father, as Lacan will mention later in his work.[2] This *pére-version* determines the modality and idealization of the modes of enjoyment. That is to say, the instauration of the law, located in the version of the father and his avatars with language, determines in itself a perverse and polymorphous output to the demand of the symbolic law in its social course.

Placed in its own scope, that is to say, perversion as transgression, Lacan observes in the figure of the law a degraded way in consonance with the fictional utilitarian use of the figure of authority, which makes possible the perverse progress of the relationship between subjects, located in this case in the figure of the bishop and faith in Genet's work, or extrapolating hastily, in the figure of the bishop, the duke, and the minister in the Sadian re-reading of *Salò or the 120 Days of Sodom* by the Italian filmmaker Pier Paolo Pasolini.

But what happens in this relationship of cultural degradation? According to Lacan (1957–1958), amid this *social rapport*, there is an "adulterated relationship [...] it is a relationship where everyone has failed, in which nobody finds himself. [...] Despite not being recognized as legitimate, it subsists, at the very least, as something linked to the existence of what one calls order" (05.03.58, p. 248). Cultural degradation sets the social order, its systematization, and the guidelines that deny it, although this does not eliminate social order. As an imprint, the law authorizes its transgressors and transgressions to manifest a specific quasi-universal validation of perverse and phallic enjoyment—this mystifying order demarcates the desire to enjoy.[3]

In other words, the social order is anchored in the figures of the law who try to maintain a relation that fails due to the very sense of repetition. Nevertheless, this insertion of degradation pursues an insistent form of the subjects to continue reproducing the order of the law in terms of the social relations established through the possibility of transgressing the law itself. In this sense, the state of the law is framed in the plane of enjoyment since the law, as such, makes it possible. Likewise, the degradation of culture condescends to a circulating space of *jouissance* via morality and its secular committees. Therefore, the subject who enjoys amid society is the citizen, the bishop, the boss, the president, whoever has accepted the symbolic demand to enjoy. It should be briefly clarified here that the insertion of the word *jouissance* does not refer only to pleasure or the enjoyment of something but to the relation of the law and its transgression; *jouissance* is only locatable in the symbolic directives of the Other due to the lust that the term represents.

Enjoyment, therefore, is in the signifier and its chaining; in consequence of circulation, in its symbolic support, and in its framing of the forbidden assisted through culture and more strictly by its becoming legislated at the social level. Finally, a transgression set within culture also formalizes the inclusion of law and legality as primordial allegories of the State and the master to direct society. Moreover, it is precisely the position of the Other and his *jouissance* that must be enunciated amid means of the word turned into law in order to leave a trace of the limits of enjoyment.[4]

Lacan (1958–1959) remarks that "the dimension of repression and censorship exists [...] this censorship [has] a social origin" (18.03.59, p. 279). Lacan inserts there the register of the law in its symbolic efficacy and mere repressive fictional disposition. With this, Lacan allows himself to enhance the symbolic register that has taken place from the Other and its crossroads between the phantasmatic relations of the subjects; this means placing the repressive purpose of the law concerning all the *mythological dramas* motivated by repression that gives continuity to the *jouissance apparatus* through censorship and repression. The repressive function of the law, which on the one hand is destined to *jouissance* and on the other is not entirely absolute, guarantees the perpetuity of the imaginary and phantasmatic register, liberating the imposing demand of the Other and its symbolic equipment. For this reason, Lacan adjusts the conception of society by indicating that there is no place in society for the satisfaction of desire but rather for *jouissance* from the social demands on desire.

Society is systematized based on prohibitions, repression, and censorship, after which a degraded society can only find, in these impositions, stimulating mechanisms located in and from the Other in his form of master. Society obeys, adapts, and conforms due to these enjoyment mechanisms operating in the subject. These, in turn, subsist by causing surpluses of enjoyment and circulation. The subject, consequently, would be a slave of his fantasy and his perverse enjoyment, a slave of his functional and positive reason within the social demands of the master. It is a partial enjoyment sentenced to the perverse functionality of the symbolic system and its spherical cyclicality.[5]

Lacan (1958–1959) mentions, in the same session of his seminar, "the necessities of the life of a group, or sociological necessities," which "do not exhaustively explain the sort of prohibition from which the dimension of the unconscious arises in human beings" (18.03.59, p. 279). The reference is precise: If something of the unconscious order arises from the Other as an original repressive and thinking imposture through the chaining from the signifier and its social adequacy as a coercive reason. Lacan argues that it is precisely the prohibition that frames the social conditions, beyond the simple needs of the subjects, given that the subjects' necessities are regulated and produced by their social and traumatic relations with the Other. In this way, social necessities are transformed into uncanny objects of desire; they are perverted through the gears of the symbolic system of culture and regulate, using repression, the abrupt insistence of the drive to destabilize the cultural and social order.

In his point of view, Lacan (1958–1959) considers the sociological interpretation of the world to be exhaustive "inadequate," which is why it was necessary for Freud to "invent a primal myth—a pre-social myth, let us not forget, since it is the one that founds society—that [is] described in *Totem and Taboo*" in order to explain how society acts from repression, and that which culture granted as a forced decision in its origin (18.03.59, p. 279). Lacan, nevertheless, suggests that the cultural bases are, from the Freudian perspective, entirely distinct from the social order, given that they are drawn by the adjustment of signifiers and their entanglements within the structure that gives birth to enjoyment. The substantial difference between social degradation and culture is, unequivocally, the perverse tendency of the symbolic system at the social level to enjoy the circulation of objects. This is a question that will consistently arise as a consequence of the subjective uneasiness supported by culture.

Lacan (1958–1959) proposes the progression of desire and uneasiness [discontent] in the following way:

> The question of desire remains at the forefront of the preoccupations of the powers [...] I mean that there has to be some social and collective way of managing desire [...] The point is always to temper a certain discontent, the discontent in civilization, as Freud called it. There is no other discontent in civilization than the discontent of desire.
>
> (03.06.59, p. 412)

Lacan suggests a managed and *unbreakable* association exists between desire, the law of the Other, and its discontents. This interweaves desire and its enjoyment effect as a mobilizer of uneasiness and society as a perverse enterprise destined to regulate to keep the subject's desire in order and under the protection of the law. In this managed substance, uneasiness is given in the conflict between desire and ordinance or, rather, repression, framed within the productivity and governed positivity of desire in society.

In other words, desire as a negative and implanted trajectory of the subject is coupled through enjoyment to a positivity that organizes social life. As Lacan (1958–1959) puts it in his July 1 lesson in connection with the above:

"the relationship" between "culture" and "society" is "provisionally" defined as "a relation of entropy." This gives more clarity to the point of the structural function of the signifier "society" (01.07.59, p. 483), since, according to its structural expression, the signifier society is positioned in a haphazard, never-defined way. But holding and linking the network of signifiers as an entropic relation, there can only be positive and administrative regulation at the social level. It is a place of minute positions that enslave the adequate states of social equilibrium in an irreversible logic. Social entropy always homogenizes and modifies the materiality of the real; paradoxically, it does not diminish but increases rapidly in the homeostatic sense.

Lacan formulates and explains in his *Seminar VI* that society has a problematic entropic relationship with culture framed in a structural field that makes a supposedly balanced social order possible. This chance can postulate to the position of imprisonment of desire in the distinction between society and culture. Entropy is, then, similar to a physical and thermal mechanism that organizes and directs the signifiers within a structure. Thus, society is exposed as the entropy that provides the signifying chain with a reforming constancy, introducing the command and not only disorder as it could be supposed but positioning a combinatorial constant that gives a preponderant place to loss.

Lacan (1958–1959) continues:

> what presents itself in society as culture—and which has thus entered, in various guises, into a certain number of stable conditions, which are also latent, that determine the circuits of exchanges within the flock—establishes a movement or dialectic in society that leaves open there the same gap as the one in which we situate the function of desire.
>
> (01.07.59, p. 483)[6]

This is how Lacan explicates the idea that society expresses a regularized relationship with a culture based on a series of foundations of a standard order in which all subjects follow and perpetuate the possibility of normalization and social resignation-adaptation, maybe even believing in progress as a traumatic ideal. At this point, the sense of a specific adjustment of the subjects' desire through drive sublimation comes into play.

In the same class, Lacan defines "entropy" as an energy that provides constancy to the signifiers of mobility and positioning through signification and adjustment to a circuit. However, this force gives movement to the signifying social machine of subjects in a society. This offers a critical dichotomy: If entropy plays a creative and organizing role in a given social order, then, in the same way, it can be thought of from its very enclaves in a contrary, antagonistic, and disordered position or possibility in the same circular system. The above states a singular approach around a logical order within the subjects' interactions.

Nevertheless, society appears as a logical formation through which culture is degraded by the limitation and regulation of the desire of subjects to institute ordinances at the level of interaction. All this constitutes a particular ideal social order, which, in the same way, is presented as a paradox between forbidding and inciting the transgression of the prohibition. With all this, the *Hades* of the *jouissance* joins the scene since there would be no other possibility than the social condemnation of the subject to live among the extravagant order of society. In this means, entropy introduces the difference that destabilizes the *just measure* of society.

For Lacan, desire represents—like Spinoza—the fundamental key to the human substance in the subjects and their intervention in the social plane. Lacan (1959–1960) punctually takes a position around the supposed "naturalist liberation of desire," which he observes "has failed historically," moving away from *Eudaimonia*. Moreover, he adds: "We do not find ourselves in the presence of a man less weighed down with laws and duties than before the great critical experience of so-called libertine thought" (18.11.59, pp. 3–4). According to Lacan, the comprehension of the social regulation of desire and its vicissitudes is the gap that allows perversion in a social sense. Desire, as such and in terms of its undecidable internal impetus, finds in the perverse trait of the transgression of the law a partially denying mechanism to be transgressive of the ideal social order that is designated from the figures of the State or the hierarchy but that does not transform it at all. In other words, the perverse fantasy of the neurotic would be the place of a perfect scoundrel since he knows how the laws operate and thus moves among them in exchange for some of the joyful crumbs that the social organization allows him to take.

The social functionality caused by the insistence on enjoyment resides in the law as such. While that law is instated in and from the Other, it also provides for the fall and articulation of the object *a*. The viscous oil of the idiot machine is not just ordinary bullshit but a repetition of the structurally asphyxiating sense. This is nothing more than a *jouissance* and problematic surplus in the subject: A *plus-de-jouir* [surplus-enjoyment], resulting from a renouncement of an inadmissible total or eternal enjoyment.[7] It is also the term that Lacan enunciates around the possibilities of surplus value, as will be observed in Chapter 4. Suffice it to say, for the moment, that if the subject encounters a constant and mechanical death drive, it is in order to find in enjoyment a chance to approach its own void, its own lack. The machine and its void direct the four Kantian formalities that delimit morality, politics, religion, and anthropology.

The "most complicated machines," according to Lacan (1954–1955), "are made only with words." This is to say, "the machine is the structure detached from the activity of the subject. The symbolic world is the world of the machine," which is demarcated through "exchange" and the "circulation of the word." The turn forced from the machine suggests a difference between "symbolic intersubjectivity" and "cosmic intersubjectivity," a question that decenters the subject and the phenomenon of consciousness through the real into the syntax (08.12.54, p. 47). In that first term Lacan (1954–1955) suggests: "the sole object of desire which we can presume of a machine is therefore its source of nourishment." It is noteworthy that Lacan conceives from this moment that the object that feeds the machine is the object of desire. Thus, "consciousness" is nothing other than the form of the "order" that controls "the ballet of the machines" (15.12.54, pp. 54–55).[8] Pleasure and displeasure are delimited in a surplus that is tuned and dispensed through the signifying machinery.

Therefore, the body is not a machine but a substance that will depend on the autonomous machinery of the treasury of signifiers managed by the dominant juridical-political structure. Lacan engages the idea of cybernetics to explain how desire has already enrolled a sense, a syntactic link, in the very dimension of the real and concrete. It is the "procession of numbers" that "engages" the subject to link itself to the "symbolic order," hence the drive ends up being a numerical constant. A "relation of non-being to being" through which "the repressed is always there, insisting and demanding to be" through social practices managed in time, space, and movement (22.06.55, p. 307–308).[9]

As is well known, what Lacan frames from Marx is, among other things, the effect of renouncing enjoyment at the center of the demands of the signifying machinery. In Lacan's (1968–1969) words, the *plus-de-jouir*, "a function of this renunciation under the effect of discourse[,] is what gives its place to the object *a*" (13.11.68, p. 17). It is there where the subject renounces the possibility of reworking the law that the machinery of the signifier is demanded. What happens in the relation between the subject and the renunciation of *jouissance* seems destined, based on the gearing of the Other, to designate an incisively compulsive effect congregated through discourse, a discourse clogged with repetitive knowledge.

In order to understand this renouncement, this surplus is an effect of discourse, and in terms of the knowledge market, it is helpful to take as an example the function of the valorization of labor. Since exploitation is inscribed in the social modes of circulation of commodities, the compulsive mobilization of the surplus is explained as a substantial renunciation of enjoyment on the part of the subject. However, what is obtained as profit by renouncing the original enjoyment is precisely the surplus profit of the object *a*, a plus granted by the Other for having established itself as a social function in exchangeable labor.

This function also explains the uneasiness in culture due to the effect of the social demand for the commodification of labor in the structure determined amid the symbolic system of culture. If anything can generate uneasiness, it is precisely the result of what is produced by a social demand centered on exchange value. Nevertheless, in the example of labor, there is a symbolic payment, essentially speaking, that is to say a materialized signifier: Money.[10] Roughly, surplus value is that surplus earned by the capitalist from the exploitation of the concrete labor force of the worker; abstractedly conveyed, it is an economic dynamic of regulation of pleasure in function of circularity. It is not in vain that Lacan called this *Mehrlust*, the gain of pleasure and displeasure, taking Marx's *Mehrwert* (surplus value).[11]

For Lacan, the *plus-de-jouir* [surplus-enjoyment] is that which the subject gets from the cultural renunciation demanded by the social order to his primitive enjoyment that can only be understood through the circulation of the market of knowledge and from the signifying logic as a guarantee of the phantasmatic support and its articulation with power.[12] Labor, as an abstract means of exploitation of the productive force for the subjects, is entirely different from knowledge, for it is the knowledge that condemns the subject to receive only a part of what he produces, a small object that is interchangeable within the discourse of capitalism.

The difference between enjoyment and surplus-enjoyment underlines value circulation modes through the exploitative capital structure. In capitalist societies, enjoyment is the mutant substance across means by which utilitarian Hades is assembled, the mythological place with its most pointed substrate in the enjoyment of commercialization of neighbor love and the staunchly compulsive and syntactic social regularity of logical order. To enjoy the neighbor is to endorse a paradisiacal place, albeit inhibited or impotent, where all subjects enjoy the same knowledge of the master. Even when the capital imperative is "enjoyment," the subject masks himself in a restrictive social function in order to guarantee his particular enjoyment and corrupt the enjoyment of his neighbor.

From Lacan's (1959–1960) perspective, this is "the right to enjoy any other person whatsoever as the instrument of our pleasure" at the level of "social exchanges" (23.12.59, p. 98). Thus, the renunciation of an initial cultural enjoyment is made to subsist in the world and expands the perpetuity of an alienated enjoyment, in the broad and Marxian sense of the term, by which society and its subjects enjoy the external administration of bodily pleasure already confined to the demanding directives of the Other through its objects.

The subject is demanded to enjoy the forbidden tree. In this form, the historical-political nature of the capitalist economy fully recognizes how unfailing it is to have a mythical tree as the guarantor of enjoyment. Instead of letting the subject plant an apple tree, it is placed at the mercy of mercantile exchange, and its poisoned apples (whose surface constitutes the small objects to which they cause desire) are of regulated enjoyment. That apple tree, perhaps distributed by *The United Fruit Company*, exchanges the loss arising from symbolic castration for apples filled with enjoyable ideological nectar. The road of international distribution for this purpose is language and its discursive avatars. The social order includes and excludes, poisoning with its uselessness.

The subject refuses to work with their unconscious precisely because the imperatives of the law and repetition promote the mandate to surplus-enjoyment to include it in a social logic. In the psychoanalytic clinic, in fact, the repetitive mandate even accounts for the ineffable characteristic of repetition and the resistance to detach oneself from the *jouissance* order at the political level with the escape into illness. The political economic system that gives territoriality to a particular ideological Hades also makes the structural logic of the renunciation of the demand categorical. In this way, a social antinomy arises, which is proper to the actions of the subjects in collectivity, given that, although they live condemned to enjoyment, the subjects renounce full and totalitarian enjoyment in order to obtain a passport toward a liberal and individualizing hell.[13] Therein also lies the all-important emptiness of the signifying chain based on castration; the object cause of desire, the object which would consist of exchanging work for the knowledge of the *traveler checks* that allow the purchase of more and more apples.

On the other hand, Lacan also sympathizes with Marx on the use of surplus. The subject, for Lacan, imperatively seeks to plug this lack with the pieces that the Other has left him. Action, desire, and even anxiety are negative values directly opposed to the managerial positivity of the speaking being. Thus, as Lacan (1968–1969) says, "the Other is in the market that totalizes values" (13.11.68, p. 17); its eternalization consists in rendering positive those negative remnants that damage the totalization and distribution of the market of symbolic values. It is then the Other who disposes, administers, and regulates by way of exchange this surplus (dead and drive), as can also be observed in the Marxian theory of use-value and exchange-value. If the big Other is intrinsic in this surplus, it delimits the chances of its appropriation as dead labor and of its acceptance as quantity in circulation as such.

Lacan (1968–1969) suggests that "the Other offers himself to be or not to be refuted" and then delimits "the surplus jouissance" as an element that "constitutes the coherence of the subject as Ego (*moi*)" (13.11.1968, pp. 23–24). What happens then to this Ego (*moi*)? The exchange in the social bond—as discourse—is always conditioned to the position of the Other and the evocation of an enunciation subject. Although the imperative is to enjoy, the insistence of the Other will be taken up as the inclusion of the law, with its dialectic at the level of inscription in the *jouissance* field of knowledge, to which one may or may not be summoned.[14] As such, this may be the summoning of truth, the step paid by the subject to condescend to a *jouissance* economy via the small object *a*. The truth of the subject remains tied to the Other and its law of circulation, which, in a perverse form, nests in the formation of the superegoic or the conglomerate of ideals. Or, in its a-systematic rupture, it condemns to economic and libidinal ostracism the truth forcluded in the psychotic structure.

The enjoyable and idiotic machinery of the system converts the subject into an imaginary redeemer who puts all his psychic energy into the game of society's uneasiness. In this form, the law exerts a forced, stupid, and deafening imperative of the subject to his enjoyment. The machine can only function through its relation between signifiers. For this reason, the signifying machinery is cardinal for elaborating the various modes of enjoyment. It is, in Lacan's words at the beginning of the 1970s, "the necessity of the surplus enjoyment for the mechanism to turn, jouissance only indicating itself there so that one might have it from this effacing, as a hole to fill" (Lacan, 1970b, p. 434). Beyond this, the notion of the machine accompanied Lacan from the first years of his seminars.

In his *Seminar II*, Lacan (1954–1955) notes that "the animal is a jammed machine," that is to say, "it is a machine with certain parameters that are no longer capable of variation" (01.12.54, p. 31). An animal that is crossed through signifiers and thus cannot give space to its drive as a complete force but to the demanding determinations of the symbolic system. In his terms, "the subject sets itself up as operating, as human as *I* (*je*)." In this respect, for "the human subject to appear, it would be necessary for the machine, in the information it gives, to take account of itself, as one unity amongst others. That is precisely the one thing it cannot do," and in this way, the machine itself exists as "an element of a calculation" (Lacan, 1954–1955, 08.12.54, p. 85). Indeed, in bourgeois societies, the dimension of the machine can only be observed as a calculable demand that cannot be dodged. In fact, the question would be to amplify "what could be meant by the *alethes* of machines, of *Alethia*" (Lacan, 1965–1966, 12.01.66). With the latter, the real appears as a horizon of possibility before the insistence of the machines.

This latter idea is an elementary explanation for finding the mode of symptomatic traversal from the determinants of truth, such as adequacy and propulsion of the action of the lethal and its movement toward the impossible within a joyful society. This difference can be detected through Artificial Intelligence, which is nothing other than the hecatomb of the unbridled vice for regulating meaning, commodities, and the capture of *not-all* of society.[15] Where the binarism *1* and the *0* confront the probability and the systematization of the machine, there is only space left for the "society of signifiers" that tries to adjust materiality and reduce it to its mere earthly circulation, even though an imbalance may resurface there (Lacan, 1971b, 13.01.71, p. 18).

The symbolic machine induces modalities of action in the subjects to the extent that its gears, that is to say its values, are oiled. A machine produces work, but the question is the use and exchange of this work. Societies are positioned in the dimension of their work being drilled to knowledge or an imaginary determinism.[16] It is for this reason—and because of topology—that Lacan proposes a "retroactive" course which, from "mathematization," makes use of the "machine" so that the Real redirects the fascination for machinic management (Lacan, 1972a, p. 483). At this point, recall that La Mettrie (1748) attempted to formalize the material appreciation of the body as a machine. However, Lacan (1956–1957) questions this material dimension by suggesting that the problem to which psychoanalysis is dedicated lies in "energetics" and not in control or adequacy (28.11.56, p. 25).[17]

To conclude these ideas about the machine, as a signifying structure and a shaper of enjoyment, we would like to highlight a nodal key to the difference between Lacan and the desiring machines proposed by Deleuze and Guattari (1972) in *Anti-Oedipus*. There, both authors bet on Nietzsche's *On the Genealogy of Morality* instead of Mauss' *Essay on the Gift*. This difference has a remarkable implication: The philosopher's readers of desiring-machines reduce their explanation of societies to the superficial level of "creditor-debtor" relations, which makes them reduce the machinery to its interchangeable bodies and not to the dominations of the structure as such by focusing on the enjoying "debt" and not on loss or lack (p. 225).[18]

On the contrary, Lacan, from his reading of the signifying machine, emphasizes—almost two decades earlier—the signifying structure that installs the frenetic and joyful repetition of the machine, its symbolic surplus, and not the general tensions of a mere relational or corporeal forcing. The signifying machine functions by the very fact of structurally and excessively enjoying the subjects beyond their will. Although the authors recognize the segregating character of the Oedipus complex, reading the social machinery requires exploring and analyzing the dimension of structure, values, and their energetics captured by the signifiers in the symbolic system of culture. In other words, knowing that Oedipus is nomadic and not free from the impasse implied by the infernal machinery of the master society in Thebes and the retroactive direction of the Oedipal enjoyment.

The Law, the Other, and Its Dialectic in Bourgeois Society

The idea of society is intricate in its strictly abstract meaning and responds to the forms taken by the master's discourse at the historical and concrete level. A faithful approach to its genealogical conceptualization immediately refers to the law and its provisions, order, and dominant effect on the community. In itself, the notion of society is untranslatable, in whose etymological meaning it refers to the Latin term *societas*, "association, gathering, community, society," which is conjoined to "*socius*," which represents "an associate, and, [given] its etymology, undoubtedly a companion in war" (Raynaud, 2004, p. 1212).

The difference between the *koinona politike* [political community] of the Greek polis and the *societas civilis* [civil society] of the Roman *cive* can give us an explanation of the distribution/separation between legality and the communal and, above all, the emergence of historical modes of administration of populations and their vicissitudes. Additionally, the notion of civil-bourgeois society in German is called *Bürgerliche Gesellschaft*. This ambiguity between civil society and bourgeois society can be a differential example of the notion of community.[19]

Nonetheless, throughout Western thought, society has been approached from different precepts and with the vicissitudes of economic management movements. Since Thomas Aquinas (1270), the idea of society has been locked in the legal order of the city and the harmonious and stable nature of the majority based on Aristotle's ideas. In the words of Aquinas, "those things which are derived from the law of nature by way of particular determination, belong to the civil law, according as each state decides on what is best for itself" (p. 1022, Q. 95, Art. 4).[20] From this Aristotelian-ecclesiastical spirit, the dimensions of the law and the statute allows embedding a first disposition of the organization in the ancient city and of the turns that the management of the Church, and later of the State and its cities took during the following centuries, as can be observed in the empiricist and liberal invention of Locke and the enlightened and contractual vision of Rousseau. For the former,

> the reason why men enter into society is the preservation of their property; and the end while they choose and authorize a legislative is that there may be laws made, and rules set, as guards and fences to the properties of all the society.
>
> (Locke, 1689, p. 201)

In such a mode, the social and economic-legal pact founds the organizations and the safeguard of the administrative economy, an elementary issue for social reproduction. For the second author, from a contractual perspective, "for society to be peaceful and harmony to be maintained, all citizens, without exception, must be equally good Christians" because "Christian charity does not easily allow us to think badly of our neighbor" (Rousseau, 1792, p. 211). In both positions, from our point of view, two elementary principles of the conformation of society in Lacan converge: a) The principle of property and individualistic and utilitarian legislation and, b) the domination of the rights of man-centered on the neighbor.

On the other hand, the meaning of war is basic because it reveals the most incisive characteristic of the uneasiness legalized among societies or, in other words, the displeasure disguised as a servile companionship of exchange with one's fellow man and the constant war in bourgeois societies. For Lacan (1953–1954), "Every human drama [...] is founded on the existence of established bonds, ties, pacts. Human beings already have commitments which tie them together, commitments which have determined their places, names, their essences" because "if you go to war, it is so as to know which treaty will be binding" (p. 197).

In addition to the well-known Lacanian reference to Carl von Clausewitz in *The Direction of the Treatment and the Principles of Its Power*, Lacan (1958b) recovers the ideas of the German military man to show that, starting from the object *a*, in war, there is a characteristic of "heterogeneous" dye and whose "asymmetry is found to dominate the whole game between offensive and defensive" (Lacan, 1967–1968, 17.01.68). It is finally the act—revolutionary or analytical—that makes the laws and fictions by which social pacts are established to some extent shake up, insofar as the performer's strategy runs in a probabilistic way.[21]

Modern society initiated a positive arrangement over subjects from the State through its laws and institutions. The law can further enlighten Lacan's explanation about law-enjoyment-prohibition in its strict juridical sense. According to Hegel (1807), the society and the State that is organized from individuality and families does not have a "consciousness" and nor an "absolute unity," a matter that makes possible the integration of particular interests within families, which form a "totality" that in terms of its development allows us to understand the association between "State as civil society or as external State" (p. 122).

The State, as a bureaucratic manager, is shaped by the dialectical vision of the family and the totalized social association through laws, their antagonisms, and the effective models of rationalization in public activities.[22] On the contrary, the community would represent negativity from the isolation of the government and its laws and, for this reason, in the function of limiting this isolation and avoiding the "spirit evaporate," the government "has from time to time to shake them to their core by war. By this means the government upsets their established order, and violates their right to independence," aiming that people remember "their lord and master, death" (Hegel, 1807, pp. 272–273). This is how negativity becomes mobilized through the laws of the State in its constant and imperative conflictual expression for the control and permanence of the spirit.

Notwithstanding this bellicose and antagonistic logic, Lacan (1963) recalls, "Only the police have the necessary trucks, and while the police can be the State, as Hegel says, the Law is something else" (p. 660). The law is situated in the modality of a mark that means not only the social order but also the emasculated desire's course and the entailment of a symbolic and problematic conflict confabulated with enjoyment and the phallic adequacy of freedom as liberty. In contrast, if the emancipation of the subject is to be determined, the subject must move away from the simulation of bourgeois law within society.[23] This effect would be of great importance for Lacan since the inversion of the values of social liberty makes the unveiling of truth from the subject possible. Furthermore, above all, as Lacan pointed out, "human rights" succinctly "boil down to the freedom to desire in vain" (Lacan, 1963, p. 661). Freedom could, consequently, move beyond the centralized order and bet on the dimension of the not-all.

As we argued in the previous chapter, for Lacan, society is framed in a field of signifiers as a signifier and, ulteriorly, as a signifying structure. That is to say, a part of it is that which configures a specific structural ordinance in the subjects. Again, we are referring to this in order to suggest law and its closures as fiction—a fiction embedded in language and subjected to the formal sense of society. There are written laws and symbolic inscriptions beyond paper that can be obeyed and complied with to delimit and give property to objects and their social organization. In this sense, we take advantage of Bentham's (1813) classification to integrate "rights" that "are distinguished into natural, moral, and political" (p. 119).

Nevertheless, for Bentham (1813), one cannot refer to "a natural right" because there is "no such natural right to have a place." In other words, "a man is never the better for having such natural right" (p. 119). These conditions cannot be expressed symbolically within the subjects. This digression is necessary to elucidate the worth of the speaking subject and his symbolic and imaginary constructions, which are, as we have seen, signifiers. The aforementioned allows us to understand that the existence of society is intimately united to the construction of law. Lacan (1959–1960) evokes Bentham to highlight the question "at the level of the signifier" and to describe that "institutions" always have a "fictitious" framework, a "fundamentally verbal" matter, whose "search has involved not attempting to reduce to nothing all the multiple, incoherent, contradictory rights," on the contrary,

> observing on the basis of the symbolic artifice of these terms, which are themselves also creators of texts, what there is there that may be used to some purpose, that is to say, become, in effect, the object of a division.
> (11.05.60, p. 275)

Law and its measure, including its symbolic resolutions, are reduced to the circulation of goods and the domain of passions according to their utility.[24]

On the other hand, Lacan (1959–1960) argued that the establishment of the "superego" in Freud's *Totem and Taboo* is "distinguished from pure and simple social necessity" since something has to do with "the relation to the signifier" and "the law of discourse" (18.11.59, pp. 5–6). For Lacan, the constitution of a punitive superego, within the imaginary and symbolic registers of the subject, traces a function coupled with an entirely social utilitarian and domination purpose. That is to say, the superego positions itself as a guarantee of the law, in words, in fiction, in order to insist on the transgression of the adequacy of social practices. In this sense, society operates as the mediator of the subject's repression and as the instigator of transgression. Furthermore, society would be nothing more than an enjoyable mechanism from the signifying structural order that designates the moral and political status of each one of the subjects.

Lacan (1959–1960) uses—in a suggestive mode—the example of the Ten Commandments in the Bible to illustrate the shape of the laws and their strength within society: "The Ten Commandments may be interpreted as intended to prevent the subject from engaging in any form of incest on one condition." We return here to the foundational circumstance of the subjects and to what is truly important in the Oedipal myth. However, this myth could not subsist without the law, without the law of the prohibition of incest.

Curiously, for Lacan himself, this interdiction refers to "the condition *sine qua non* of speech" (16.12.59, pp. 68–69). In this way, we understand that what facilitates the law is an incitement to break it and leave a symbolic trace as an inscription of the automatism of repetition at the level of the fantasy of transgression, mainly in neurosis. "Reality" is expressed through "the commandments" on a powerfully "tyrannical" path (Lacan, 1959–1960, 25.11.59, p. 30).[25] These "ten commandments" constitute the regular "acceptance" of exclusion in the "whole of the civilized community" because of its reproducibility in the social and political hierarchy (Lacan, 1959–1960, 16.12.59, p. 69).[26]

The relationship and the supposed association between subjects in the symbolic world insistently frame the inclusion of a law system here. This also establishes a conditional Other's enjoyment from the alliance of social statutes in the signifying machinery as an axis of mythical knowledge. As fiction, it compels the subject to enjoy and thus continue repeating the foolish sense of the death drive. As Lacan (1959–1960) says: "We spend our time breaking the ten commandments, and that is why society is possible" (16.12.59, p. 69). If we understand here that the law is the cause of a neurotic position in the psychic process of the subjects, we find, in this idea of Lacan, the senseless and pathological game of society and its forbidding states.[27]

The exchange between the law and the subject is degraded in its purpose since society has relied on the renunciation of enjoyment as the remainder of its unfinished structure. Transgression and excess thus make the duo rationalize social practices. This last logic implies that the Other's perverse wager provides subjects with a multiplicity of objects that allow them to cover this lack due to rejecting their enjoyment at the social level. This socialized section of excess that originated in the word and the signifier leads to the effective replicability of the object *a*, properly speaking. Because of the exchange laws, society makes its fiction consistent with its legal and utilitarian modes of truth production.[28]

According to Lacan (1959–1960), "It is only too clear that not only do societies live very well by reference to laws that are far from promoting, their universal application, but even more remarkably [...] societies prosper as a result of the transgression of these maxims" (23.12.59, pp. 77–78). Lacan presents here a distinctness between the nature posited in Kant and a society as such. The most obvious example is found in the argument that society for Lacan is made possible and articulated through the law. Yet, Kant (1785) points towards a restriction and command of the law and thus to be able to amplify the ferocity of the command and law itself in its "categorical" and "objectively necessary" sense (p. 31). If society structures the law through forbidding, it is the prohibition itself that poses its transgression, and it is there that we find enjoyment in its insistent and practical form and a counter-nature of society.

For Lacan, the law places us face to face with our desire; this throws us into the immediate fate of enjoyment. In more straightforward words, the expression of the law is framed as a relation between the subject and their covered desire. Nevertheless, the presence of a maxim as a law instituted within society is made so that the subject has stiffened in the law itself. This essential transgression produces an approach to death, and, in such a way, enjoyment is enunciated as a categorical imperative. Thereupon, the ethical background here arises from the passage of ethics through which Kant is "measured" by the "universal range" in social acts and the rules of systematic adequacy of desire (Lacan, 1967–1968, 17.01.68).

Again, let us return to Kant (1788) when he argues,

> a practical rule is always a product of reason because it prescribes action as a means to an effect [...] this rule is an imperative, that is, a rule indicated by an "ought," which expresses objective necessitation to the action and signifies that if reason completely determined the will, the action would inevitably take place in accordance with this rule.
>
> (p. 18)

From our point of view, the Kantian position enunciates an imperative close to the action proper to the moral and rational condition. Suppose the subject is reduced between good and evil. In that case, the rule of ought-to-be is included within the designs of reason, and with it, society proclaims a fence of the universal in the adjustments of a transcendental mandate: *Enjoy!* An insistent crisis that recalls how "a tyrant is someone who appropriates the power to enslave the Other's desire" (Lacan, 1963, p. 662). This fatal fortune, of course, cannot be possible without the "positivization" of the I in the utilitarian and dramatic "imperative" of modern societies (Lacan, 1966–1967, 11.01.67).

In a genuinely ingenious and seditious tone, Lacan (1963) links Kant with Sade and mentions that "in coming out of the Other's mouth, Sade's maxim is more honest," and one can understand that in this maxim "the discourse of the right to jouissance clearly posits the Other qua free—the Other's freedom—as its enunciating subject" (pp. 649–650). We now find the paradigm of Sade's perspective from the point of view of the one who can give space to the Other and become the punisher, the sadist. What is interesting at this moment is that the subject is in contact with the imperative to enjoy, which is fabricated within the possibility of the moral law, a law that a damaged culture has given. The libertine character expressed in Sade, from most of his writings, is that of the transgressor of the law who is enunciated by the great Other—a subject who, paradoxically, is not limited to the social rules but emerges in a new position before the Other by putting into play his own body in a transgression.[29]

The radical point here is that if the laws have been assembled through the Other's regime and its *jouissance* at the social level, they are being put forward in their possibility of being transgressed at the moment when the Other is having a precise enjoyment in the same way. They amplify the pathology of the objects. The setting up of a social system, to call it in some way, has the outlawing of a subject's splitting as a chance of the complex desire. That same desire is the one that delimits the action of the imperative to enjoy the social norms that the imperative has drawn up. In fact, in the Marquis de Sade's (1795) words, "upon those foundations all the laws repose; they justify the punishments inflicted upon him who abuses his liberty; in the same way, they authorize the imposition of conditions" (p. 409).

Here, we find legalized auspices from the Other's signifiers and socially permissible acts. The design of moral laws is then a coalition of circumstances defined in the imaginary and symbolic registers that introduces the echoes of social corrosion determining the imperfect modes of the ordinance of freedom. From the above, society fabricates a legalized model of "alliance" of subjects that cannot but be predestined to a particular social inflection that, due to freedom, can put in suspense a particular purpose of "society". Beyond this, the effectiveness of moral laws within the culture can also propose and insist on the fantasy perversion of the subject and, therefore, a supposedly libertarian adequacy to the conservatism evoked via the social degradation marked by the imperative to care for one's neighbor is increased.[30] Consequently, there is a complex "analogy" between the "exigency of the liberty of jouissance in Sade, with the universal Kantian rule of behavior" (Lacan, 1961–1962, 28.02.62).

The main animadversion of the moral imperative impinges on the logic posed through the phantasm and its imaginary frames. The law builds the design of utility and happiness partially adapted to the social representation of domination structures. As Lacan (1959–1960) demonstrates, "society takes some comfort from the mirages that moralists, artists, artisans, designers of dresses and hats, and the creators of imaginary forms in general supply it with" (13.01.60, p. 99). These imaginary statutes admit the launch of prohibitions by the mark of the signifier, and with it, there is an insistence on distorting the forms of coexisting in society.[31] There is a forbidding outline so that enjoyment can be announced in the social development of the subjects and their driving force of work be disposed.

The perversion offered from the Other's surface will always have to find refuge in discourse to enable its existence and the subject's adaptation to its desire. At the same time, it needs devices and cuts where transgressive enjoyment can never be absolute, inciting the enjoyment of desire in itself. In this way, the subject in its social sphere is subsumed in obeying the categorical conveniences of morality or moving towards giving an account of the desiring path in its ontological-social certitude. Of course, in society, as we have observed, man is a sacrificial animal and trades his sacrifice, sometimes even imploring modes of domination marked by the superego. In effect, it is cardinal that "a society sanction a right to *jouissance*, by permitting everyone to lay claim to it, for its maxim to thus be legitimated by the imperative of moral law" even if this does not remain "universal" but in the order of the "general" (Lacan, 1963, p. 649).[32]

From a Lacanian point of view, the role of the Other's *jouissance* and its existence in the practices of the subject's enjoyment and their socialization persists in a dialectic of recognition, transgression, and support of ideals, many of them progressive. The distinction must be based on the fact that the subject uses the Other as the medium through which it enjoys (*Che vuoi?*). The Other places rules and commandments in a symbolic and imaginary imperative.[33] These rules refine man to gradually move away from his condition as a horde animal, as Freud (1921) observed, to become a mere horde.

There are serious consequences here since the human animal, due to its status of regulated subordination, behaves in its affection as a "porcupine crowded"—Freud took the quotation from Schopenhauer—that cannot "tolerate a too intimate approach to his neighbor" (p. 101). Perhaps with Lacan, the intricacy of the relationship with the similar is indeed characterized in a poem by the Spanish writer Luis Cernuda (1932): "Men one day felt their cold. And they wanted to share it. Then they invented love. The result was, you know, as in hedgehogs" (p. 186).

The above demonstrates the aspects across which a subject is tamed through symbolic splits and imaginary totalities. A phallic *jouissance* enraptures them and proposes to desire an already fragmented and inhibited ulterior pleasure. The freedom to desire is socially bound due to the limits of human rights and their legitimizing entropy. It is indispensable to discern here whether "male homosexuality" insists on being "a sort of entropy moving in the direction of a degrading of the community" or, on the opposite, whether "feminine homosexuality" comes as contrary to the "counter to social entropy" dictated by the inscription of male bourgeois civility (Lacan, 1962, p. 620).[34]

The dialectic between the Other's enjoyment, laws, and range will invariably reach a juncture grounded in the legal relations of *jouissance* as an imperative of exchangeable value. Suppose the subject is capable of the Other's *jouissance* and the latter of *jouissance* due to the subject's castration. In that case, it is evident that the order of the relationships between the two would form an essential part of the conjunction of what we can call society.

That is to say, the Other makes the use of signifiers possible for each subject and thus shapes a society engraved by its fictional enjoyment possibilities. There is no possibility of a society without laws; the central point here is precisely the use given to the controls of the superego and the support of guilt amid the social management of transgression. In such a way, the mediation of this enjoyment is the renunciation of enjoyment itself, which has a surplus for the subject. Therein lies the disturbance of his social existence, which we will continue to review later on.[35]

To conclude this subsection, we must remember that even if the subject finds a renunciation of enjoyment, the perverse position shall always be present in the imaginary dimensions of the subject. Although the perverse form can be found in the subject and in the Other, the limitation and problematic mediation of the law will permanently be a producer of *jouissance*, even if it is in its plus form. The neurotic will always find, in perversion, a staging of the design of the imperative to socially enjoy its juridical and structural existence. Or, in Lacan's (1962–1963) words, "Other's *jouissance*," which only emerges under "a modalized form, which moreover stayed at the level of a question mark" (12.12.62, p. 69). This vicissitude suggests that, despite the bourgeois domination of desire and laws, there will remain a powerful point of fragmentation impossible to weld.

Ideology and Neurosis: On the Repetition and the Working-Through

We have briefly introduced the notion of ideology. Although we allude to Althusser, we should also confront the meaning of ideology, as Lacan has suggested, and will seek to relate it to the constitution of society. We start from the point at which ideology emerges in the relation between the symbolic and imaginary registries. These two registers primarily play a fundamental role in the structuring of the ideology and their function of that which can be founded as the ideal. However, it is worth asking what the nucleus of this ideology is. Furthermore, where can we articulate the servitude of ideology to the repetition of societies?

We know that for Lacan there is a fundamental distinction between repetition as *Tuché* and as *Automaton*. The former is an intricate "encounter with the real" (Lacan, 1964b, 12.02.64, p. 52). This means reaching beyond the organizational limit proposed by Aristotle. On the contrary, the *Automaton* "is what really thinks by itself without any link to that beyond, the ego, which gives thought its subject" (Lacan, 1955–1956, 27.06.56, p. 307). In addition to being the instance that reproduces the frenzied enjoyment of thinking, the *Automaton* restrains the working subject's insistence in order to grant him/her the uneasiness of immobility and the annulment of their labor force through submission to the "network of signifiers" and all its machinery (Lacan, 1964b, 12.02.64, p. 52).[36]

It is well known that ideology's dynamics tend to be a precise repetition—as *Automaton*—and thus reproduce the ideal dimensions of the master's discourse as a form of social bond. Ideology persists in societies because it subjects the neurotic to greed and a deeply lazy inhibition. The *tuché* that gives rise to the random and contingent is subdued by neurosis as a structure and modality of enjoyment that deactivates and subjects the subject to procrastination. The function of *jouissance* here is the annihilation of the potency of desire in order to cause an enjoying ritual of immobility subjected to the presence of the same thing over and over again.

Alluding to the reading of his teacher Clérambault, Lacan (1966b) already observed the automatic insistence of "metaphor" and a "mechanistic ideology" (p. 51) that directed the treatment of psychosis. Ideology in its mechanical form can only be seen in the uses of the signifier value and the encounter with a mode of social action already determined in functionality. Consequently, ideology can only operate if it lacks history and focuses all its efforts on sustaining a specific mode of social development, mainly at the level of adequacy to a paranoid and programmatic self.

Beyond this, Lacan proposes that, although ideology has a differential basis in language, its omniscient solidity is found in the function of imaginary form and reproducing its ideals. From this logic, Lacan (1960c) suggests that "Psychology transmits ideals: the psyche therein no longer represents anything but the sponsorship that makes it qualify as academic. Ideals are society's slaves" (p. 705). Lacan presents us here with one of the unconscious functions. As we have distinguished above, consciousness is a stance of unknowing, a paranoid position if we can think of it as such.

The relative autonomy of the consciousness makes it a participant in exchanges that largely escape the designs of the unconscious. Lacan (1964–1965) identifies, in the "developmental psychology" praxis, and also in "philosophy," an "ideological" endeavor that puts "the human spirit" before "discourse" (02.12.64). That is to say, the relations of ideas are placed before inter-significant relations. From that line, loss vanishes in a territory of fatuous completeness that subsumes the subject—primordially the neurotic—in the apolitical forms of stability arranged in the social edification of their illusions.[37] Without encountering the centrality of his existence, the subject makes ideological representations of their own as the only possible horizon of their inhibition.

The ideological prism is linked with the imaginary spectrum that tries to fix a model of feedback that demarcates the ideas that found designs and conjectures. If social ideals plague the world, it is because they operate a reality framed and encapsulated by the Other and the fantasies that slow down the drive by constraining it to the maintenance of a despotic social bond. There is little we can understand or glimpse of "that marionette called man, the human being or human dignity" that is not already channeled by some "revolutionary or reactionary ideology" (Lacan, 1966d, p. 43).

As Lacan notes in the conference that we quoted, science and its acceleration confine—almost as an unbreakable rule—that the greater the acceleration of science, the more relevant the decrease in the cultural drive of the obsessive neurotic who delimits his social reality as that of the ideology of the scientist, of the bourgeois, or of both.

Here, we understand social and ideological reality as something that is not entirely inherent to the subject but is made possible to the extent that the designs of other satisfaction models are limited to the subjects. Ideology is a social order for the ideals of capitalism from its pre-industrial epoch to the present day. The social and ideological order, however, is not wholly encompassed by culture, although the latter attempts to unite, in a certain way and with conditions, the subjects; society, as a signifier, poses the formation of a structure framed in the drawing of an ideological undermining that guides the relational manifestation of the subject. Obsessive neurosis, as Lacan (1960–1961) has observed, causes the phallic function to emerge under ideological and "degraded forms" that do nothing but reproduce powerless enjoyments (26.04.61, p. 253).

This illusory ideological trickery, subsequently and as soon as they meet with society and the patterns given by culture in capitalism, becomes a struggle between *Eros* and death as drives where the subject positions their desiring existence. Both drives are in cahoots and are even antagonistic since they allow the subject to be exploited through their enjoyment. Finally, every condition of the subject will find itself submerged in the margins of its desire, cultural renunciation, repetition, and *jouissance*.[38] In the same sense, the symptom, with its undeniable uselessness and firmness, expresses the opposition between the compulsion to repetition remarked through social practices and the desiring drive that can only be resolved in a conflictual or even pathological pathway.[39]

According to Lacan (1958b), it is in "the unconscious" where the "first ideal marks in which the tendencies are constituted as repressed in the substitution of the signifier for needs" can be discovered (p. 253). The signifiers and their concatenation lengthen the function and transformation of organic life to be disposed of in the waters of the dominant ideology reproduced in the collective.[40] Repression, the angular vicissitude of neurosis, usually exploits this metamorphosis to install the asphyxiating rigidity of subjective uneasiness. The neurotic fantasy is usually solved between inhibitions or impotence that make it choose the sameness of automatic exploitation rather than exploring the contingent existence of cultural creation. Lacan (1959–1960) submits that "transformation of the energy of desire which makes possible the idea of the genesis of its repression. [...] it is at the origin of a higher complexity, something to which the realm of civilization owes its development" (18.11.59, p. 6).

Due to the insistence of the symbolic system of culture—as the architect of the movements of structure—the neurotic tries to respond to its call by employing a social reproduction of the paternal debt and its guilt-ridden character. In other words, the income ideology is relevant because it expresses an idyllic and phallic model for the subject. A representation that is chained from exchanges of signifiers accumulated in the Other. There, the subject is often unable to find that "the only thing one can be guilty of is giving ground relative to one's desire" (Lacan, 1959–1960, 06.07.60, p. 321).

Ideology has then a role closely linked to neurosis due to its suffering and indebted mechanism. Ideologies dominate across constructing forms of servility before the guarantee of the fantasy fixed on the unknown and its repetitive yields and find opposition to divergent contingency in centralized finitude. In this logic, Lacan (1973a), following Freud, reminds us that "it is not evil, but good, that engenders guilt" (p. 544). Thus, an ideology of social welfare is ipso facto economically solipsistic and alienating.

In the same way, ideas come to mobilize a fantasmatic recreation within the imaginary of the subjects. The confabulation of particular psychologies, as so much is said of those that evoke an entire knowledge of the self, does nothing but appease and control the critique of the social order, of the designs of society that stretch to ground a univocal and idyllic relationship between subjects through fetishizing their world. This relationship is diametrically opposed to desire as such. The social order, held hostage within the Other, participates in the degradation of culture through ideology and its alienated performance. If we assume that culture is the first feature that can create an immixion of the social, then the design of the repetitive autonomy of consciousness often shortens the drive and destined desire towards an almost impasse recognized through fetishized ideas and ideals governed by the Other.

To live with ideology and reproduce it automatically is the function of many modern psychologies but not of psychoanalysis, which attempts to decenter the subject from its viscous relationship with the commodity-object. There, the Other, in its castrating capacity, regularly carries out the functions that also make possible the desiring contingency of the subject from the unconscious and its equivocal repetitions, its uncontrollable and incommensurable lapses. In plainer words, ideology and ideals for subjects are only an imaginary, managed, and automatically repetitive representation of how life should develop in its regulated normality. However, a differential knowledge can be found in the symbolic system of culture from the dislocation of social prohibitions that reproduce a pattern of behavior perfected in standards within the directness of social modes of production that subdue unconnected and deviant relations with objects.

Based on the above, the domination of the Other and the ideological conformation through which the subject is interpellated respond to the recreation of social ideals as an abstract foundation for its constant reproduction. The dominant ideology is everywhere; it subdues beliefs in its praxis, and it is precisely there where we find the attempt of capital to reduce culture to exhaustive repetition. Society is that fictionalized place where signifiers circularly mobilize the subject and through which an ideology construction supports, with its grandiloquent nuances, a specific mode of exploitation of pleasures and its reverse. As Lacan (1968–1969) would put it, "ideology" is "dependent on a certain number of conditions, especially social, those of production" (30.04.69).[41]

In the predominant position of ideology within modern societies, the subject still has the self-sacrificing possibility of recovering something of that original lack, produced through symbolic castration. However, the subject will always be prey to the interpellation of the Other in its imaginary form and symbolic character. If the subject is imprisoned by ideology and signifiers, it is precisely because, in their consciousness, it has tried to find something to replace their lack, something that satisfies from the small object *a*. There is involved, at the social level, the incitement to progress and normality, as a "generous ideology" that is rooted in "bourgeois" ideals (Lacan, 1959–1960, 04.05.60, p. 208).

It is in the boundaries of "perfection" well diffused about the "soul," where the "masters of the spiritualist ideology" become the "dregs of our society" for they only amplify the "mark of progress" (Lacan, 1965–1966, 09.02.66). In this sense, Lacan's highly subversive critique of psychology, complementing what has been discussed before, resizes the limiting position of psi techniques that have permeated current societies and their functionality. The critique of ideology also entails an analysis of society dilapidating its supposed union and integrity. In parallel, it also criticizes psychology—positive in many cases—whose *psy* techniques try to reduce the subject to an individual condition and to the automatic way of repeating and remaining in repetition. It is in this frenetic repetition that "an elaboration" psychic "through critique and construction" can emerge (Lacan, 1966f, p. 303).

Lacan (1960–1961) argued that amid "the schema of the relationship between perversion and culture, insofar as culture is distinct from society," there is a differential aspect because "while society leads, via censorship, to a form of disintegration which is called neurosis, perversion can be understood, contrariwise, as a kind of elaboration, construction, or even sublimation" (23.11.60, p. 31). If culture disturbs the concrete circumstances of the subjects, as the receiver of the signifiers where they emerge, there is also a point where society has been explicitly related to the possibilities of *working through*. Society has in neurosis the command of petrification from the origin where the symbolic castration forces the subjects to understand themselves with an uneasiness inserted from castration because of language. However, there is undoubtedly something about the transgressive trait that would be highly opportune to break the social dikes of normality to *re-elaborate* and not *automate*.

This latter is because castration produces in the subject an original prohibition and additional repressions that are delimited in the social order of the Other. If neurosis can be taken here as a generality in the production of social subjects, the chance of emancipation from the established order must remain in the subject. As Lacan (1955–1956) elucidated,

> the point of convergence of the libidinal dialectic that the mechanism and development of neurosis refer to in Freud, is the theme of castration. It is castration that conditions the narcissistic fear. To accept castration the subject must pay as elevated a price as this reworking of the whole of reality.
>
> (04.07.56, p. 312)

On the contrary, perversion, according to Lacan (1961–1962), "contributes elements that shape [*travaillent*] society, and neurosis favors the creation of new cultural elements" (23.11.60, p. 31). Perversion, as such, can endow the subject with specific knowledge about his enjoyment and, in this way, cause the signifiers ordered by the Other to be in constant movement. If the neurotic is condemned to enjoyment and to limit his *jouissance*, to suffer the good with uncertainty because they do not know the purpose for which they do not know, the perverse, on the other hand, would enter into the minuscule space of knowing something of their enjoyment in order to subvert the prohibitive law of the Other.

Thus, the brothel of ideologically reproduced society is full of bliss and goodness, of selfish gifts from and to the subject. Therein is found on the social reality aimed at exchanging pleasures and dead objects. It is not only the dominant ideology but domination through ideology that is responsible for the channeling of a libidinal economy that idealizes and covers the social world with false beauty.[42]

Under the gaze of the Other, there is the possibility of finding him or her as a kind of fetishistic observer if we may be allowed the approximation. Nevertheless, what does this Other observe? It seems that we are entering a kind of panoptic power. We can enjoy the Other from the insertion of the law and the social circulation of ideas and their liberal foundation. However, we are also faced with its moralizing designs and reduction to repetition.

The Other observes every minute and grants us the possibility of transgressing its laws in order to strengthen the paranoid and social persecution of the self. It is relevant that the Other designates the subjects' actions by being placed as vigilant and, as such, as a chance of punishment. The domination of subjects in societies is the determination of their conscious thoughts and the extractivism of their neurotic relation to labor. As Marx and Engels (1846) observed, "the class which is the ruling material force of society is at the same time its ruling intellectual [spiritual] force" (p. 67).

The neurotic society finds in the bourgeois class ideology the perversion of the symbolic system at the moment of channeling its work to the repetitive circulation of commodities. The current assertion will allow us to raise two points in our interpretation of society in Lacan. On the one hand, the presence of the Other and a (repressive) gaze that conceals the knowledge of who is being observed are a condition similar to the one who is imprisoned in the panopticon proposed by the English philosopher Jeremy Bentham.[43] The prisoner assumes that someone is lying in wait, watching everything he does, pointing out the law to him. However, the inspector of this prison may still need to arrive. Has any of the subjects seen the Other? Bentham's wager looks similar to Lacan's position regarding the insertion of the Other, who is nowhere to be found in any physical condition but agglutinated in some social personification. Its materiality can only emerge through its enunciation of language and power distribution.[44]

Likewise, freedom is limited by the Other; what we may call a *free society* is the state of slavery to the imperatives of the symbolic system. If the functioning of the generalized panopticon rehearses its power in contemporary society, it is precisely because we find the subject unknowing of the Other and the knowledge it possesses. Society is based on the displeasure produced by the signifier and the death of labor.[45] Consequently, the idea of the panopticon should not only be limited to the interpretation of the gaze but also to its fiction, as Lacan observed. Voyeuristic and exhibitionist practices thus delimit social relations to the extent of the possibilities of discourse where the subject is an indispensable actor.

In this respect, and as a conclusion to this chapter, the reach of the Other on the subjects and the social setup traced in its concrete work can change direction through a different laboring logic. If neurosis is the basis for the breakdown of activity due to the cavil of thought and ideals, then the disruptive unconscious labor restores the force that was not subsumed in the lazy redundancy of ideology. Indeed, the ideological emphasis attempts to limit labor in order to generate a social bond beneficial to the master. This introduces neurotic apathy, which is reduced to utility and functionality. At this point, repression, in its strict social sense, can only lead to what Freud (1914) determined as an "ostrich-like policy" that rejects the bond with the social body (p. 152).[46]

The *working thought* [*Durcharbeiten*] is a paradoxical laboral and performing discontinuity in the *continuum*. It is not only resumed to clinical practice but admits that the laboring force of the event and language reorganizes the modes of signification in another modality of non-conclusive repetition as another "metaphorical effect" (Lacan, 1959, p. 596). The working thought not only changes the direction of identification but also mobilizes the subjection to *jouissance* repetition. It is there that "the whole series of events, the whole history, is relived and re-worked several times" (Lacan, 1953–1954, 27.01.54, p. 20).

Society and the imperative of identification with a punitive superego amplify the oppressive drive management in a social bond aimed at repetitive exploitation. However, as Lacan (1964b) points out, "the loop must be run through several times. There is in effect no other way of accounting for the term *durcharbeiten*, of the necessity of elaboration, except to conceive how the loop must be run through more than once" (24.06.64, p. 274).

Lacan (1968–1969) also distinguishes the German term "*Durcharbeitung*" to specify a "working through something," and this triggers new possibilities in the orientation of identifications and the relationship between the Ego-ideal and the superego (05.02.69, p. 152). In this sense, the idyllic chaining between society's signifying objects and dynamics of enjoyment can undergo a traumatic cut that redirects neurosis to other modes of action in social life. As we see, neurosis (particularly obsessive neurosis) is presented as the panacea of redundant social enjoyment and directed at the futility of the aspirational and progressive thinking of bourgeois ideology. On the contrary, working thought assigns force as an activity to a contingent possibility hooked to materiality and its eventual principle.

Notes

1 See Milner (2011a).
2 See Chaumon (2004) on the relationship of law, ethics, and politics in Lacan, discussed in chapter VII.
3 Allouch (1984) suggests that "desiring desire differs all the more clearly from obtaining its enjoyment" and that "enjoyment is an ultimate way of avoiding desire" (p. 108).
4 In this respect, *Jouissance*, according to Scott Wilson (2008), "is located therefore as the end and meaning of work and thought, but it is always sacrificed to, or taken by, the Other that represents the law precisely in the form of enjoyment" (pp. 6–7).
5 From Will Greenshields' (2017) perspective, "the law that prevents access to a forbidden realm of absolute jouissance is not an external barrier to desire but is instead written into the very structure of desire itself" (p. 159).
6 See also about entropy and repetition in the circuit of the signifier in Rouse & Arribas (2011, p. 216).
7 See Dylan Evans' (1998) idea about "drained jouissance" (p. 12).
8 In a remarkably homological form, for Marx (1867a), the "mechanical monster whose body fills whole factories, and whose demonic power, at first hidden by the slow and measured motions of its gigantic members, finally bursts forth in the fast and feverish whirl of its countless working organs" (p. 503).
9 John Johnston (2008) suggests that "Lacan also realized that the new cybernetic machines do not simply exist outside of us." Thus, "human being assumes an in-mixing of many kinds of information-processing machines." Likewise, "Lacan accepted the challenge that cybernetics posed to traditional human boundaries" (p. 106). See also Moncayo (2018), specifically Chapter VI: The Symbolic in the early Lacan as a Cybernetic Machine, as Automaton and Tyché, and the two forms of the Real.
10 Pierre Bruno (2012) mentions in this respect that "money arrives at the exact place of the loss of enjoyment that the entry into language seals while it configures the demand for enjoyment" (p. 79).
11 Marx (1867a) describes surplus value as "the amount by which the value of the product exceeds the value of its constituent elements" (p. 320). Thus, it is a particularity that introduces excess into the value system.
12 According to McGowan (2013): "The onset of capitalism inaugurates a significant change not just in the structure of the economy and of social relations but also in the nature of social authority" (p. 167).
13 In the view of Calum Neil (2011), "Enjoyment is not a social accident, nor is it a 'natural' fact. It is rather, as Lacan states, an assumed place from which and in relation to which the self can emerge" (p. 51). We can add that it is also the subject's direction and drive to subsume itself into an Ego.
14 Derek Hook (2018), for his part, posits in parallel that "imposing laws on others" and "dispensing judgment or enacting punishments" is part of a "libidinal excess" as an excess of enjoyment. This further produces "'subterranean' reinforcements of codified rules and proscriptions" in societies (p. 126).
15 See Matthew Flisfeder (2021), in particular chapter one: "Social Media Does Not Exist!"

16 Ed Pluth (2007) suggests that "the whole machine, when set to working, produces a little ghost. This is what I am calling the signified effect" (p. 35).
17 See Jan de Vos (2013) to expand on the consolidation between *psy* disciplines and the control and use of bodily machinery (his chapter one).
18 Another interesting critique can be found in Žižek (2012), which discusses the idea of "becoming machine" and the problem of societies' founding antagonism.
19 We have already discussed this difference in the entry "Society" included in the volume *The Marx Through Lacan Vocabulary* (Juárez-Salazar, 2022, p. 237).
20 In *Lituraterre*, Lacan (1971a) alludes to Thomas Aquinas to remind us of the relationship between the sewer and culture.
21 See Carl von Clausewitz (1832, p. 584).
22 For Charles Taylor (1979), from a Hegelian perspective, "Modern society [...] is Romantic in its private and imaginative life and utilitarian or instrumentalist in its public, effective life" (p. 71).
23 See Claude Lefort (1986, p. 281) on the link between law, power and social relations.
24 See, for example, Albert O. Hirschman (1977) on "socially useful behavior" and passions (p. 62).
25 Silvia Lippi (2012) points out that "transgression brings to our minds disorder, indetermination, and freedom. But this freedom, paradoxically, depends on the law, on the forbidden" (p. 19).
26 Ferdinand Tönnies (1887) advised—almost similarly to Lacan—that "Both humans and animals have a maternal instinct, but in human beings the instinct has also been developed into a sense of duty" and "this order of things is made more weighty and venerable through being embodied in commandments and prohibitions." But, for Tonnies, there is a difference with "civil law" and its "global system" (pp. 216–217).
27 Žižek (1997), from Kant's ethics, indicates: "Law does not tell me what my duty is, it merely tells me that should accomplish my duty" (p. 284).
28 With certain differences, these ideas can be contrasted with the historical relationship between truth, law, religion, and the management of the soul in Michel Foucault's thought (Foucault, 1973).
29 On the libertine body, its domination and exclusion, see Hénnaff (1978).
30 As Žižek (1998) has summarized it: "Sade is not the entire truth of Kantian ethics, but a form of its perverted realization" (p. 20).
31 Žižek (2005) has suggested that "If God is dead, the superego enjoins you to enjoy, but every determinate enjoyment is already a betrayal of the unconditional one, so it should be prohibited" (p. 96).
32 Dany Nobus (2017) states, in this regard, that "the Law [...] feeds itself on the disjunction between needs and desires: in establishing human rights on the basis of what it regards as essential human needs, it elicits human desire, and so once again shows itself to be sustaining desire rather than eradicating it" (p. 104).
33 Althusser's (1970) elementary notion of ideology serves as an example: "[A] representation of the imaginary relation of individuals to their real conditions of existence" (p. 162).
34 In fact, for Hook and De Kesel (2022), "Jouissance is also destabilizing: libidinal enjoyment routinely over-rides instinct" (p. 57).
35 As McGowan (2020) mentions: "The superego licenses brutality in the name of morality. It enables subjects to believe in the necessity of their transgressions while still enjoying the experience of guilt for what they do" (p. 143).
36 To expand on this differentiation, see Recalcati (2008, pp. 316–317) and Lombardi (2015).

37 For Žižek (1989): "The illusion is therefore double: it consists in overlooking the illusion which is structuring our real, effective relationship to reality. And this overlooked, unconscious illusion is what may be called the ideological fantasy" (p. 30).
38 Freud (1897) had already noted this cultural renunciation in his *Draft N*, which he sent to Wilhelm Fliess in a letter dated May 31.
39 It is there where a social "normopathy" can be found, as mentioned by McDougall (1978, pp. 43–44).
40 In this respect, Althusser (2005) suggests that "an ideology is a system of ideas only insofar as it refers to a system of social relations. It is not an individual fantasy but a socially established body of ideas" (p. 64).
41 As Žižek (2006) highlighted, from Althusser, the "ideological interpellation" is the symbolic identity conferred on us as "the result of the way the ruling ideology 'interpellates' us—as citizens" (p. 35).
42 For Michael Schneider (1979), "neurosis" would be "the proper psychological reflection of a society" through which a "misrepresentation of consciousness" emerges as a "consequence of the fetishistic character of the commodity" (p. 349).
43 Bentham's (1787) ideal was socially reformist: "Morals reformed, health preserved, industry invigorated, instruction diffused, public burthens lightened, economy seated, as it were, upon a rock, the Gordian knot of the poor-laws are not cut, but untied, all by a simple idea in Architecture" (p. 95).
44 According to Bentham (1781) "The community is a fictitious body, composed of the individual persons who are considered as constituting as it were its members. The interest of the community then is, what is it? —the sum of the interests of the several members who compose it" (p. 15).
45 For Helmut Dahmer (1983), "the world of displeasure imposes its recognition by consciousness," and the "pursuit of pleasure," in effect, "does not accord with the increase of 'usefulness'" (p. 161).
46 We have explored this idea in the chapter "Politics" in *The Marx Through Lacan Vocabulary*. See Gómez Camarena & Juárez-Salazar (2022).

Chapter 4

Subversion, Social Bond, and Political Economy

Subversive Homosexuality and Social Genesis

In his book *Los muros de agua*, the Mexican communist writer José Revueltas (1941) predicted that there would be "some land of defeated men, whose heads are bent over time, embracing in their arms, without containing, all the condemnation" (p. 38). It would seem that, in the history of the subject of capitalism, society has stealthily imposed tentacles and scales to navigate in its sea of misery and individualistic alienation, arriving at a sterile land populated by dead merchandise. From this imposed redemption, Lacan's reading of society in capitalism can give some clues about the conditioning factors of such martyrdom.

It is unquestionable that Lacan, toward the end of his work, does not give much attention to the exploration of society and concentrates more on discourse as a modality of the social bond and the conversion of "force" toward "political economy" in a new revision of Freudian theory since Marx. This renewing turn of the politics of the unconscious is already located in two cardinal sentences: The unconscious as "the ideal worker" (Lacan, 1973, p. 518) and in the declaration that "the unconscious is politics" (Lacan, 1966–1967, 10.05.67). Both guidelines relate to the unconscious with an archaic economy of pleasures and its historical, social, and political changes. Lacan has a more detailed approach to Marx's work throughout this last stage of his teaching and is challenged by the various political events during those years, such as the French May.[1]

Like most of the matters related to psychoanalysis, the development and genesis of society are also based on the problem of sexuality and its commerce. These two issues involve discursive formations that allow for the management of interacting subjects. Which could be the most singular and conflictual encounter of the subjects? The immediate answer would perhaps be "the sexual relationship." However, something in Lacan's teaching will make us doubt such a design. It is precisely one of Lacan's most enigmatic and controversial slogans that we propose *ab initio* to frame this chapter: "There is no sexual relation." Because, not in vain, Lacan (1964b) recalls that

DOI: 10.4324/9781032673837-5

"the reality of the unconscious is sexual reality—an untenable truth" (29.04.64, p. 150).

The first point we will take here is the examination of homosexuality and its relationship with the social dynamics from Lacan's point of view. It is well known that something must be intricate within the homosexual act, since the very enunciation of the signifier expresses a plurality of representations. To begin with, Lacan resorts to the Greeks to account for love, particularly in his seminar on transference. There, Lacan (1960–1961) alludes to Plato's *Symposium* as a homosexual "assembly," that is, a political place where the transcendence of love is discussed in intimacy (25.01.61, p. 133). If at the origin it was love, since it is the starting point of that seminar, in *The Symposium*, we find that the birth of what we call culture would be intricate *ab initio* with homosexuality. For Lacan (1960–1961), in the same seminar, society contains a certain degree of "censorship" in that form of "disintegration which is called neurosis." In this respect, culture, according to Lacan, would be a kind of singular amalgam of society insofar as it finds, in homosexuality, its original, but not natural, bond. In his own words, "While it is true that psychoanalytic theory points to fraternity among men as the basis of the social bond—homosexuality attaches man to the neutralization of the bond" (23.11.60, p. 31).

In a retroactive form, Lacan returns to the Freudian origin of society. However, for him, this relation is a fact of culture, which reaffirms the primitive position of the cultural bond that the mythical exchange formalizes in the light of the symbolic universe. Society would not have to deal with culture alone but would have to sustain itself in relation to prohibition and the perversion that society makes possible. Culture is then the main engine of a subjected encounter that is somewhat disarticulated and reorganized by society. Lacan (1960–1961) states that "homosexuality still was what it is, a perversion" (23.11.60, p. 31). However, Lacan moves away from the derogatory view of homosexuality and proposes not an apological reading of homosexuality but a revision framed in the subversive origin of culture and its phallic determination. The distinction between Greek and contemporary homosexuality, Lacan (1960–1961) indicates, can only be found in the quality of the objects: "In Greece, the conditions were favorable for their being objects of homage, without it being necessary to go find these objects in dark alleys or in the gutter" (23.11.60, p. 31). That is to say, there is a tension in the forms of exchange and exploitation of the sexed and symbolic circulation of the subjects that homosexuality articulates in a revelatory manner to the social order.

According to Lacan, homosexuality is a subversive encounter where the subject inverts the domination of the ego ideal within society and its phallic enjoyment. Its perverse formation is on the side of disruptive knowledge in the subject, an original cultural condition that escapes the censorship of society but is tinged by the mark of culture. Lacan (1962–1963) thus poses homosexuality as "the root of social adhesion" and that "libidinal adhesion of the social bond, in so far as it only occurs in the community of males, is linked to the side of sexual miscarriage that is especially allotted to the male due to the fact of castration" (05.06.63, p. 269). Thus, we see that Lacan here takes up Freud's interpretation of the primordial horde to account for the homosexual origin of culture as a form of radical protest against the reductionist and inhibiting implications of the social order and its heterosexual hegemony.[2] What is relevant in Freud's indication is that, in this way, the foundation of the impossibility of sexual intercourse in its natural sense is situated. For the subject want-to-be, the subject "castrated" by the Other, a sexual exchange emerges as a result of the loss of the hegemonic phallic position of the father and his omnipotent enjoyment. This generates a castration that does not refer to an organ as such but to a symbolic and imaginary exchange that borders on the real that can have a sexual encounter and socialization.[3]

The previous idea expresses that the first encounter with society is found in a libidinal relation that is directed toward homosexuality and protests its castration. This also indicates the distinction of enjoyment between men and women. If one does not enjoy it in the same way, it is because the signifier of the phallus is structured in different orders of sexuation and particular directions as a result of the inscription of the signifier.[4] In this sense, Lacan (1962–1963) mentions that "what is called female homosexuality might hold great cultural importance, but it has no value as a social function because it pertains to the field specific to sexual rivalry" (05.06.63, pp. 269–270). Consequently, the possibility of a social bond has, for Lacan, the support of the phallus, its repressive condemnation, and the censorship of enjoyment, together with the discursive articulation that the phallus signifier brings into play. This leads us to question the place of the heterosexual union between a man and a woman in society. We can understand the fact that the libidinal function of the male is what summons the only social bond; however, the relationship is within a form of impasse in today's capitalist society that delimits the *healthy* enjoyment of sexual encounters.[5]

Lacan delves into the integration of marriage within the structuring of contemporary societies. That is, he explores the archetypal and heteronormative social status of the institution of marriage: The legalized union of the male position and the female position. According to Lacan (1961–1962), in his *Seminar IX*,

> the necessities of marriage prove themselves to be, for us, a properly social trait of our conditioning; they leave completely open the problem of the dissatisfactions which result from it namely the permanent conflict in which the human subject finds himself, just because he is human, with the effects, the repercussions of this law (of marriage).
>
> (14.03.62)

In his view, the subject seems to continue to reproduce the social and institutionalized figure of bourgeois marriage, even if this encounter is only embodied in the imaginary and the symbolic. Society repeats and congeals the construction of marriage as a form of social union legitimized even within same-sex relationships. Marriage becomes a fundamental gear in the structure of society because it adapts identifications to the positivity of the normative logics of heterosexuality and the regulation of social bonds administered by the determination of commodities and because of the fantasy of deception that underlies the encounter with the other and fidelity.

At this moment, for Lacan, marriage becomes a nodal signifier to construct the social in the elemental and inter-significant bond and thus loses all conditions of naturalness or perpetuity.[6] Marriage thus constitutes a type of censorship, a civilizing cut-off suitable for bourgeois social performance, since it disposes the authorized terms proper to the grouping of subjects and, in the same way, condemns them to monogamy and the reproduction of the dynamics of structural exploitation of the capitalist system. Marital monogamy, in turn, also proposes the possibility of infidelity and even its enjoyment located in the Other and its laws.

As a sequel to what was said in previous chapters about the family, we now see that the insertion of monogamy within Western bourgeois culture is simultaneously a possibility of enjoyment in the symbolic and imaginary trading status of family cohesion. The law or the assumption of the violation of monogamy condemns the subject to a phallic, unitary, and complementary enjoyment that, in effect, goes beyond the supposed affirmation of free sexuality. Returning to Lacan and the law of the Judeo-Christian commandments, they state: "You shall not commit adultery," and it would seem that this is the injunction to enjoy from the great Other with the fellow human being. In this way, the law is formulated to be socially transgressed and not to regulate links.

However, not all enjoyment is centralized in phallic and vigorous reproduction; on the contrary, there is a passive modality that calls for discernment and subversion against the phallic function. In fact, from set theory, Lacan suggests that, in "the class"—the definable dimension of the set that does not necessarily end up being elaborated—"everything that is pinpointed with an attribute, is something that has to do with sexual relation," and "there is a transition through the intermediary of this one-to-one correspondence" which assumes that "there are as many on one side as on the other, and some people ground the idea of monogamy on this." However, due to "social catastrophes," it was determined that "that sexual relation would not have to be bi-univocal," regular, and joyful because its elaboration can also unfold in a bijective way; that is to say as a form of one-to-one and in undefinable and infinite random relation or correspondence beyond its enclosure at the social level (Lacan, 1971–1972, 17.05.72, p. 166).[7]

From Lacan's (1961–1962) teaching, "the institution of marriage" is validated "itself because of its persistence" amid its "lower middle-class traits [*petit-bourgeois*], throughout a society which at the beginning believed it could go further in the putting in question of fundamental relationships, I mean in Communist society" (14.03.62). Lacan's critique, at this point, is exciting because it raises the significance of the power of marriage within a measurable economic and social exchange. The identification with the phallic mandate of bourgeois societies gradually became a social bureaucracy of the regular heteronormative order plagued by a supposed liberal openness. It is a taxable and manageable institution preceded by a class struggle and the precision of the hegemonic petty bourgeoisie that insists on maintaining a form of social union of phallic and individual guidelines. If anything is evident even at this point, it is that, for Lacan, the interference of the Other has primitive characteristics that are subsequently economized in sexed social exchanges because they have a cultural basis misrepresented by society as an imaginary binary and complementary relation. We thus discover the social and subjective expression of repetition in the conflict of the forced link in the juridical codes of exchange. Marriage is substantially instituted in pre-existing cultural conditions in the structure of the Other, and it enjoys dynamics through which the subject feels the impossible relations of their incomprehensible encounter with the other.

As opposed to the neurotic mechanisms of the heterosexual relationship, perversion would be a form of protest to the onslaught of the Other and the channeling of desire since it is a way in which the social order (in which the subject is immersed) can be disturbed. It is a complex response to the social system that condemns the abyss of the prisons, of the chaining of the jouissance, and the disaggregated repetition of neurotic desire. As Lacan (1961–1962) mentions, "the relationship of desire to the subject, of the subject to the desire of the Other has nothing to do with anything whatsoever that can be intuitively supported from this register" (04.04.62). Lacan alludes here to a psycho-sociological register suggesting that order precisely disguises desire for us, which determines a disposition of consciousness. That is to say, the repetition comes to be installed in a constant return to the regulated position of desire. It is the social condition that causes repetition in a specific course toward the perspective of individual segregating enjoyment between subjects because through the social "circuit," the "perversion" logically achieves, "through a series of gradations," a "protest that, with regard to conforming, arises in the dimension of desire, insofar as desire is the subject's relation to his being" (Lacan, 1958–1959, 01.07.59, p. 484).

In this regard, Lacan (1964b) was very explicit when he said that "the fundamental exchanges take place and it is there that we find once again that the most elementary structures of social functioning are inscribed in the terms of a combinatory" of adequacy and circulation between elements and functions (29.04.64, p. 150). In this singular encounter, there is an elaboration beyond the biological, concatenated, and particular order. This surface, close to the combinatorial, is of the entire "play of the signifier" and belongs to the reduction of the encounter to structured forms of the subject's utterance (29.04.64, pp. 150–151). It is because of the above that, in the bijective function of the valorized elements, Lacan integrates, problematically, the spectrum of the social link. This reading starts from the elemental and signifying structure insofar as it has made possible the fictitious and deformed reality of the sexuality of each of the subjects, their phantasmatic social perversions, and their neurotic scope.

Hence, in the permutation of symbolic values, what is found in the unconscious is a socially lost knowledge that causes desire in another trajectory. It is essential to mention that in the protestant scope of homosexuality in the subject, there is a random domain susceptible to the combinatorial in which the subject has been structured at the disposal of signifiers, and its history is put into play. Homosexuality protests the bond from the real of the murder of the totemic father, drawing the re-inscription of the singular one-for-one in collective action that opposes the segregation of the neurotic social bond that insists on supposing the relationship between two, omitting the effects of the thirdness that, in specific terms, allows for multiplicity.[8]

As Lacan (1965–1966) observed, "It is precisely on the side of the slave that *jouissance* remains, and, precisely, because he renounces it. It is because the master erects his desire that he comes to grief on the margins on *jouissance*" (08.06.66). This brings us back to the position we questioned in a previous passage. Insofar as he is embedded in a society, the subject has his enjoyment as an imperative. However, he renounces it in order to make his existence in the world possible and reduces his social situation to the imaginary and symbolic insistence on completeness. The possibility of this renunciation, as Lacan (1965–1966) says, is

> the cement of the society of masters; while Freud gives the solution just like that: it is quite simply homosexual. It is the desire, that is true, not to undergo castration, which means that the homosexuals, or, more exactly, the masters are homosexual and this is what Freud says. The starting point for society is the homosexual bond, precisely in its relationship to the prohibition of *jouissance*, the *jouissance* of the Other.
> (08.06.66)

If we posit that the renunciation of enjoyment produces a surplus located in the lack, thinking of the homosexual as master proposes to us a condition that turns against an enjoyment that has originated from the action of castration and has left him in lack. The homosexual subject tries to avoid this castration to which he is condemned due to its barred position and its access to the symbolic world and the normative framework of heterosexist society.

The unequivocal situation by which the subject is involved in an original homosexual society is the onslaught and resistance to castration. The homosexual who binds himself to his brothers in that murderous potency with which they attack the father is nothing but the condition of refusing to be castrated and, in the same way, is the refusal to be deprived of the only object in which he can include his object relation: The impossible possession of the woman.[9] We must, on the other hand, specify that as soon as the homosexual links himself to this primitive and mythical clan, he is addressing his protective capacity for castration and also the eventuality of possessing something that has remained within the absolute control of the Other. That which is the privilege of the Other is precisely the surplus enjoyment to which he can only have access through renunciation and through the perverse or neurotic act in which he is placed in his structure.

What Lacan (1966–1967) asserts regarding the above is that

> If the *homme-il* is not recognized in the status of the sexual act in the sense that it is foundational in society, there exists "a society for the protection" of *homme-il*. This is even what is called masculine homosexuality.
>
> (12.04.67)

Nothing is more accurate to clarify the idea of the position of the homosexual and to explain the refuge of man in the absence of meaning of the sexual relation. We thus understand that, for Lacan, the function of the sexuality of the male subject is articulated by an impasse caused by a social deviation in neurosis. Symbolic castration making social symptom comes to produce, in the homosexual society, not only the origin but also a search for the true difference of his desire before the command of the Other and his supposedly absolute and universal jouissance. What we call "social symptom" is a redoubt assembled from the renunciation of enjoyment, the signifier castrated from the exchange of labor power.

This same social symptom is disposed of in a dialectic proper to renunciation of an absolute jouissance, a symptom that is also "a particular symptom" (Lacan, 1974–1975, 18.02.75). As an expression of a disruptive and differential truth, it is also an *aletheia* in the social order and in the frenetic co-opted circulation of the drive. Indeed, this short-circuit produces a *plus-de-jouir*, a surplus under the order of the signifier. We find, in labor force, the social uneasiness par excellence in the renunciation of the subject in its social determination. Despite this, the refuge of homosexuality for the subject remains linked to a drive deviation, which becomes a difference in the subject's desire. We thus understand that society has degraded the cultural condition of the subject, and homosexuality is the evident form by which the subject aspires to protest against the neurotic symptom, which is nothing but how rational society has been configured and instituted. The social symptom is, therefore, a homosexual symptom of the proletarian brother's clan.

It seems then that we also find ourselves thrown into the problem of fantasmatic sexuality in the subjects. On the one hand, the man configures himself by drawing in the woman that fantasmatic object in which to articulate his enjoyment; however, on the other hand, the woman is to enjoy her own body and, subsequently, enters differentially into the maw of phallic enjoyment. This is found in the possibility of a symbolic exchange due to the traumatic and deadly structure of enjoyment where the woman carries a substantial preeminence since the man can only display a virility conducted toward the individualized and obsessive segregation of phallic enjoyment.

Lacan (1966–1967) mentions that "the introduction of the subject, himself an effect of significance, is properly to put the body and *jouissance* into this relation that I defined by the function of alienation" (31.05.67). Before our reading, an antecedent disposition of separation between the enjoying bodies materializes. There is only one sexual partner invoked in the symbolic realm, with whom there can be a particular exchange within the fantasy. We have now understood that the subject's relations will be aligned through its *jouissance*, and the impossibility of enunciating the sexual act as such is nothing other than to find a subject split by the Other and his symbolic castration. There is a subject who pushes to recover the significance of its existence from his fantasmatic recreation with his/her sexual *partenaire*.[10] We thus find the subject faced with the proposal of sexuality confronted in the indeterminacy of the real. However, when the subject is in the exchange of sexuality, they show themself to be structurally and socially limited by the limitations and effects of the lack of being.[11]

Because of these commercial circumstances, the pursuit of meaning for the sexual partner always constitutes a logical problem in conjunctive relations. The *partenaire*, from Lacan's (1957b) point of view, accounts for "an intimate strategy" that "is not necessarily encountered among the individuals [in the neurotic's entourage], the only points currently accepted, since they are united by relational vectors on the maps onto which modern social psychology projects its schemas" (p. 377). In this field, it leads us to suppose that if something is elucidated concerning sexual relation, the absence of meaning [*au-sens*] is regulated in the frivolous adequacy of the socialized individual—a break between fantasies that aspire to position the symbolic and the imaginary founded on the impossibility of the real. Accordingly, Lacan (1962–1963) reminds us that "the woman's *jouissance* is within her. She does not conjoin it to the Other" (19.06.63, p. 304). We find, then, a woman who is at the differential antipode to the Other since what is at stake within the sexual relation is precisely that the man has been castrated. From his symbolization, he surrenders to enjoying the "expired" organ, as Lacan calls it, which is precisely found in the Other, its redundant and metastatic enjoyment. In brief, the signifier movement of a fallen organ from the origin encloses the real of absence via the regulation of signifying relations.

The response to the father's poisonous *jouissance* that is proposed through homosexuality is singular and, at the same time, collective.[12] What is at play is to go against castration itself, and it is a random response to the commodification of the sexed society and its normative purposes. To comprehend this, we must depart from the problem of the introduction of language, castration, and, therefore, the subject's lack. In this regard, Lacan (1966–1967) refers, "in the field of the sexual act, what it discovers, is the introduction of what I called *jouissance-value*, namely, the cancellation of the *jouissance* most immediately involved as such in sexual union; what it calls castration" (31.05.67).

As a result of this, and taking the symbolic castration around the non-possibility of sexual intercourse, the impasse in the origin of society is shaped via a form instituted as a vestige of the differential possibility of the link between subjects. In Lacan's words, castration

> does not solve anything. [...] it explains to us how it happens that the simplest and the clearest legal form of the sexual act—in so far as it is instituted in a regular formation which is called marriage—was first of all, at the beginning, only the privilege of the master. [...] [I]f you know a bit of history and specifically Roman history, even opposed to the pleb. Not everyone who wants it has access to the institution of marriage, only the master.
>
> (Lacan, 1966–1967, 31.05.67)

All these adjustments, at the cultural level, owe to Venus Cloacina, which adopted an administrative reliability of married life in the elementary forms of the culture distributed from the waste [*déchet*] in the "cloaca maxima" and its relation with the "culture" (Lacan, 1967b, p. 66).

We must explain at this point that the scope and aspiration of the subject may obey the possession of something, a knowledge perhaps, which can only be made possible to the extent that the position framed in marriage is the domination of the man—and of a specific phallic and enjoyable knowledge—that has been socially instituted because he/she is supposedly the one who possesses the phallus in a literal sense of the organ and also in its imaginary and symbolic reminiscence that attempts to fill in or restock structural gaps.[13] It is because of structural containment that, according to Lacan (1967c), "profound rearrangements of social hierarchies which constitute the characteristic of our time" (10.11.67) have arisen.

Nevertheless, we cannot but be surprised by such aspiration because as soon as this social institution of marriage designates its conditions, it is nothing more than a smokescreen where the subject aspires to place him/herself within a place that will always be fragmented and in demand. If we associate the condition of the master between the homosexual clan and marriage, we can see two axes that are embroidered in different fabrics. The first is emancipation against the law, and the second is an infertile yearning to acquire the position of domination of the Other. For Lacan (1966–1967),

> that marriage shows itself there—I would not say, more resistant, it did not resist—more established [*institué*] than elsewhere. And that, in the field in which the aspirations are articulated, in a thousand effective forms, in all the fields of art, of cinema, of the word, without counting in that of the great neurotic discontent of civilization, marriage, of course, remains at the centre, not having budged by an inch in its fundamental status.
>
> (31.05.67)

From the above, we account for the symbolic articulations that marriage produces in the glare of its reproduction in contemporary hierarchical societies. We thus find that marriage, as such, is destined to be one of the supports of neurosis and social symptom. The latter's scope has only had to find the means to continue to elaborate itself. Even if today's society desists from or criticizes the meaning of joining in marriage, it is evident that this, as a signifier, will continue to grant political-economic marital positions and segregations to thriving subjects in society's uneasiness.

To finish this passage, we want to make it clear that the ritualized society in capitalism, since the 19th century, has prioritized fetishized mechanisms of the neurotic and mercantile union through which social subjects attempt to symbolize the indiscernible and always already deviated sexual act. As an accurate reflection of the search for meaning and support, all this signified the social encounter. It seems that, for Lacan, the non-sexual relationship grants the subject a detachment not only from the sexual act but also from his political action within society. From our point of view, Lacan's approach to society during the second half of the '60s reflects not only that there is no sexual relationship but also that homosexuality, from the structure and subversion of the *pére-version*, reaches into question the relation of the subjects insofar as they are entirely symbolized and are the effect of castration. For this reason, the essential part of the subjects' alliance is found in homosexuality, seen as the ontogenetic passage to culture and as a drive coalition toward impossibility and the real. It is here that Lacan rescues the homosexual partnership as the revelation that makes the social bond since, from his perspective, homosexuality is, above all, a radicalizing perversion of subjects' social genesis.

Lacan as an Economic Homologue of Marx: The Structure of the Social Bond

The homology that we propose for this chapter should be familiar to us after the previous sections if we consider the relevance of Lacan's homological mode in many of his theoretical studies. Lacan's speculative perspective, seen from its relationship with the economic system within which culture and subjects appear, had a pivotal stimulus in the German philosopher Karl

Marx, who sought to understand the social and exploitative mechanisms in which the links between individuals are woven.[14] From his theoretical development of surplus value and within its scope, Marx continued to produce approaches not only to the economy but also to the factor of exchanges between individuals and the interweaving between thought and society. The reading of Marx and his economic-political optics will serve as an axis to propose an interpretation of society similar to that suggested later by Lacan and embedded in the structuring causalities of the social modes of production.[15]

For Marx, the history of society is the spectrum of processes that dialectically bring about transformations of nature and modify people's social relations in their historical determination and causality. In their critique of Max Stirner and his limited conception of meaning, Marx and Engels (1846) propose:

> Since the "word '*Gesellschaft*' [Society] is derived from *Sal*'" (which, incidentally, is not true, for the original roots of all words are verbs) then "*Sal*" must be equivalent to "Saal". But "Sal" in old High-German means a *building; Kisello, Geselle*—from which *Gesellschaft* is derived—means a house companion; hence "Saal" is dragged in here quite arbitrarily. But that does not matter; "*Saal*" is immediately transformed into "*salon*", as though there was not a gap of about a thousand years and a great many miles between the old High-German "*Sal*" and the modern French "*salon*". Thus society is transformed into a salon society, in which, according to the German philistine idea, an intercourse consisting only of phrases takes place and all real intercourse is excluded.
>
> (p. 242)

This extensive quotation poses, in the beginning, the explicit linguistic problem in the sense of verbal action rather than the signified definition of societies. What subsists in the social salon is, pointedly, the exchange that is usually discarded. In the synonymic speech of St. Max, Marx and Engels find the ominous conspiracy between the language of meaning and the knowledge of the bourgeoisie that amplified all forms of economic exchange.[16]

In parallel, if we follow a method of recovering Freud similar to Lacan's, we find that the subject's progress in bourgeois society is inherently intertwined with a shadowy economic course. Freud (1924b), in *The Economic Problem of Masochism*, came to suggest this based on the analysis of a singular exchange in libidinal unfolding. Freud mentions that "the existence of a masochistic trend in the instinctual life of human beings may justly be described as mysterious from the economic point of view" (p. 159). That is to say, the mystery of the libidinal gain within the drive exchange of the pain inflicted on one's own body lies in the libidinal traffic of the subjects that will be inexpugnably linked to the ways of producing unpleasant surpluses from the social dynamics and their morality. In fact, for Freud (1923) himself, morality, in its economic context, acts as a "decomposition" due to the superego (p. 57). In other words, it is a degrading element of the organic.

This is why the neurotic, in bourgeois society and their problematic and inhibited link with the other, stumbles upon the "moral tortures" that turn out to be the efficient framework of an economy of displeasure in their "*jouissance*" (Lacan, 1973b, p. 78). The economy of internalized *plus-de-jouir* replicates the abstractions of the extensive economic exchange of bourgeois societies in psychic causality. There is, consequently, a relationship between the enigma of the neurotic masochistic aspiration and the secret of commodity fetishism that lies in the social and external significance of the circulation of subjective and reified mercantile exploitation.

Lacan relates several of his ideas—principally from the 1960s—to the positions of Marx and of economics and even uses, as we have already observed, some Marxian proposals regarding the exchange between subjects to explain his postulates. Already in his *Seminar II*, he questions "the imaginary economy" because it "has meaning," and "we gain some purchase on it, only in so far as it is transcribed into the symbolic order, where a ternary relation is imposed" (Lacan, 1954–1955, 01.06.55, p. 255).[17] There is, consequently, no economy that is not related to the thirdness and to the globalized economy of the signifier that constitutes the autonomous dimension before the subject. Marx (1858) noted,

> the real subject retains its autonomous existence outside the head just as before; namely as long as the head's conduct is merely speculative, merely theoretical. Hence, in the theoretical method, too, the subject, society, must always be kept in mind as the presupposition.
>
> (p. 34)

Consequently, for Marx, "Bourgeois society is the most developed and the most complex historic organization of production," and its "categories" describe "its relations" and "the comprehension of its structure, thereby also allows insights into the structure and the relations of production of all the vanished social formations" (Marx, 1858, p. 38).

In the same circumstances, Lacan (1965–1966) indicates, with respect to dialectical materialism, that

> Socrates did not engage in social criticism nor did Freud. It is no doubt because both one and the other had the idea from where there was situated an extraordinarily important economic problem, that of the relationships of desire and of *jouissance*.
>
> (20.04.66)

For Lacan, desire intersects with enjoyment as a death drive found in an entangled economic reciprocity that grounds the vicissitudes of subjects in society and their exchanges. Consequently, the question of modern society and the contemporary economy enter into a logic of constant circulation and determinations stiffened in commodities. As Marx (1858) well glimpsed in the *Grundrisse*, "political economy has to do with the specific social forms of wealth or rather of the production of wealth. The material of wealth, whether subjective, like labour, or objective, like objects for the satisfaction of natural or historical needs, initially appears as common to all epochs of production" (p. 771).

Based on the previous idea regarding the common effect of the dialectical interactions between desire, enjoyment, and profit, there is something of the materiality constructed and divided from the exchange of these factors and the use of labor power. The formation of the subject in society is entwined in an economic sense on the grounds of the values symbolized through the Other, and it is there where it is appropriate to ask ourselves, is the subject not a commodity of exchange in economic relations from its driving existence? The division of human labor—the concrete and the abstract—thus proposes a dynamic of opposites in the face of the vicissitudes of use and change in the fields of knowledge and enjoyment. In this sense, it is for all workers and capitalists that there is something symbolic in the making of a bond. The main problem that we will have to question is the origin of payment and administration in the symbolic exchange as such. Marx knew perfectly well that what was received as payment was inferior to what was at stake in the subject: Labor power, its abstractions, and its dissatisfaction.[18] From this, everything appears to be a circular bond between renunciation and monetary circulation.[19] Thus, "there is a certain way of approaching the distribution of money which indeed constitutes something coherent within society and which has very precise characteristics in terms of this mode of articulation and superimposition" (Lacan, 1972b, p. 203).

For Marx (1867a), "wealth" in the capitalist world appears to us as an "immense collection of commodities," which is why, for the capitalist system, the commodity is the "elementary form" (p. 125). This demonstrates that the current social and economic order is determined by the exchange of commodities by the subjects in a fetishized world. According to Marx, these commodities circulate through the relation between use and exchange values. Marx (1867a) thus indicates that the "material substratum" of these commodities is "use-value," and this value is also the material support of "exchange-value" (p. 139). In other words, the material basis can be considered a commodity's use value. This use value will have an exchange value in its social exchange, and surplus value will be produced. In this sense, Marx (1867a) proposed that

> the value of a commodity represents human labor pure and simple, the expenditure of human labor in general. And just as, in civil society, a

> general or a banker plays a great part but man as such plays a very mean part so, here too, the same is true of human labor
>
> (p. 135)

and the exploitation of the laborer. There where the "body" enters into an "economy" whose "pleasure is a defense against access to *jouissance*" (Lacan, 1967e, p. 357).

From our Lacanian reading of Marx, we conceive use value as a value intricately embedded in social bonds to be exchanged. Therefore, there preexists an abstraction within exchanges that disperses and prescribes the modalities of death to subsist in the gain of surplus value and, in that vicissitude, emerges the position of the signifier value that has eaten away at the force of living labor. The accumulation of signifiers and values settled inside language economize drives through the circulation of enjoyment. That dilated condition is precisely the passage from a libidinal economy to an economy of enjoyment supported by bourgeois society.

If we assume that no symbolic condition exists in the real, use value and exchange value are related to Lacan's (1956) symbolic field situated in the social market whose retroactive result is "the subjective economy, commanded as it is by the unconscious"; "it is, in effect, a signification that is evoked only by what I call a metaphor—to be precise, the paternal metaphor" (p. 463). There is a situation of the *Mehrlust* that demarcates the abstract and surplus substance of regulating pleasure as sin as an effect of the structure.[20] What appears in the libidinal economy as ordinary exchange performs in Lacan's enjoying bourgeois society as an excessive suture of the enjoyment of the structure.

Lacan (1966–1967), amid the social and bourgeois economy of jouissance, stipulates that "*jouissance*-value" is the "cancellation of the *jouissance* most immediately involved as such in sexual union; what it calls castration" (31.05.67). The exchange of values between the Other and the subject based on enjoyment is already an economic deformity of rentability on the subject. It seems then that this enjoyment value, earned in castration, is related to an exchange value in the meaning used by Lacan. That is to say, the subject's division is intricate and reduced in the signifier materiality fed by language and its signifiers in the economic vicissitudes favored by the social bond. Thus, and in his words, where there is "discourse," there is also a "social bond" to which "bodies submit" to capital and its bourgeois conditionings (Lacan, 1972a, p. 474).

In the same way, Lacan (1966–1967) also suggests that

> if that is hidden, it is because the woman, who in the sexual act is founded as a subject, in fact takes on the function of exchange value, covering what is already instituted as value in what psychoanalysis reveals under the name of castration complex.
>
> (07.06.67)

The male subject is supported by a socially alienating enjoyment conclusive through the incisive precept of the Other from the loss in the phallic dynamics of society. Women, on the contrary, are embedded in the order of the Other, but their enjoyment, as a function of castration, is not always phallic since they can direct their freedom toward another logic through society because they have nothing to lose. Thus, as Marx and Engels (1848) remarked,

> the bourgeois sees in his wife a mere instrument of production. He hears that the instruments of production are to be exploited in common and, naturally, can come to no other conclusion than that the lot of being common to all will likewise fall to the women.
>
> (p. 227)[21]

As Lacan (1966–1967) pointed out, in his *Seminar XIV*, the

> social exchange, in the foundation of the material, as I might say, destined for the sexual act. This leaves no less in suspense whether we can, by reason of this external element, situate something about the woman in her function as metaphor, with respect to a jouissance that has passed to the function of value.
>
> (07.06.67)

The insertion of the woman into the exchange of symbolic values allows her access to various possibilities of the enjoyment of the Other and not only to the subsumption of phallic logic. The exchange value that modulates women in the economic aspects of managing masculine force is nothing more than the exchange of a value broken by the Other for the tiresome reason that women are tied to the goal of receiving something. Because the woman is incorporated into this dialectic, the exchanges of the Other produce an effect of a signifying structure that socializes a phallic regulation of economic passivity. This directly does not imply anything other than the placement of an ideological and bourgeois fantasy of cumulative completeness in which both man and woman are chained in socially normative heterosexuality. In bourgeois society, it seems that dancers enjoy the sound of the channeling of their image.[22]

From a social and structural viewpoint, Lacan (1968–1969) wondered himself:

> Was surplus value there before abstract labour, I mean what this abstraction is separated out from, I mean as a social means, resulted from something that we will call—I am not guaranteeing the exactitude of the first word but I want to say a word that has weight—the absolutization of the market.

For Lacan, we can understand surplus value as the effect of social encounters through the absolutization of the market. That value of labor that is not paid to the worker and administered with the politics of enjoyment. In "whose fruits," Lacan tells us, "the capitalist discourse is constituted" (20.11.68, p. 37). It is in the economy of capital that regulates, at this historical moment, the forms of the market and of subjectivity exploited by the replacement of the objects that cause desire, which subdue the capitalist social bond.

Lacan's economic logic concerning surplus value, which he relates to the object *a*, makes it clear that we are faced with the avatars of discourse, that is to say the dialectic of the subject with the Other and the direction of death in commodities. This supposes that, in the exchange of labor and its production of surplus value, the subject is articulated in the function of knowledge, a value that remains chained around him, and the disposition of the market. Lacan (1968–1969) illustrates in a direct way that "knowledge is the price" and "the price is sometimes incarnated in money," and this does not have an individual implication but an inherent relation to its market and the economic relations of exploitation that it engenders. For Lacan, "knowledge has nothing to do with labor," so for it to exist, there must be "a market of knowledge" where it is necessary that "knowledge becomes a merchandise," is exchanged, and dimensions the forms of the social bond (20.11.68, p. 39).

Following the same homological reading, Marx (1867a) already mentioned in the same sense that "the product is transformed from the direct product of the individual producer into a social product" (p. 643). We assume then that, for Lacan, there is a market of exchange to relate the commodity and to subdue the dimensions of labor in its abstract and socialized condition. Knowledge as such is, from Lacan's point of view, a commodity which, like all commodities, is fetishized and has found itself in the jaws of surplus value, a surplus jouissance exchangeable for the effect of discourse. This commodity product offered in the knowledge market makes the subject's labor emerge in the form of discourse as a specific mode of exploitation and circulation. It is in this way that the domination of bourgeois society has been able to take good advantage of the subject's enjoyment through the passionate management of its interests. If the Other provides the subject with a discourse and intertwines it in its courses, we can easily understand that the signifiers are infected with the virus of the bourgeoisie at this historical moment.

As Marx (1867a) insinuates,

> use-value is certainly not *la chose qu'on aime pour lui-meme* in the production of commodities. Use-values are produced by capitalists only because and in so far as they form the material substratum of exchange-value, are the bearers of exchange-value.
>
> (p. 293)

That support where use value finds its exchange is the market. Society then rotates within an economic exchange dominated by the capitalist system, which designates how this use value can be a vehicle of enjoyment generated from creating a bond centered on production. Lacan reaches, consequently, to locate in Marx's surplus value [*Mehrwert*] a *plus-de-jouir* [*Mehrlust*] that can only be obtained as a refusal of primitive enjoyment in the repressive circulation of pleasure and its concupiscence (Lacan, 1968–1969, 20.11.68, p. 29).[23]

The capitalist discourse, its significance, and enjoyment are incarnated in the subject, joining together a social bond measured in the use of commodities as a concentrated axis of the movement of desire. In Lacan's (1968–1969) words,

> the way in which each one suffers in his relationship to enjoyment in so far as he does not insert himself into it only through the function of surplus enjoying, this is the symptom, and the symptom in so far as it appears from the fact that there is no longer anything but an average social truth, an abstract truth.
>
> (20.11.68, p. 41)

It is pertinent to infer that, for Lacan, what promotes the renouncement of enjoyment, that surplus, is what forges the economic sense of the symptom and the logic of dissatisfaction or inhibition. The above suggests a surplus of dead object in the labor performed within the subjects in their becoming and their exchange with the Other, generating a profitability of uneasiness at the social level. Thus, surplus value, Lacan (1970b) mentions, is "the cause of desire from which an economy makes its principle, that of the extensive and therefore insatiable production of lack-in-joying [*manque-à-jouir*]" (p. 435).

Due to the movement of commodities and the division of labor, society manifests a continuous and frenetic conflict. Nevertheless, according to Lacan (1968–1969), "in a strike, the collective truth of labour is manifested and what we have seen in May, was the strike of truth" (20.11.68, p. 41). Lacan's statement is highly suggestive since it places the possibility of a collectivity that unveils the stultified by the commodity and its production process as a mark of uneasiness. If work is left behind, then the insistent orientation of the *plus-de-jouir* can also be suspended for a brief moment. Society, as we know from Marx, alienates the worker in class antagonism by reducing his thought and his labor to dead and exchangeable commodities. In effect, in capitalist society's production mode, one can read the clear homology between Marx and Lacan concerning the circulation, break, and distribution of death from the mercantile distributions of commodities and their surplus value. Lacan thus speaks of an arrest of the machine constructing surplus enjoyment and a logic of sense.

Yet, as Lacan (1968–1969) himself mentions, "no discourse can tell the truth," only the symptom at work bursts forth as a chance to open it (20.11.68, p. 42). It is pertinent that the strike in its suspension of labor—quite simply—is a summons to the social and symptomatic truth of the subjects who stop that deadly surplus enjoyment turned into merchandise. As Marx (1843a) notes, "the people must be taught to be terrified at itself in order to give it courage," that courage of truth which can only express itself symptomatically in the temporary withdrawal from the production of death and excess (p. 10).

What, then, is the subject reduced to in the economy of capitalist society and its measures? In our encounter between Marx and Lacan, for the latter, the subject is rooted in their surplus enjoyment and, in turn, tied to the discourse of capital. A discourse that has in the knowledge its articulation to the lack of being of the subject ($\$$ — S_2) and the resolve of an economy reduced to consumption propitiated through the nihilistic Master's truth (S_1) whose reproductive product is the surplus value of the object (*a*). From the same perspective, for Marx (1844), "The misery results, therefore, from the essence of present-day labor itself" (p. 27). And also from "the numberless individual acts of circulation [that] are thereby immediately grouped together in their characteristic social movement as a mass circulation between major economic classes of society" and to the "object" as "one part of the total product" and "the labor" (Marx, 1867b, p. 435).

In this last way, social uneasiness is framed in labor since, for Lacan, it is related to the unhappiness produced in social abstraction in the enjoyment of capital and the circulation of surplus. We understand this last issue as that which stays gliding in the exchange value: Surplus value in Marx and in Lacan surplus enjoyment. As Marx (1867a) observed,

> the society of capital and wage-labor, a certain change takes place, or so it appears, in the physiognomy of our *dramatis personae*. He who was previously the money-owner now strides out in front as a capitalist; the possessor of labor-power follows as his worker.
>
> (p. 280)

And, with it, the libidinal economy of conflict is centered on transforming the death drive into knowledge and exploiting the force of socialized enjoyment labor in the bourgeois key. From a similar perspective, this social uneasiness, as Lacan (1972c) also noticed, "can only increase because of something completely new in the social bond itself": The "scientific discourse" (p. 20).[24]

While homogenizing science and exploitative economics reproduce the action of the structure at the social level, Lacan (1969–1970) demonstrates that

> what psychoanalysis enables us to conceptualize is nothing other than this, which is in line with what Marxism has opened up, namely that

> discourse is bound up with the interests of the subject. This is what, from time to time, Marx calls the economy, because these interests are, in capitalist society, entirely commercial.
>
> (18.02.70, p. 96)

The capitalist discourse captures the subject in its productive recesses since the dialectical exchange of values marks everything they (the subject) trade and whose social liberty is buried in the production and excessive consumption of commodities, a social agreement in the presence of exploitation. This supposes beforehand that the unstable relations between subjects are rooted between knowledge and its expression as merchandise that has transformed needs into desire based on the demand of the symbolic system. It is there where discourse, as a formalization of "social bond" and a political economy of enjoyment, implies a "pact" that involves at least a place of "truth" (Lacan, 1975b, p. 46).

Lacan (1969–1970) relates that

> This is what Marx calls the economy, because these interests are, in capitalist society, entirely commercial. It is just that since the market is linked to the master signifier, nothing is resolved by denouncing it in this way. For the market is no less linked to this signifier after the socialist revolution.
>
> (18.02.70, p. 92)

With the above, we do not suppose Lacan is attached to domination. On the contrary, we believe that his interpretation, in terms of the capitalist discourse, does nothing but highlight the misery of the subject in capitalism insofar as the exchange of its plus-de-jouissance always falls under the domination of the Master. What is at the bottom of all this is the transformation of the ancient gluttonous and insatiable Master into a modern master who distributes his gluttony and speculates with his profits and his crises based on the enigmatic economy of signifying exchange in modern societies.

In *Radiophonie*, Lacan (1970b) states: "in other words, it is from the unconscious and the symptom that he [Marx] claims to prorogate the great Revolution: it is from the discovered surplus value that he precipitates the consciousness said to be of class" (p. 424). Surplus value, as a Marxian enunciation for Lacan, is the only means by which discourse can intrude and dominate the subject with a social bond that transforms the archaic knowledge of the primitive into the actuality of the signifying speculation of the knowledge of the modern Master propitiated to a great extent by science. Nevertheless, something remains in the order of protest against the imposition of the renunciation of enjoyment that must be articulated to produce the advent of the subject, and with it appears the option of the *us* in the face of the society of enjoyment of the great capitalists.

Lacan (1969–1970), based on the homology between surplus value and surplus jouissance, defines that "What is masked at the level of Man: is that the master to whom this surplus *jouissance* is owed has renounced everything, and *jouissance* first up because he has exposed himself to death" (11.03.70, p. 107). Marx's function of surplus value is found in a fortunate conflict with Lacan, since for the former the one who gets the commodification and accumulation of surplus value is the capitalist watching the slave enjoy their social and sexual liberty, whereas the latter states that it is in the slave where *jouissance* as such is found in its rawness and its compulsion.

In this way, the worker is separated from the slave since they have renounced jouissance in their work. This key has at its core the idea that the genesis of the social order that expresses the Marxian position on society is bound up with *Lust* as greed, avarice, expenditure, and their respective enjoyments. The subject is the effect of the social relations of exploitation and the antagonism of the distribution of labor under a structure historically determined by socialized enjoyment in individual and unproductive misery.[25] The point that stands out in Lacan's reading is that the problem resides in a new master who may even appear friendly to the worker in order to circulate accumulation—a new master who associates science with capital.

Suppose there is a chance of a new radical social advent of the subject beyond the mercantile limits indicated in the previous paragraph. In that case, it can only appear through the ideological and subversive critique of the Master's knowledge through social shame in the face of the compulsion to enjoy and by *hystericalizing* the *jouissance* effect of knowledge. As Lacan (1969–1970) describes, in his elocution on the discourse of the hysteric, she "fabricate[s] a man as best she can[,] a man who would be animated by the desire to know" (17.12.69, p. 34). The above reveals that revolutions have a particular hysterical characteristic and that knowledge about society is alterable and dialectical. Thus, the revolutionary subject can be understood as hysterical, beyond the fact that merchandise continues to do its thing in the market. In the end, it is convenient to ask ourselves: Is it possible that hysteria and shame reveal to us something of the Master's knowledge and thus lead the subject to another horizon of emancipation?[26]

For Lacan (1971b), it is evident that within our society, there is not "a society of masters," but instead distributions of the signifier and its instruments of circulation as *jouissance* values, units of value without shame. Consequently, what is remarkable about a social structure from the signifier refers to "a discourse that will not be a semblance" which for Lacan "concerns something that deals with an economy" (13.01.71, pp. 17–18). Lacan refers at this point to the economy of discourse. In his words, discourse "appears (*fait semblant*)." However, the semblance of discourse we find entangled in terms of individual signifying enjoyment and the ideological support of unified reality. That is to say, when discourse appears in the subjects, it is only that which gives the semblance of something that distances itself from the truth and the public thing. Society invents its private, joyful, and shameless world in order to distance itself from the "public," which always "arises from the shameful" (Lacan, 1976, p. 267).[27]

Shame appears beyond the social semblance because it introduces the reduction to a mere object that exchanges social identification with the entire and guilty *jouissance* of the modern Master. While for Lacan (1970–1971), shame is somewhat charged with identification and "*hontologie*" (17.06.70, p. 180), for the young Marx (1843b), on the contrary, "shame is already a revolution" because "it is a kind of anger turned in on itself" (p. 441). The problem thus does not lie in assuming shame or curing it but in recognizing in it a differential and discursive economy, an economic and social discrepancy from the excessive movement of the object overturned in the external and personal recognition as an economy that has its own Moebius band course that decenters the social economy of individuals. The economic combination between Lacan's idea of shame and Marx's goes beyond the opposition between guilt and shame, of the capitalized semblant or of the community.[28] From our perspective, this mixture is an economic redeployment of enjoyment toward a fragmentary excess that inscribes the impossible in the social bond for another possible service of death.[29] A social and radical loss that would make it possible to imagine "each sphere" of "society" as the "*partie honteuse*" (Marx, 1843a, p. 10).

From this last perspective, discourse as a social bond and its ordering is nothing more than a fictitious position of truth. A truth that does not exist only in the wealth of capital but only on the side of the economic-management framing of the signifier. This is why, for Lacan (1971b), "the unconscious can be half-said as a language structure"; as a pure "effect of discourse" which can only be found through that which we observe through the "surplus enjoying" (13.01.71, p. 21). Thus, the discourse amplifies the question of truth and its struggle with knowledge and explains how the structuring of this surplus jouissance represents the subject as a desire economized through knowledge knotted to a symptom that is economically determined by the "sign" and the "knot" of a "political" character that Marx proposed (Lacan, 1973c, p. 13). This knotted desire will always be intrinsic to the position of the mercantile exchange of knowledge, and this will order the discourse. The semblance, in discourse, aspires to eliminate shame and is thus another device of the economic aspect that causes the encounter of the drive with the determinations of the signifier as an effect of truth.

Lacan (1971–1972) emphatically suggests that "social bond" is the "current state of what is grounded" as "discourse." From his perspective, the subject's discursive position "does not get it in the slightest" concerning what is introduced through discourse but only weaves tensions and symbolic demands that introduce impotence (03.02.72, p. 62).[30] Where we see a social bond, there is also a semblance that provides the discourse and its movements. This lets us glimpse that if society has an order, a structure, and a social function, it is from the semblance that it is granted and condemned to a set of forces. There is no such thing as a society if it is not positioned through discourse and its economy. The truth is located through the exchange of the driving force for the effect of truth that determines the social bond. Because of its economic and discursive components, the social bond is not the same as the social link since the former reflects an economy of the strict and essential relation between elements, and the latter expresses a disengaged connection. The economic management of the signifier is specified in the void of meaning between the sets that make the semblance of the social bond and direct the structure's knowledge.

In the vicissitudes of the semblance, it is undeniable that we are embodied and exploited on the premise of labor, its bifaceted character, and the discursive structure that mobilizes commodities as a particular mode of death and knowledge. As Lacan (1973–1974) mentions,

> the question is to know what unconscious knowledge [...] I posit it as what works. And what works can work—there is no kind of grip on work except in a discourse. It is a matter of grounding what is working in the analytic discourse. If there were not this social bond and this social bond in so far as it is founded by a discourse, the work would be ungraspable.
>
> (15.01.74)

Consequently, the social bond is purely economic, for it is nothing other than labor management to constitute a libidinal economy and a further distribution of passions, desire, and pleasures under the auspices of the chrematistic insistence of the Other's knowledge. It should not be forgotten here that knowledge is nothing other than dead and stagnant labor, just like any other commodity.

Beyond all that has been reviewed in the issues between the economy, the commodity, the abstract relation, and the signifier and between Marx and Lacan, we cannot now refuse to review a little into that which represents the class struggle and the constitution of society founded on the distinctions it summons up. Already from the famous phrase of Marx and Engels (1848) in the well-known *Communist Manifesto*, "The history of all hitherto existing society is the history of class struggles" (p. 123), we can perceive the sense of the antagonistic and administrative organization of the social world. This class struggle is embedded in the relations of exploitation by the bourgeois class of the proletariat, managing its labor power at the psychic level. The origin of society is precisely the exchange of the subject and its relations of exploitation by a scientific distribution of accumulation. This exploitation cannot exist without the dimension of signifying machinery that designates the "constant capital" which is "the value of all the means of production applied to production in this branch," whose "fixed capital," in addition to the machinery, is also the libido as a constant (Marx, 1867b, p. 472).

The economic convergence between Lacan and Marx hinges on the connection between the concept of work and the aggregation of a class such as the bourgeoisie and the proletariat, which is not the same as the master and the slave, given that there are random circumstances through discourse that structure the direction that each of the classes takes. The bourgeoisie, in this sense, is the one who can dictate in this historical and determined moment the prevailing discourse in society. If the Other is the one who articulates the signifying machinery and suggests its meaning, it is evident that at the center of the discourse of exploitation by the bourgeoisie, there is a logic of domination of the driving workforce. For Lacan, from our point of view, the dominant discourse is that of the one who has and uses the knowledge and the economic order produced by the relations of signifying exploitation of driving force, causing variable capital to set in motion and orient the "social labor force" thought to essentially extract "living labor" (Marx, 1867b, p. 472).[31]

In other words, what we can find in Marx is the dialectical reading of the social world based on the how and the reasons for the productive operation from different concrete and abstract levels. All this is understood as structure and correlation between subjects from a sequence of production relations that result in labor exploitation. Something evident is that the *plus-de-jouir* in Lacan is a complex concept framed in the relations of production. It is not strange that Lacan discovers in this surplus enjoyment that is deprived of the subject's social truth. The background of social reality is nothing more than the elucidation of the relations between classes and the historical and dialectical antagonism of the political world. It is there that the logic of "enraged sullenness of petit-bourgeois" forms "social progress that misrecognizes its mainspring" that prevents us from contradicting "what contradicts the vast dialectic that makes us serfs of history" (Lacan, 1957b, p. 372). The dialectical sense of antagonism makes possible not only the psychic conflict but also the economic class conflict that introduces the laboring malaise as an indicator of the drive exploitation in the social sphere. Or, as Lacan (1971–1972) notices it, the "worst" in the problem of the "social bond" is the "sexual exploitation of the bourgeoise" (17.05.72, p. 159).

From Marx's (1858) position, "bourgeois society is the most developed and the most complex historic organization of production" (p. 38). That is to say, at this historical stage, society is fused to the development of the means and the productive forces that determine the course of a diversified force of labor. The history of bourgeois society has a reversal toward the predecessor forms that have configured its existence because it has sequentially administered the living labor of the subjects. The transcendental object at this point is that bourgeois society can only exist as such because it is restricted via class struggle and the circulation of drive labor in the libidinal economy and its correlation to an enjoying economy. Social productions, beyond this, are defined in specific relations of social production, between commodities and the alienation of the subject employing a jouissance surplus that ultimately determines them and invents the sense of the "average person" that "does not exist" and is only a "statistical fiction" in the social bond of the modern master (Lacan, 1974, p. 19).

Therefore, the imaginary linkage of what could be defined as society refers to the conformation of the economic structures connected with its paradigms of structure. That is to say, not just any economic condition can be a determinant of society since society, if it can be thought of as such, is elaborated in the modes of production and accumulation of wealth from historical-structural modalities.[32] The subject does not make the social bond, but the structures autonomously determine it. That is to say, bourgeois society appears as soon as labor and exploitation of the worker are articulated in discursively determined economic relations, and the other approximations to a possible subjective social encounter would undoubtedly be just imaginary, a semblance in "where the economy of jouissance is disguised" (Lacan, 1967f, p. 29).

As Marx (1845) elucidates, "the ideas of the ruling class are in every epoch the ruling ideas: i.e., the class which is the ruling material force of society is at the same time its ruling intellectual force" (p. 67). The above expresses the distinction of the relations of the subjects between the ideas of the dominant class and the ideological reflex as an imaginary and idealistic link that supports almost totally the material and signifying exploitation. If we return to Marx with Lacan, from a materialist and economic reading, the associations of signifiers propose to us a hilarity of the univocal "Ego" prisoner of an economy that is no longer only libidinal but also enjoyable. Alongside this, if the ruling class's ideas configure the subject, we find here the guideline of an order of domination that realizes the avatars of the subject's drive exploitation in society; therein lies the importance of making social malaise profitable and marketable. This indicates that production relations are conditioned according to those who possess the capital of circulation.

To conclude this section and after considering the economy as part of a structure and its regional and superstructural determination—following Althusser's words—we can discern a subject that is not entirely determined by economic relations but by the weft and systematization of structural relations, evidently rational and in constant contradiction.[33] On the contrary, the subject is imbued with something that escapes, at least in a singular feature, all economic determination, betting on the lost cause. This recalls, in the same way, the chance of an aleatory redirection that poses elementary conditions in the structure because in Marx's (1867a) words, "the structure of the fundamental economic elements of society remains untouched by the storms which blow up in the cloudy regions of politics" (p. 479).

In addition to the social division of labor, the family distribution, as a repressive and commercial determination of labor and sexual exploitation, and the scope of the commodity become values in the significant and social wefts in the face of the uncertainty of the real. Let us remember that, for Marx (1867a), in the last instance, "the general form of value" appears as "mere congealed quantities of undifferentiated human labor, [and] shows by its very structure that it is the social expression of the world of commodities." In such a way, "it is made plain that within this world, the general human character of labor forms its specific social character" (p. 160). Does the psychic economy of jouissance not function in this mode in the repressive and commercial facets of society?

This can be reflected in any form of social structuring that we find in the contemporary socio-political sphere and the psychic and corporeal subjects' uneasiness. Society is a division between beings through the signifier, its value, and the enjoyment of exchange. Actually, the subject's sexuation can give us an account of this because, as Lacan (1974a) remarked, "the body is introduced into the economy of *jouissance*" (p. 22). Thus, the real of the commodified body takes on significance and consistency. Beyond this, any institutional form or redoubt interpenetrated by language and economy can be a referent.[34] This last position indicates that the whole social formation will always have a sense and knowledge intimately bonded to the economic structure where the avatars of signifying value unfold in its framing on the chessboard.

Then, the final proposal suggests that society does not find a definitive or impenetrable economic articulation but a transitory one according to the management of the *plus-de-jouir*. And, as much for Lacan as for Marx, its conformation is derived from the relations of the material signifiers and the economic relations of production in the vicissitudes of the sexual encounter, the commodity, and the family. For Lacan, culture, as the production of social subjects, would define what can be understood as society at the level of a planetary economy from signifier values. For Marx, the economy would be the stronghold where the social relations of production that forge modes of utilization of culture are exchanged. Both homologically combine a "theory of language as a structure of the unconscious" that "can be considered implied by Marxism" only under the logical condition of a "material implication"; that is to say that the "theory of language is true whatever the sufficiency of Marxism, and is necessary to it, whatever the defect it transmits to it" (Lacan, 1966a, p. 208).

There Is No Social Relation: A Marxian-Lacanian Exegesis

In 1987, Margaret Thatcher mentioned in the magazine *Women's Own* in an accurate way: "There is no such thing as society."[35] Nothing could be further from the title of this section for two reasons. The first one is that the sentence that gives the section its title does not focus on the fact that there is no society; what there is not is relation. On the other hand, emphasizing that there is no social relation implies recognizing the failure of the structure, its real element, and not only the complex ontological objectivity of differences.[36] In fact, Jacques Lacan (1969–1970) seems to have answered this Thatcherian sentence some years before when he mentioned:

> In the Master's discourse, since it is, all the same, there that surplus-*jouissance* is situated, there is no relationship between what will more or less become the cause of desire for a character like the master who, as usual, fails to understand anything about it and what constitutes his truth. As a matter of fact, there is a barrier here, on the lower level.
>
> (11.03.70, p. 108)[37]

The expression *there is no sexual relation* is logically different from the phrase *sexual relationship does not exist*. In the first one, the real vortex between sets is highlighted, and in the second one, a void representation is assumed as a function of ontological and universal disencounter. This linguistic issue can only be resolved if we consider that the void gives rise to the impossible—not to the incomplete—and, in the second sentence, only a position of rupture emerges, of identity fragmentation and subsequent encounter. Hence, in the phrase, *there is no social relation*, as a homological Lacanian-Marxian formula, the becoming of the impossible real and the redirection of lack in the problematic conjunction of society are at stake.[38] On the contrary, in the statement *society does not exist*, there is only a cut between the mass and the politics of hegemony that excludes the ambivalent value of the signifier and its enigmatic encounter with the pre-ontological real.[39]

To emphasize and sustain this previous nodal disparity, we must mention that Lacan's echoes concerning the social bond and society in the final part of his oeuvre are very singular. However, if we look for a definition of society *stricto sensu* in his work, we would limit the articulatory possibilities of the signifier. In fact, due to sexuality, we stumble upon a particular deviation that does not correspond to the relation between subjects. The passage and the relation among sets is undoubtedly a semblance of exchange for the sustenance of a truth regulated and produced by the master signifier. This does not imply that sex is not linked in its contingency with the subject and its corporeality. On the contrary, "this relation [*rapport*] is impossible to write" and "it is not affirmable but moreover not refutable: under the heading of truth" (Lacan, 1973d, p. 310).

Sexuation, which includes corporeality without being reduced to it, expresses a logic through which the subject will define its limits to *jouissance* and otherness. In this way, from the formulas of sexuation themselves, society is a remnant of signifiers and positions that have been elaborated and directed through the supposed binary dynamics of the social relations of production. To find society as a signifier articulated through sexuality reflects the ongoing search for subjects' meaning, a way of explaining what one is in a set of human beings. However, it is cultural formations that have given society a position in the signifying chain by inscribing the subject in an elementary division due to his sexuality, which, as Lacan (1964b) said, "is established in the field of the subject by a way that is that of lack" (27.05.64, p. 204).

From a Lacanian perspective, there is a material dialectic traversed through enjoyment, reminiscences, surpluses, and mutations in society. *Enjoyment*, as such, is attached to speech and discourse. For this reason, the social being is condemned to fragmented enjoyment via socialized exchange in the capital codes. Taking into account that the figure of jouissance is delimited in the jaws of the Other, Lacan realizes that it is thanks to the imperative of enjoyment that the subject finds its restrictive marks and its laws, which call for a renunciation of *jouissance* in the destinies of sexed life. As Lacan (1972a) himself indicates, "life, it is probable, reproduces, God knows what and why. But the answer only becomes a question where there is no relation that sustains the reproduction of life" (p. 456).

In this regard, it is engaging to argue that the Other also enjoys the social order in which it is inserted. We propose that if the Other is found managing and controlling social exchanges, it is thus who introduces the frames of voluntary servitude. Society is lodged in the dialectic of the Other and the subject's desire through the exchange of values, ideals, and mandates that justify the modalities of sexuality. In such a way that, from the generalized uneasiness [*malaise*] of civilizations, Lacan refers:

> in connection with sexual relationships, some fatality is inscribed that makes necessary in it what then appear as being the means, the bridges, the *passerels*, the buildings, the constructions, in a word, which at the deficiency, at the deficiency of this sexual relationship [...], any possible discourse will only appear as a symptom, within this sexual relationship.
>
> (Lacan, 1971b, 16.06.71, p. 166–167)

That is to say, for Lacan, there are no bridges or social constructions between reality, society, and the subject, only commensurable city abysses that symptomatically return in relation to value and the surplus enjoyment from the imaginary geolocations in civil society. Consequently, the social bond is only a differential distribution of agency and the signifier to determine the destructive logic of impossible social encounters.

It is the Other, as the symbolic system of culture, who directs and masks the subject's desire and manipulates them—with the help of the signifier society—into the mercantile trace through which the other has to articulate all their discursiveness on the political plane. That is to say, a formation of the social bond that designates the modalities of the agent in relation to the production and the stronghold of truth. The transindividual condition of the unconscious reflects that it is social and discursive relations that distance and distort subjects as a whole. As Marx (1858) enunciated it, "universally developed individuals, whose social relations, as their own communal [*gemeinschaftlich*] relations, are hence also subordinated to their own communal control, are no product of nature, but of history" (p. 92). In this way, we see that social relations are produced in a fictional and historical way, where radical and cultural differences, not complementary or univocal capitalistic differences, mark sexuality. The point is clear: If the subject is in a discourse, it is the Other who puts on the table the signifiers through which the social chaining can be recreated in a libidinal economy that configures its motricity and in an economy of jouissance that points toward death in the social and sexual norms and the lust.

From Lacan's point of view, the Other discovers in society the recreation of all the artificially binding precepts that have been devised as a result of the signifiers that appear in the diatribe of the social and sexual order. Society is embedded in economic designs that adjust the subject to push to relate fantastically and ideologically in the social world. If Marx proposes as the base of existence the social relations as producers of the individual as family and division of labor, in Lacan, we find that the division of the subject materializes as opposed to the determination of the enjoyment of the symbolic system harnessed through social relations of production. In both cases, subjects connect with *individualized unity* via the imaginary and utilitarian closure of the social and sexual relation. As Marx (1867a) foreshadowed, for capital, in its self-absorbed fantasy, "all men are alike in the face of capital—a milliner [woman] and a blacksmith [man]" (p. 364).

Besides, Marx and Engels (1848) also taught that due to "social relations" and their vicissitudes, "history does not end by being resolved into 'self-consciousness' as 'spirit of the spirit', but that each stage contains a material result, a sum of productive forces"; in this way, "this sum of productive forces, capital funds and social forms of intercourse, which every individual and every generation finds in existence as something given" which is nothing other than "substance" and which, from Lacan's point of view, can be related to the jouissance core of the symbolic system traversing and extracting, through social exploitation, the laboring and driven corporeality of the subject (p. 62). Where "there is no sexual relation," there also surfaces an enjoyment that "supplements" it and that is related to the "*plus-de-jouir*" (Lacan, 1972a, p. 460).

Likewise, in *German Ideology*, Marx and Engels (1846) oppugning Bruno Bauer relate: "This unique sex [put forward by Bruno] is explained on page 121, in the sense that 'sensuousness, like a vampire, sucks all the marrow and blood from the life of man; it is the insurmountable barrier against which man has to deal himself a mortal blow'"; to which they both reply: "But even the saintliest man is not pure! They are all sinners and lack the glory that they should have before 'self-consciousness'" (p. 114). Is it not plausible to link this with the metaphor of the capitalist as a vampire who has a unique sex? Is it not also connected with the insurmountable barrier without jouissance and before the death drive and phallic enjoyment? Thus, we discover that the sexual relation lies in an absence produced through the jouissance effect of the symbolic castration to which language summons us and its socialized adequacy that tries to be binarily and unitarily tamed by capitalist society. *Il n'y a pas de rapport sexuel* is not non-existent, but the effect of the radical and absolute difference in societies and beds is due to the consequence of the social bond.

Thus, the social mobility of signifiers through the Other and the master's social bond is not a fixed instance at the historical level but a changing one. In it, the word representations are provisionally installed, in which culture and society are mixed, as well as the assembly of the bond of political-economic interest. As Marx and Engels (1848) observed, "man's ideas, views, and conceptions, [...] man's consciousness, change with every change in the conditions of his material existence, in his social relations, and in his social life" (p. 229). The family, being the first sexually alienated amalgam of society, produces a social whole determined by the lack filled by the mercantile productive excess, where there is no social relation but a movement of the signifier value concerning the law. This is how the modern master dictates, from the bourgeois family reason, the forcing of a distancing from the unnatural subject posed by culture, which feeds the economic conditions that make the social symptom possible. Lacan (1972–1973) confirms this when he mentions that

> culture, insofar as it is distinct from society, does not exist. Culture is the fact that it has a hold on us (*ça nous tient*). We no longer have it on our backs, except in the form of vermin, because we do not know what to do with it, except to get ourselves deloused.
>
> (13.02.73, pp. 53–54)

Around this vertiginous voyage and arriving at the last stage, the notion of society in the final part of Lacan's oeuvre can be regarded as the discursive conjuncture that, as a social bond, puts in place diverse paths and impasses of the Other to collect representation, exchange, and normative articulation. Moreover, it must be said that there is no whole relationship between subjects either sexually or socially. The homology between *there is no sexual relationship* and *there is no social relation* is because the signifier, as value, in its diachronic and synchronic movement and determination, obeys an impossible design as a horizon of possibility. There is nothing that encrypts them either universally or in the last instance, and both remain at the mercy of the commodity-object that, as surplus, as circulating knowledge, fills subjective existence through the modalities of the social bond.[40] According to Lacan (1970b),

> the unconscious *ex-sists* only by revealing itself clearly in the discourse of the hysteric, everywhere else there are only grafts: yes, surprising as it

> may seem, even in the discourse of the analyst where what is made is culture.
>
> (p. 530)

From its foreign policy, in the analysis, a culture gives rise to a punctual and differential narcissism of the lost cause. In this way, both Marx and Lacan agree on the normalizing deformity of social relations through the brutal modes of *extimate* enjoyment and production that are in the midst of a response to a historically located master.

From all this, the question about there being no social relation refers to the uncertain link between the subject and their truth. The symbolic character in which discourses function as a bond reflects the inscription through which the subjects confine their existence to an economically profitable dynamic and avoid, in a particular manner, problematizing their original condition as mere corporeality. Furthermore, they evade their uneasiness by surrendering themselves to surplus enjoyment, avoiding the inquiry of the alienation in the consumption of things.[41] Perhaps the subject could recover something of their corporeal existence mechanized by the signifier and turn toward culture, and as Lacan (1972–1973) mentions, "I recommend that you keep it [culture], because it tickles and wakes you up" (13.02.73, p. 54). In this way, the subject finds in language their first point of union and the point of separation inherent in the relations between signifiers and, consequently, concerning the "if there is no such thing as a sexual relationship, we must see in what respect the jouissance of the body can serve a purpose here" (Lacan, 1972–1973, 20.02.73, p. 71). A reading of society in Lacan unveils the fatuous stability of the social mechanisms of repression. As a signifier structure, society also proposes random exchanges that do not fully capture culture. Society, according to Lacan, incites us to shake the onslaught of the Other and to divert conditioning and its efficacy culturally.

Within the framework of discursive relations, the phantasmatic social relation also proposes and manages a field of knowledge and the meshing knowledge styles aimed at the direction of the epistemological drive. As a means of jouissance, knowledge reduces the subject to the signifier exchange and the identification with the master. For this reason, the sentence "there is no social relation" expresses not only a lack but the preamble for relations in society to produce relational enclaves of utilitarian fiction of knowledge. The desire to know, as Lacan (1973–1974) regarded, "takes substance from the social group" and is thereby linked to the jouissance dynamics of the prevailing political-economic system (09.04.74). From the inclement cunning of knowledge, the formula that there is no social relation expresses a negative position in the face of the managerial design of knowledge and the governance of the drive and the vicissitudes of the body. In this respect, a social body is only the reflection of a discursive peculiarity that positively designates the becoming of the subjects and, with it, social science designates the functional cuts that fix the supposed existence of a relation via the serialization of scientific discourse.

In the final stage of Lacan's work, dynamic junctures of explanation and elucidation of the scope of a social bond remain. Lacan's final and adjacent approach to society resides in finding it as a signifier and as a signifier structure that allows the demand of the Other to be described in the subject from a social bond demarcated in a quaternary logic. It is precisely in this structure of society that for Lacan (1974a), "there is only one social symptom: each individual is really a proletarian, that is to say, he has no discourse with which to make a social bond, to use another term semblant. This is what Marx put an ending to, and in an incredible way," and this is the reason why "a sexual relation is lacking in all forms of society" (p. 18). The emergence of a difference before the repressive master caused a lack in the constitution of society. There is a prior and ontological lack that can only be explained by the impossibility and permanence of the uncanny certainty of social beings. As Lacan (1976–1977) noted, "between the social delirium and the idea of God, there is no common measure. The subject thinks he is God, but he cannot justify that he is produced from the signifier, from the signifier S_1" (17.05.77).[42]

The progress of Lacan's thought points to the relevance of discourse for the subject and accounts for the social pressures in which the subject is positioned at the level of the social semblance. The quest for a fixed or univocal concept of society loses pertinence because society is only represented in its combinatory elements, and in this way, we can understand the insistence on the semblance, frustration, and inhibition before the truth prevalent in the forms of social bond and the conformation of knowledge. In a similar logic, the social relations of production, elucidated by Marx, preserve a homology with the sexual non-relation due not only to his examination of the natural principle of the relation with the fellow human being but also to the ambiguous and never closed form of equivalence traced by social and political dispositions in the management of social life.

As Lacan (1975–1976) indicates, in his *Seminar XXIII*, from a topological point of view, "when there is equivalence, there is no relation" (17.02.76, p. 82). This equivalence of a social and bourgeois character is configured in the extensions of individualistic liberalism and the impossibility of equality in the semblants.[43] From the impossibility—different from the unrealizable—of the social relation can arise repression of meaning, of the indeterminate where "freedom, equality, property, and Bentham" (Marx, 1867a) reign or the continuous horizon of social emancipation as the alliance of the impossible (to govern, to teach, to psychoanalyze).[44]

In the axiom, there is no social relation so that one can clarify the managerial setting of enjoyment preserved in support of the need as well as the sexual relation. In this way, the condition of necessity is close to the real, as shown by sexuality as such. For Lacan (1971b), the need in the sexual relation "is not measurable, and it is indeed in this element of indetermination that there is signed what is fundamental, which is very precisely that the sexual relationship is not inscribable, cannot be grounded as a relationship" (19.05.71, p. 121). If the sexual relation can only reflect the "inter-symptomatic" because the "symptom" is of the "signifier order" and if Marx is the inventor of the symptom, then the social structure of the non-relation is inherent to the value that unveils the class antagonism and the failure of sociological knowledge (Lacan, 1978, p. 220).[45]

Likewise, the needs of Marx's dispositions are based on a historical character that does not have ultimate satisfaction due to the transformation of the production conditions.[46] Consequently, what we have is a management of needs and drives that do not find sufficient satisfaction in the problematic link between a subject, the structure, and commodities. There is only a punctual deviation of material need and sexuality. Thus, there is no sexual and no social relation because of the incessant value engendered in the knowledge and measure of the management of pleasures and needs through the symbolic system of culture. Indeed, capital is woven in the closed relation because its relation of values makes it appear as a "relation with itself" that can only express itself if the real difference is excluded by reducing everything to exchange as a perversion of needs (Marx, 1867c, p. 139).

Finally, to comprehend society as impossible and from its negativity in Lacan, the expression of the event and its emergence in a site of event is cardinal.[47] Since it is not a fixed instance, society can be analyzed from a materialistic approach that prioritizes the indeterminacy of sexuality while recovering the historical and symptomatic conditions that make the identification that has determined it stumble.[48] If we leave open the road of the impossibility of conjunction in the social relation, a polymorphous orientation emerges there through the exception and the force of truth. The representation of the social must be random, contingent on the encounter, just like the gears that make it up. No sexual relation implies, in an unassailable form, that there is no social relation but attempts at complementarity between emptiness and supposed unity. The determination of the existence of society as a bond is different from the social bond because, in the former, the fullness is granted by the link of the imaginary and the structuring thrust of the signifier, whereas, in the latter, there are only modalities of the economy of value and the material support of exchange as a set.

Notes

1 About Lacan and the French May, See Livio Boni (2012) and Rabaté (2009).
2 For a detailed discussion of the Freudian view of homosexuality, see Hertzmann and Newbigin (2023).
3 In Robert Samuels' (2000) words: "to paraphrase Lacan, there is no natural sexual relation. Heterosexuality as well as homosexuality is something that has to be created and constructed" (p. 112).

4 For a detailed exploration of Lacan's formulae of sexuation, see Le Gaufey (2020).
5 According to Yves Depelsenaire (2008), "sexual relationship is like asceticism" because "the real has no meaning whatsoever" and neither does "sexual relationships" (p. 28).
6 Marx's ethnographic review is similar to Lacan's since he considers that no institution, i.e., the family, marriage, or capital, is produced in natural or perpetual conditions but is socially mutable. In this regard, see Lawrence Krader's (1974) extensive review of Marx's ethnological notes and Lewis Henry Morgan's (1877) influence on Marx.
7 Indeed, the modern episteme can only be conceived as an "intimate relation of mutual exclusion," and psychoanalysis discovers the universal exception (Milner, 1995, p. 53).
8 This association of thirdness or trichotomy is also elementary to Charles Sanders Peirce's (1958) logical and linguistic elaboration.
9 In Stephen Frosh's (1994) words: "Lacan claims that the essentially patriarchal organization of culture, or properly speaking the phallic structuring of language, means that woman takes up her place as the Other, as something which stands outside the Symbolic as its negative, giving it its presence through her exclusión" (p. 118).
10 As Badiou and Cassin (2017) note: "Sex proposes—nakedly, if I may put it this way—the real as the impossible proper: the impossibility of a relationship. The impossible, hence the real, is thus linked to ab-sense and, in particular, to the absence of any relationship, which means the absence of any sexual meaning" (p. 50).
11 For Žižek (2006), "Every subject has to invent a fantasy of his or her own, private formula for the sexual relationship—the relationship with a woman is possible only inasmuch as the partner adheres to this formula" (p. 48).
12 This feature of singularity in the collective ensures that the subject is not "dissolved in the classes and the masses" and is located in an "internal transindividual constitution of the collectivity" (Pavón-Cuéllar, 2022, p. 79).
13 In fact, from a Laclausian point of view, "The people, as such, is the result of a radical construction and implies an insuperable gap between the real (heterogeneous) and the contingent modes of its symbolization" (Biglieri & Perelló, 2020, p. 336).
14 The link between Marxism and psychoanalysis, from a historical and political perspective, is not recent. From the most classical Freudian-Marxist traditions connected materialism and forms of exploitation in their dialectical and critical direction of ideology (Reich, 1972; Fenichel, 1967), in their vicissitudes in the face of the drawbacks of capital and repressive and rational psychological formations (Fromm, 1970; Bernfeld, 1973), or even from the viewpoints of the Critical Theory of the Frankfurt School (Marcuse, 1956; Horkheimer, 1972) and the materialist critiques of the Freudian perspective (Sève, 1973). For a specific and detailed exploration, see Pavón-Cuéllar (2016) and the compilation of authors close to critical psychology, psychoanalysis, and Marxism (Parker and Pavón-Cuéllar, 2017).
15 The study of the connection between Marx and Lacan has also achieved a relevant place in academic and militant discussions. See, for example, Soueix (1992), Regnault (2005), Landman and Lippi (2013), Pavón-Cuéllar (2013), and Soto van der Plas et al. (2022).
16 For Shlomo Avineri (1968), what "the Industrial Revolution" made "possible was a socio-political revolution in late medieval Europe: the emergence of a civil

society, bürgerliche Gesellschaft, i.e. an autonomous sphere of economic activity, unimpeded by political and religious restrictions. [...] According to Marx, the communal movement created a sphere of autonomous economic activity, unrestricted by political and religious tutelage which might limit its freedom of economic choice" (p. 155).

17 Leonardo Arrieta (2013) also points out how Lacan recognizes, in his *Seminar V*, in Marx a "precursor" of the "mirror stage" in relation to "value" (pp. 225–226).
18 On dissatisfaction and its relation to enjoyment, see Jean-Paul Hiltenbrand (2005).
19 About this and its relation to capital, see Alemán (2018a).
20 As Ignacio Ellacuría (1990) writes, from Liberation Theology's perspective, "there are social and historical structures that are the objectification of the power of sin and, in addition, convey that power against men" (p. 356).
21 See Sharon Smith (2015).
22 See Norbert Elias (1991).
23 A detailed exploration on the origin of the *plus-de-jouir* can be read in Barrios and Filippini (2021).
24 In fact, for Glynos (2002), "the natural scientist" focuses "on pushing back the boundaries of knowledge—a knowledge whose exponential, multidirectional, and virtually uncontrollable expansion is fast becoming a typical feature of today's capitalist liberal democratic societies" (p. 14).
25 On expenditure, the unproductive, and loss, see Bataille (1933).
26 About the relevance of shame as a political factor in Lacan, see Danelinck (2018).
27 In this regard, Joan Copjec (2006) offers a brilliant and political elucidation of the relation between Lacan and the students of the French May.
28 For a more precise discussion of the relation of guilt and shame to society, see Piers & Singer (1953).
29 It is not only Lacan's idea of dying of shame that is relevant here. Additionally, the thoughts of Norbert Elias (1985) about the problem of knowledge and death can be considered parallel. See also Gros (2021) on shame and societies.
30 Since *Seminar XVII*, according to Dominiek Hoens (2006), Lacan distinguishes "psychoanalysis qua social bond from other discourses. Besides this differentiation, Lacan is also reflecting on how psychoanalysis depends on other discourses and the historical context in which it originated and exists" (p. 90).
31 As Althusser (1969) mentions: "He [Marx] understands abstract economic reality (which Smith, for example, rediscovers in the laws of the market as a result of his work of foundation) as the effect of a deeper, more concrete reality: the mode of production of a determinate social formation" (p. 110).
32 From Lukács' (1978) perspective, "Marx's presentation of the two specific and qualitatively distinct commodities, money and labor-power, provides in full detail a closed and seemingly complete picture of the first truly social production" (p. 44).
33 According to Marcuse (1960), for Marx, "the history of civil society" is "the history of the irreconcilable antagonisms inherent in this social order" (p. 259 ff).
34 For example, Poulantzas (1975) remarks that "the relative autonomy of the various institutions (power centers) in relation to social classes is not due to the fact that they possess a power of their own distinct from class power, but to their relation to the structures" (p. 115).
35 This notion, and Thatcher's political outlook in general, was deeply influenced by Friedrich August von Hayek's (1944) perspectives about economic liberalism in his book *The Road to Serfdom*.
36 From Ernesto Laclau's (1990) point of view "society does not 'exist' insofar as objectivicy, as a system of differences that establishes the being of entities, always

shows the traces of its ultimate arbitrariness and only exists in the pragmatic—and as a consequence always incomplete—movement of its affirmation" (p. 183).

37 Tomšič (2024) even notes, in Thatcher's statement, a crisis of the notion of society and the historical and structural trouble of antisociality sustained by capitalism.

38 As Tomšič (2015) points out: "[T]he dialectical materialist method, following modern epistemic ideals, discerns the structural real, which amounts to Marx's central hypothesis in *Capital*: there is no such thing as social *relation*" (p. 9) [Italics in the original]. From our reading, this link between the two sentences is not an equivalence but a homology focused on the relation.

39 See Appleton (2024) and Laclau and Mouffe (1985) to amplify this debate.

40 The capitalist and globalizing "market," according to Sauret (2009), is the "supreme value" that rejects "culture, the social" and even the "political" (p. 296).

41 Milner (2011a) suggests that the subject, in their "politics of things," finds no "limit," a politics of "unlimited" enjoyment from the excess of socialized jouissance (p. 148).

42 There is a pure value relation and how one "value is represented for another value" (Milner, 2011b, p. 90).

43 See Morton Fried (1967) in *The Evolution of Political Society*.

44 From Alemán's (2012) viewpoint, "the social bond is not constituted on the basis of a 'common ground.' The common ground is the impossibility of the relation that imposes that we respond to this impossibility with the invention of a supplement constituted by the social bond" (p. 25). Allouch (2017), in agreement, argues that the "non-existence of sexual relation is not a given"; it is a "non-existence that is either conquered or not" (p. 133).

45 From Alemán's (2018b) perspective, there are three "names of the common" in "the Lacanian non-there is: there is no sexual relation, there is no metalanguage, there is no other of the Other" (p. 122); here one could well add: there is no social relation.

46 On needs in Marx, see Agnes Heller (1976).

47 For Badiou (1988), the "void" names what is "in common" between the site and the "situation" around the event (p. 206).

48 As Badiou (2005) notes, we must "illuminate the value of the exception. The value of the event. The value of rupture. And this against the continuity of life, against social conservatism" (p. 15).

Conclusions

A Lacanian *Sociologery?*

Throughout all these chapters, it was possible to glimpse the scope of the notion of society in Lacan's words and *écrits*. The first approaches elucidated the importance of the tripartite function in which the subject finds itself: The individual, the structure, and the social tension. These are mechanisms through which, for Lacan, the composition of the socialized and normalized personality in society is founded and through which we can understand the relevance that the social tension had for Lacan within the conformation of personality.

What we consider at this point as substantial is the condition for the individual to be inserted within the social tension itself, since it is thanks to it that a configuration mode of the exterior that causes the psyche can also be engendered and thus produces a series of inscriptions of the social functioning well-focused on the distribution of populations. This is why Lacan's doctoral thesis materializes the first encounter with the function of society and its relevance at the level of psychic manifestations. Lacan knows that it is primarily in a society where one finds something that conforms to social reality in the subjects. For this reason, social tension invites us to think of an individual produced by the three functions already mentioned.

Another core point of this exploration within Lacan's early approaches to society is the distinction between nature and culture. Although at first sight it may seem obvious, for Lacan, the opposition of culture to the natural life can be observed in practices that may seem natural to us but are indeed encrypted from before birth by the function of laws and the marks left by the symbolic register of culture. The accumulation of complexes is a revelation of the tension between the drive and the cultural world, which refers to psychic conflict. This foundational antagonism is mainly responsible for the conflicts of the family institution. It cannot be removed from the elementary encounters between the structural hierarchies that make a subject emerge. From the Lacanian point of view, in the early years, society was an intermittent arrangement of the subjection of social relations to culture itself to account for individually socialized mythology.

Lacan's inquiry into the social and economic exchanges of the subject is equally engaging since it gives us an interpretation far removed from what is

DOI: 10.4324/9781032673837-6

natural as such. The subject is necessarily subjected to culture; all their deeds and movements are, for Lacan, a remnant of the cultural precepts in which the subject is abducted. The distinction between nature and culture is key to comprehending the subject's acts in society within the cultural maw of the economic system. For this reason, Lacan's examination of the counter-natural function of the subject allows us to see that culture is the background that governs, creates, sickens, and subdues the individual, differentiating it from himself, employing identification and the advent of his subjectivity.

Lacan amplifies the relevance of Freud's primitive horde while challenging one of the main contributions of psychoanalysis in the social and cultural spectrum. Lacan disputes that Oedipus is a totalizing entity for the subject's endeavor and studies it as a conflicting expression between social demands and the possibilities of socialized knowledge. This version is revelatory and contrary to the universalist representation that Freud gave to the figure of the incestuous desire of the subject. The prohibition of incest in societies is cardinal because it only shows the efficacy of the law and the reproduction of the management of the sexuality of bodies.

Lacan thus postulated that the Oedipus complex is a catalyst of culture. Due to its relentless determination, the subject displays cultural exchanges that demarcate the subjects' acts. In the prohibition of incest, there is a social and original cut that grounds the forbidding in an enjoying framework belonging to the culture. Lacan, therefore, proposes that Oedipus is a social variable and, as such, is the object of many distributive resonances due to social demands and their antinomies, which can account for a society that is structured due to the desire that mobilizes the prohibition. For the so-called young Lacan, it is undeniable that the formation of the family, in its conjugal aspect, is the cornerstone of the exchanges characterized by culture. The family, understood by a couple of men and women, reinterprets the conformation of a totalitarian origin of man from a primordial horde. For Lacan, the demarcation of the family by culture raises the structure of the Freudian myth of the horde. Lacan remarks that the most relevant aspect of this horde is the cultural dialectic that arises from the parricidal act of the clan of brothers: Guilt, inheritance, and debt.

After 1953, Lacan focuses on language and its abstraction, the possibilities of exchanging subjects with everything, and his exploration of the original formation of society. From his point of view, from language, we find the conformation of the symbolic universe, in which the institution of norms between subjects is made possible. Language is, for Lacan, a transcendental axis through which the subject is structured and desired, and this has its original effect since all human interactions depend on the positioning of the symbolic, which is framed by the subject's castration at the moment of being split by language.

From Lacan's perspective, the structure of language, and its metaphorical and metonymic motions, is the elemental distinction between animals and subjects, marking differences and traffic between values that are never usually similar due to their order. In an anthropological vein, Lacan relates his ideas to Lévi-Strauss to contrast nature with culture through language and the production of desiring social beings subject to unease. It is precisely thanks to language that the subject is encrusted into the law of the symbolic. Therein lies, for Lacan, what is truthfully elemental for the cultural subject, the law of culture as demand and degraded organization in the society. Due to the symbolic efficacy, language and the subjective mythical condition affect subjects' socialized existence. Regarding the social order, Lacan relaunches the importance of myth as it makes the chaining of signifiers possible, which must be captured on a social and symbolic base before the subject is born into the culture. Lacan calls this place, this system, "the treasury of signifiers," and from then on, the surface of the Other conditions the direction of the drives, and the desire of the subjects within their surrounding world.

It is then undeniable that the subject finds in language all the realization of its prevailing parsimony to symbolize his world and to meet the movements that modulate its encounter with the other. Society thus becomes a symbolic support. With this, Lacan does nothing other than mobilize the totalitarian sense of society to situate the gift's social fact as a centralized order mechanism and the influence of the symbolic. From this logic, a new movement reorganizes the certitude of social facts and the supposed biological-normative stability of societies. The signifier turns animal societies into human societies as symbolic entities. Lacan attaches great matter to the signifier since society is conveyed as a signifier and a signifying structure. For Lacan, society is a structure of signifiers that have joined the subject, but as such, in a solitary way, this signifier represents absolutely nothing. In the end, Lacan's way of disturbing society is related to the social bond demarcated through demands and discursive positions and the impossibility of the sexual relation as a fact that gives rise to the void and is unmeasurable in social relations.

Already in his last seminar, Lacan (1977–1978) hints that "analysis is a fact, at least a social fact, which is founded on what we call thought that we express as best we can with the '*lalangue*' we have" (11.04.78).[1] That social fact, what is given and circulated, is nothing other than the differential exchange of the not everything in language; a path that can only be followed in the singular drawing of the unary trace within the conformation of social dynamics and the demand to enjoy on the part of societies. Amid the societies of jouissance, there is only one way of annoying the stability of society, and it cannot be carried out without a signifying trace.

Due to all this, the final premise, as an inconclusive mystery of knowledge, resides in thinking of society and its machinery as a *sociologery* related to Lacanian *linguistery*. [2] To explain this proposal, the notion of *lalangue* is nodal because it insists on the expression of negativity and the difference built between an ordered and foundational system that is usually expressed structurally in language and the mistakes and differences manifested through the speaking being [*parlêtre*], that place of the common language.[3] For Lacan (1973a), "the signifier battery of *lalangue* provides only the cipher of meaning" (p. 516). In its minimal cipher, randomness, difference, and eventuality can only be found, redefining the enjoyment of action in language.

If there is *lalangue* in *linguistery* it is only because both situations manifest the force of the impossible as a differential horizon and not a submission to concepts or to the scientific conclusion of knowledge and its measurements.[4] *Lalangue* proceeds beyond the mere imaginary and symbolic management of subjects and, as Lacan (1972–1973) mentions, "serves purposes that are altogether different from that of communication" since it expresses the non-dominable particularities of the management of meaning (26.06.73, p. 158). With *lalangue* is indicated the differential revelation of the encounter with language and the arrangement of an elemental knowledge that cannot be fully captured since it is the mode of inventiveness produced as a non-all in the face of the real.[5] In *lalangue*, the differential feature of the bijection of language is framed and, consequently, resolves, not without loss and void, a differential relation to the symbolic structure and its social function.

From Lacan's point of view, *linguistery* is a neologism that summons *lalangue* but also hysteria and the not-all; it places the guidelines to understand that the symbolic system of culture that is barred and that certainly cannot submit to the unpredictability of the real and its randomness because its base, *lalangue*, is always enigmatic and thus escapes any purpose of the social bond of science.[6] Lacan (1973a) mentions: "under the term *linguistery* [*linguistricks*] I group whatever claims—and this is new—to intervene in men's affairs in the name of linguistics. Linguistics being the science that concerns itself with *lalangue*" (p. 511). From this logic, the neologism *sociologery* works with social ties and the material randomness of their encounters. In this sense, we propose *sociologery* as a reading that Lacan himself makes of society and social relations in order to extract, in an undoubtedly anti-philosophical way, the indeterminable remainder that is knotted here in the keys of the adage that there is no social relation, and also as a peripeteia of reading social reality—a punctual shaking of the functional, fictitious, and profitable knowledge of sociology as a science of the social practices.

From the reading of the minimal element of the structure that functions through the wedge of language in the body and subjective existence, it is feasible to find a *sociologery* that grounds the open dynamics of the exteriority of the signifier to discover new points of anchorage in the relation between the master signifier, knowledge, production, and truth. Thereby, we find the disturbance of insight that in the no social relation, there are impossible modalities that direct society not toward exploitation of the drive but toward a social reconfiguration of the *parlêtre* in its collective becoming. Where the subject of the unconscious emerges, there also appears a differential chance at the level of social demands and normativity. Consequently, a *sociologery* describes the random signifier conditions of society that make space not only for differences but also for a negentropic and subversive horizon of the impossible as a point of advancement of other prospects of *jouissance* in the social bonds of production and against social sciences as the discourse of the university.

Throughout his oeuvre, Lacan never ceases to hystericize society. This dimension becomes increasingly more emphatic as he uses the social bond as a modality of extraction that sharpens the indeterminate of the signifier to propel an emancipatory and subversive principle of the classical ways of understanding society, either from the continence of the signifier, passing through the disaggregation, or the surplus jouissance, and going through the movement of social bonds as discourses. After all that has been expressed, *sociologery* outlines the contingent stratagem of the signifier society—as a contraption—through an archeology—a crafty antiquarian praxis—that explores all that resists a closed understanding of social norms, the civilized management of bodies, and the economic contortions of culture.

Notes

1 The term *lalangue* is a result of Lacan's play on words to express *Langue* [Language or tongue] and the article *la* [The]. Bruce Fink use the English neologism *Llanguage*. We chose to keep the original French.
2 Bruce Fink's used the word *Linguistricks* to translate Lacanian *linguisterie*. Joan Copjec used *linguistery*.
3 The common, singular, and contingent in *lalangue* directly realize the interrogation of the Sinthome. See Alemán (2014, pp. 50–52).
4 For Milner (2001), the "sociologizing device" realizes distinct "dichotomies," including that of nature and culture, and requires the minimal unity of the "signifier" that "only represents for." It is because of this that "*linguisterie*" is delimited by a "suffix [erie]" which is "reserved for certain groups whose members are dispersed, despised, rival among themselves and are condemned to a deplorable old age: swindling, gallantry, loutishness, piracy." In this suffix, the collective "adventure" of "some subjects" (pp. 23–28) can be noticed.
5 Vladimir Safatle (2023) proposes in these same lines the social and "solidary" assumption of an "impossible" toward a "non-phallic form of jouissance" (p. 47).
6 As Alemán (2024) points out, "no social tie exists outside of discourse because the subject and the other do not have any medium that would establish their bond in language" (p. 76).

References

Alemán, J. (2006). *El porvenir del inconsciente.* Buenos Aires: Grama.
Alemán, J. (2012). *Soledad: Común. Políticas en Lacan.* Madrid: Clave Intelectual.
Alemán, J. (2014). *En la frontera. Sujeto y capitalismo.* Barcelona: Gedisa.
Alemán, J. (2018a). *Lacan y el capitalismo. Introducción a la soledad: común.* Granada: EUG.
Alemán, J. (2018b). *Capitalismo. Crimen perfecto o emancipación.* Barcelona: NED Ediciones.
Alemán, J. (2021). *Ideología. Nosotras en la época. La época en nosotros.* Barcelona: NED Ediciones.
Alemán, J. (2024). *Lacan and Capitalist Discourse. Neoliberalism and Ideology.* London: Routledge.
Allouch, J. (1984). *Letra por letra. Transcribir, traducir, transliterar*, M. Pasternac (Trans.). Buenos Aires: Edelp.
Allouch, J. (2013). *Prisioneros del gran Otro. La injerencia divina* I, S. Mattoni (Trans.). Buenos Aires: El cuenco de plata.
Allouch, J. (2017). *No hay relación heterosexual*, J. Huerta (Trans.). Mexico: Epeele.
Althusser, L. (1968). Préface: du Capital à la philosophie de Marx. In: L. Althusser and E. Balibar, *Lire le Capital I* (pp. 9–86). Paris: François Maspero.
Althusser, L. (1969). *For Marx*, B. Brewster (Trans.). London: Verso, 1965.
Althusser, L. (1970). Ideology and Ideological State Apparatuses. (Notes towards an Investigation). In: *Lenin and Philosophy and Other Essays* (pp. 127–187), B. Brewster (Trans.). New York: Monthly Review Press, 1921.
Althusser, L. (1978). The Underground Current of the Materialism of the Encounter. In: *Philosophy of the Encounter: Later Writings* (pp. 163–207), G. M. Goshgarian (Trans.). London: Verso, 2006.
Althusser, L. (1992). *L'avenir dure longtemps.* Paris: Stock, 2007.
Althusser, L. (1993). *Writings On Psychoanalysis: Freud and Lacan*, J. Melhman (Trans.). New York: Columbia University Press.
Althusser, L. (2005). *Filosofía y Marxismo. Entrevista por Fernanda Navarro.* Mexico: Siglo XXI.
Appleton, T. (2024). *A Lacanian Conception of Populism. Society Does Not Exist.* London: Routledge.
Aquinas, Th. (1270). *The Summa Theologica.* London: Burns and Washbourne, 1922.
Aristotle (1932). *Politics*, H. Rackham (Trans.). London: William Heinemann.

Arrieta, L. (2013). Marx et le significant de la valeur dans la clinique des psychoses de l'enfance. In: P. Landman and S. Lippi (Eds.), *Marx, Lacan: L'acte révolutionnaire et l'acte analytique* (pp. 225–240). Paris: Érès.

Avineri, S. (1968). *The Social and Political Thought of Karl Marx*. Cambridge: Cambridge University Press.

Badinter, E. (2010). *L'amour en plus: histoire de l'amour maternel, XVIIe-XXe siècle*. Paris: Flammarion.

Badiou, A. (1988). *L'être et l'événement*. Paris: Seuil.

Badiou, A. (2005). *Filosofía del presente*, F. Alejandrina (Trans.). Buenos Aires: Libros del Zorzal.

Badiou, A. and Cassin, B (2017). *There's No Such Thing as a Sexual Relationship*, K. Reinhard (Trans.). New York: Columbia University Press.

Baños Orellana, J. (1995). *El idioma de los lacanianos*. Buenos Aires: Atuel.

Baños Orellana, J. (2013). *La novela de Lacan. De neuropsiquiatra a psicoanalista*. Buenos Aires: El cuenco de plata.

Barrios, F. and Filippini, S. (2021). *De cuando Marx importunó a Lacan. Una genealogía posible del plus-de-jouir*. Montevideo: Escolios.

Barthes, R. (1957). *Mythologies*, A. Lavers (Trans.). New York: The Noondays Press, 1991.

Barzilai, S. (1999). *Lacan and the Matter of Origins*. Stanford: Stanford University Press.

Basualdo, C. (2011a). Lacan maussien. In: *Revue du Mauss*, 1 (37), 187–192.

Basualdo, C. (2011b). *Chronique d'une rencontre ratee*. Paris: Bord de l'eau.

Bataille, G. (1933). *La notion de dépense*. Paris: Éditions Lignes, 2011.

Bentham, J. (1781). *An Introduction to the Principles of Morals and Legislation*. Kitchener: Batoche Books.

Bentham, J. (1787). *The Panopticon Writings*. London: Verso, 1995.

Bentham, J. (1813). *The Theory of Fictions*. London: Routledge, 2011.

Bernfeld, S. (1973). *Sisyphus or The Limits of Education*. California: University of California Press.

Bétourné, F. (2002). *Lacan-l'index: Les complexes familiaux (1938)*. Paris: L'Harmattan.

Bianchi, P. (2012). From the Representation to Class Struggle. A Reponse to Samo Tomšič. In: *S: Journal of the Jan van Eyck Circle for Lacanian Ideology Critique*, 5, 114–126.

Biglieri, P. and Perelló, G. (2020). Populism. In: Y. Stavrakakis (Ed.), *Routledge Handbook of Psychoanalytic Political Theory* (pp. 330–340). London: Routledge.

Bion, W. R. (1961). *Experiences in Groups and Other Papers*. New York: Routledge.

Bolaño, R. (2011). *2666*. Barcelona: Anagrama.

Bonald, L.-A.de (1796). *Teoría del poder político y religioso*, J. Morales (Trans.). Madrid: Tecnos, 1988.

Bonald, L.-A.de (1826). Recherches philosophiques sur les premiers objets des connaissances morales. In: *Oeuvres de M. de Bonald* (Vol. IX). Paris: Librairie d'Adrien Le Clere.

Bonald, L.-A.de (1830). *Démonstration philosophique du principe constitutif de la société*. In: *Oeuvres de M. de Bonald* (Vol. VIII). Paris: Librairie d'Adrien Le Clere.

Boni, L. (2012). La conjuration. Lacan autour de 68. In: *Cahiers du GRM*, 3, 1–20.

Bottici, C. (2014). *Imaginal Politics. Images Beyond Imagination and the Imaginary*. New York: Columbia University Press.

Bou Ali, N. (2018). Measure against Measure: Why Lacan contra Foucault? In: N. Bou Ali and R. Goel (Eds.), *Lacan Contra Foucault. Subjectivity, Sex and Politics* (pp. 9–44). London: Bloomsbury.
Bruno, P. (2012). *Lacan, passeur de Marx. L'invention du symptôme.* Paris: Érès.
Cassin, B. (2020). *Jacques the Sophist. Lacan, Logos, and Psychoanalysis*, M. Syrotinski (Trans.). New York: Fordham University Press.
Castoriadis, C. (1975). *L'institution imaginaire de la société.* Paris: Seuil.
Castoriadis, C. (1986). *Domaines de l'homme: Les carrefours du labyrinthe.* Paris: Seuil.
Cernuda, L. (1932). *La realidad y el deseo (1924–1962).* Madrid: Alianza, 2018.
Chaumon, F. (2004). *Lacan. La loi, le sujet et la jouissance.* Paris: Michalon.
Clausewitz, C. von (1832). *On War*, M. Howard and P. Paret (Trans.). Princeton: Princeton University Press, 1976.
Cléro, J.-P. (2017). *Lacan et la langue anglaise.* Paris: Érès.
Comte, A. (1875). System of Positive Polity. *General View of Positivism and Introductory Principles*, J. H. Bridges (Trans.). London: Longmans, Green and Co.
Copjec, J. (2002). *Imagine There's no Woman. Ethics and Sublimation.* Cambridge: MIT Press.
Copjec, J. (2004). *Read my Desire. Lacan Against the Historicists.* Cambridge: MIT Press.
Copjec, J. (2006). May '68, The Emotional Month. In: S. Žižek (Ed.), *Lacan: The Silent Partners* (pp. 90–114). London: Verso.
Copjec, J. (2016). The Sexual Compact. In: A. Cerda-Rueda (Ed.), *Sex and Nothing. Bridges from Psychoanalysis to Philosophy* (pp. 107–138). London: Karnac.
Cortázar, J. (2007). *Historia de cronopios y de famas.* Madrid: Punto de lectura.
Dahmer, H. (1983). *Libido y sociedad*, F. Blanco (Trans.). Mexico: Siglo XXI.
Danelinck, D. (2018). *Debería darte vergüenza. Ensayo sobre álgebra lacaniana.* Buenos Aires: Heterónimos.
De Vos, J. (2013). *Psychologization and the Subject of Late Modernity.* London: Palgrave.
Deleule, D. (1972). *La psicología, mito científico*, N. Pérez de Lara and R. García (Trans.). Barcelona: Anagrama.
Deleuze, G. and Guattari, F. (1972). *L'anti-Œdipe. Capitalisme et schizophrénie.* Paris: Les Éditions de Minuit.
Depelsenaire, Y. (2008). Il était une fois… le rapport sexuel. *La cause freudienne*, 3 (70), 19–28.
Derrida, J. (1992). *Given Time: I. Counterfeit Money*, P. Kamuf (Trans.). Chicago: The University of Chicago Press.
Derrida, J. (2005). *Force de Loi: Le fondement mystique de l'autorité.* Paris: Galilée.
Dolar, M. (1993). Beyond Interpellation. In: *Qui Parle*, 6 (2), 75–96.
Dolar, M. (2014). Wittgenstein and Psychoanalysis: The Speaking Lion. In: *European Journal of Psychoanalysis*, 1 (2), 1–14.
Dosse, F. (1997). *History of Structuralism. Volume I: The Rising Sign, 1945–1966*, D. Glassman (Trans.). Minneapolis: University of Minnesota Press.
Durkheim, É (1892). La famille conjugale. In: *Textes 3. Fonctions sociales et institutions* (pp. 35–49). Paris: Les Éditions de Minuit, 1975.
Elias, N. (1985). *The Loneliness of the Dying.* New York: Continuum, 2001.
Elias, N. (1991). *The Society of Individuals*, E. Jephcott (Trans.). New York: Continuum.

Ellacuría, I. (1990). Historicidad de la salvación cristiana. In: I. Ellacuria and J. Sobrino (Coords.), *Mysterium Liberationis. Conceptos fundamentales de la teología de la liberación* I (pp. 323–372). Madrid: Trotta.
Engels, F. (1876). *The Part Played by Labor in the Transition from Ape to Man*. New York: International Publishers.
Engels, F. (1878). *Anti-Dühring. Herr Eugen Dühring's Revolution in Science*. In: *Karl Marx and Frederick Engels Collected Works* (Vol. XXV, pp. 5–312), E. Burns (Trans.). London: Lawrence and Wishart, 2010.
Engels, F. (1884). *The Origin of the Family, Private Property and the State*. Sydney: Resistance Books, 2004.
Engels, F. (1886). *Dialectics of nature*. In: *Karl Marx and Frederick Engels Collected Works* (Vol. XXV, pp. 313–589), C. Dutt (Trans.). London: Lawrence and Wishart, 2010.
Espinas, A. (1878). *Des sociétés animales*. Paris: Librairie Germer Bailliére.
Evans, D. (1998). From Kantian Ethics to Mystical Experience: An Exploration of Jouissance. In: D. Nobus (Ed.), *Key Concepts of Lacanian Psychoanalysis* (pp. 1–28). New York: Other Press.
Falquet, J. (2006). *De la cama a la calle: perspectivas teóricas lésbico-feministas*. Bogota: Brecha Lésbica.
Fauconnet, P. (1928). *La responsabilité. Étude sociologique*. Paris: Alcan.
Federici, S. (2004). *Caliban and the Witch*. New York: Autonomedia.
Fenichel, O. (1967). Psychoanalysis as the Nucleus of a Future Dialectical-Materialistic Psychology. *American Imago*, 24 (4), 290–311.
Flisfeder, M. (2021). *Algorithmic Desire: Toward a New Structuralist Theory of social Media*. Evanston: Northwestern University Press.
Flower McCanell, J. (1986). *Figuring Lacan. Criticism and the Cultural Unconscious*. London: Croom Helm.
Foucault, M. (1966). *Les mots et les choses. Une archéologie des sciences humaines*. Paris: Gallimard.
Foucault, M. (1969). *L'archéologie du savoir*. Paris: Gallimard.
Foucault, M. (1973). *La verdad y las formas jurídicas*, E. Linch (Trans.). Barcelona: Gedisa.
Foucault, M. (2001). Le sujet et le pouvoir. In: *Dits et écrits II, 1976–1988* (pp. 1041–1062). Paris: Gallimard.
Fourier, C. (1822). *Théorie de l'Unité universelle* (Tome I). Paris: Les presses du réel, 2001.
Freud, S. (1895). Project For a Scientific Psychology. In: *Standard Edition of the Complete Psychological Works of Sigmund Freud* (Vol. I, pp. 283–398), J. E. Strachey (Trans.). London: The Hogarth Press, 1981.
Freud, S. (1897). Draft N. In: *The Complete Letters of Sigmund Freud to Wilhelm Fliess, 1887–1904* (pp. 249–252). Cambridge: Belknap Press, 1985.
Freud, S. (1900). The Interpretation of Dreams. In: *Standard Edition of the Complete Psychological Works of Sigmund Freud* (Vol. IV), J. E. Strachey (Trans.). London: The Hogarth Press, 1981.
Freud, S. (1908). Civilized Sexual Morality and Modern Nervous Illness. In: *Standard Edition of the Complete Psychological Works of Sigmund Freud* (Vol. IX, pp. 177–204), J. E. Strachey (Trans.). London: The Hogarth Press, 1981.
Freud, S. (1913). Totem and Taboo. In: *Standard Edition of the Complete Psychological Works of Sigmund Freud* (Vol. XIII, pp. 1–163), J. E. Strachey (Trans.). London: The Hogarth Press, 1981.

Freud, S. (1914). Remembering, Repeating and Working-through. In: *Standard Edition of the Complete Psychological Works of Sigmund Freud* (Vol. XII, pp. 145–155), J. E. Strachey (Trans.). London: The Hogarth Press, 1981.
Freud, S. (1918). The Taboo of Virginity (Contributions to The Psychology of Love). In: *Standard Edition of the Complete Psychological Works of Sigmund Freud* (Vol. XI, pp. 191–207), J. E. Strachey (Trans.). London: The Hogarth Press, 1981.
Freud, S. (1920). Beyond the Pleasure Principle. In: *Standard Edition of the Complete Psychological Works of Sigmund Freud* (Vol. XVIII, pp. 7–65), J. E. Strachey (Trans.). London: The Hogarth Press, 1981.
Freud, S. (1921). Group Psychology and the Analysis of the Ego. In: *Standard Edition of the Complete Psychological Works of Sigmund Freud* (Vol. XVIII, pp. 67–143), J. E. Strachey (Trans.). London: The Hogarth Press, 1981.
Freud, S. (1923). The Ego and The Id. In: *Standard Edition of the Complete Psychological Works of Sigmund Freud* (Vol. XIX, pp. 3–68), J. E. Strachey (Trans.). London: The Hogarth Press, 1981.
Freud, S. (1924a). The Dissolution of the Oedipus Complex. In: *Standard Edition of the Complete Psychological Works of Sigmund Freud* (Vol. XIX, pp. 173–182), J. E. Strachey (Trans.). London: The Hogarth Press, 1981.
Freud, S. (1924b). The Economic Problem of Masochism. In: *Standard Edition of the Complete Psychological Works of Sigmund Freud* (Vol. XIX, pp. 156–172), J. E. Strachey (Trans.). London: The Hogarth Press, 1981.
Freud, S. (1927). The Future of an Illusion. In: *Standard Edition of the Complete Psychological Works of Sigmund Freud* (Vol. XXI, pp. 3–57), J. E. Strachey (Trans.). London: The Hogarth Press, 1981.
Freud, S. (1930). Civilization and its Discontents. In: *Standard Edition of the Complete Psychological Works of Sigmund Freud* (Vol. XXI, pp. 58–151), J. E. Strachey (Trans.). London: The Hogarth Press, 1981.
Freud, S. (1939). Moses and the Monotheism. Three Essays. In: *Standard Edition of the Complete Psychological Works of Sigmund Freud* (Vol. XXIII, pp. 2–139), J. E. Strachey (Trans.). London: The Hogarth Press, 1981.
Fried, M. (1967). *The Evolution of Political Society.* New York: Random House.
Fromm, E. (1970). *The Crisis of Psychoanalysis. Essays on Freud, Marx and Social Psychology.* New York: Henry Holt.
Frosh, S. (1994). *Sexual Difference: Masculinity and Psychoanalysis.* London: Routledge.
Frosh, S. (1999). *The Politics of Psychoanalysis. An Introduction to Freudian and Post-Freudian Theory.* London: Macmillan.
Frosh, S. (2013). *Hauntings: Psychoanalysis and Ghostly Transmissions.* London: Palgrave.
Galiussi, R. and Godoy, C. (2013). La declinación del padre en la enseñanza de Lacan (1938–1961). In: *Anuario de investigaciones*, XX (2), 105–111.
Geertz, C. (1973). *The Interpretation of Cultures: Selected Essays.* New York: Basic Books.
Geertz, C. (1983). *Local Knowledge: Further Essays in Interpretive Anthropology.* New York: Basic Books.
Giocanti, S. (2008). *Charles Maurras. Le chaos et l'ordre.* Paris: Flammarion.
Glynos, J. (2002). Theory and Evidence in the Freudian Field: From Observation to Structure. In: J. Glynos and Y. Stavrakakis (Eds.), *Lacan and Science* (pp. 13–50). London: Karnac.

Gómez Camarena, C. and Juárez-Salazar, E. (2022). Politics. In: C. Soto van der Plas, E. M. Juárez-Salazar, C. Gómez Camarena, andD. Pavón-Cuéllar (Eds.), *The Marx Through Lacan Vocabulary. A Compass for Libidinal and Political Economies* (pp. 162–176). London: Routledge.

Greenshields, W. (2017). *Writing the Structures of the Subject. Lacan and Topology.* London: Palgrave.

Gros, F. (2021). *La honte est un sentiment révolutionnaire.* Paris: Albin Michel.

Gross, O. (2018). *Más allá del diván. Apuntes sobre la psicopatología de la civilización burguesa.* Madrid: Irrecuperables.

Guchet, X. (2010). *Pour un humanisme technologique. Culture, technique et société dans la philosophie de Gilbert Simondon.* Paris: Presses Universitaires de France.

Hadar, U. (2013). *Psychoanalysis and Social Involvement. Studies in the Psychosocial.* London: Palgrave Macmillan.

Hadot, P. (2004). *Wittgenstein et les limites du langage.* Paris:Vrin.

Hayek, F. (1944). *The Road to Serfdom.* London: Routledge, 2006.

Hegel, G. W. F. (1807). *Phenomenology of Spirit,* A. V. Miller (Trans.). Oxford: Oxford University Press, 1979.

Hegel, G. W. F. (1894). *Philosophy of Mind,* W. Wallace (Trans.). Oxford: Clarendon Press.

Heller, A. (1976). *The Theory of Need in Marx.* London: Verso, 2018.

Hénnaff, M. (1978). *Sade. L'invention du corps libertin.* Paris: Presses Universitaires de France.

Hertzmann, L. and Newbigin, J. (2023). *Psychoanalysis and Homosexuality. A Contemporary Introduction.* London: Routledge.

Hiltenbrand, J.-P. (2005). *Insatisfaction dans le lien social.* Paris: Érès.

Hirschman, A. O. (1977). *The Passions and the Interests. Political Arguments for Capitalism before its Triumph.* Princeton: Princeton University Press.

Hjelmslev, L. (1957). Pour une sémantique structural. In: *Essais linguistiques* (pp. 96–112). Copenhagen: Nordisk Sprog-og Kulturforlag, 1959.

Hobbes, T. (1651). *Leviathan or The Matter, Forme and Power of a Commonwealth Ecclesiasticall and Civil.* New York: Oxford University Press, 1998.

Hoens, D. (2006). Toward a New Perversion: Psychoanalysis. In: J. Clemens and R. Grigg (Eds.). *Reflections on Seminar XVII. Jacques Lacan and the Other Side of Psychoanalysis* (pp. 88–106). Durham: Duke University Press.

Holmes, A. (2021). Lacan's Critique of Jaspers. Understanding and The Problem of Meaning in Psychoanalysis. In: *Lamella. It Thinks!* 5 (6), 89–100.

Hook, D. (2011). Psychoanalytic Contributions to the Political Analysis of Affect and Identification. In: *Ethnicities,* 11 (1), 107–115.

Hook, D. (2018). *Six Moments in Lacan. Communication and Identification in Psychology and Psychoanalysis.* London: Routledge.

Hook, D. and De Kesel, M. (2022). The Function and Field of Speech and Language in Psychoanalysis. In: D. Hook, C. Neill and S. Vanheule (Eds.). *Reading Lacan's Écrits: from 'Logical time' to 'Response to Jean Hyppolite'* (pp. 56–140). London: Routledge.

Horkheimer, M. (1972). *Critical Theory. Selected Essays,* M. O'Connell (Trans.). New York: Continuum.

Horkheimer, M. and Adorno, Th. (1987). *Dialectic of Enlightenment: Philosophical Fragments,* E. Jephcott (Trans.). Stanford: Stanford University Press, 2002.

Jameson, F. (2002). *A Singular Modernity. Essay on the Ontology of the Present.* London: Verso.
Jaudel, N. (2014). *La légende noire de Jacques Lacan. Élisabeth Roudinesco et sa méthode historique.* Paris: Navarin.
Johnston, A. (2006). Ghosts of Substance Past: Schelling, Lacan, and the Denaturalization of Nature. In: S. Žižek (Ed.), *Lacan: The Silent Partners* (pp. 34–55). London: Verso.
Johnston, J. (2008). *The Allure of Machinic Life: Cybernetics, Artificial Life, and the New AI.* Massachusetts: MIT Press.
Juárez-Salazar, E. M. (2022). Society. In: C. Soto van der Plas, E. M. Juárez-Salazar, C. Gómez Camarena, and D. Pavón-Cuéllar (Eds.), *The Marx Through Lacan Vocabulary. A Compass for Libidinal and Political Economies* (pp. 225–238). London: Routledge.
Kant, I. (1785). *Groundwork for the Metaphysics of Morals*, A. Wood (Trans.). New Haven: Yale University Press, 2002.
Kant, I. (1788). *Critique of Practical Reason*, M. Gregor (Trans.). Cambridge: Cambridge University Press, 2015.
Karatani, K. (2020). *Marx: Towards the Centre of Possibility*, G. Walker (Trans.). London: Verso.
Khan, M. (1987). *Alienation in Perversions.* London: Karnac.
Kojève, A. (1947). *Introduction à la lecture de Hegel.* Paris: Gallimard.
Koyré, A. (1957). *From the Closed World to the Infinite Universe.* Baltimore: Johns Hopkins Press.
Koyré, A. (1966). *Études galiléennes.* Paris: Hermann.
Krader, L. (1974). *The Ethnological Notebooks of Karl Marx.* Assen: Van Gorcum.
Kristeva, J. (1988). *Etrangers à nous-mêmes.* Paris: Fayard.
Kropotkin, P. (1892). *The Conquest of Bread.* New York: Vanguard Press, 1926.
Kurzweil, E. (1996). *The Age of Structuralism. From Lévi-Strauss to Foucault.* London: Routledge.
La Boétie, É. de (1574). *Discours de la servitude volontaire.* Paris: Mille et une nuits, 1995.
La Mettrie, J. O.de (1748). *L'homme machine.* Paris: Luzac.
Lacan, J. (1932). *De la psychose paranoïaque dans ses rapports avec la personnalité.* Paris: Seuil, 2015.
Lacan, J. (1936). Beyond the Reality Principle. In: *Écrits* (pp. 58–74), B. Fink (Trans.). New York: W. W. Norton and Company, 2006.
Lacan, J. (1938a). Intervention sur le rapport de R. Loewenstein « L'origine du Masochisme et la théorie des pulsions », 10ème conférence des psychanalystes de langue française. In: *Revue Française de Psychanalyse*, X (4), 750–752.
Lacan, J. (1938b). Les complexes familiaux dans la formation de l'individu. In: *Autres Écrits* (pp. 23–84). Paris: Seuil, 2001.
Lacan, J. (1945). Le nombre treize et la forme logique de la suspicion. In: *Autres Écrits* (pp. 85–99). Paris: Seuil, 2001.
Lacan, J. (1946). Presentation on Psychical Causality. In: *Écrits* (pp. 123–160), B. Fink (Trans.). New York: W. W. Norton and Company, 2006.
Lacan, J. (1947). La psychiatrie anglaise et la guerre. In: *Autres Écrits* (pp. 101–120). Paris: Seuil, 2001.
Lacan, J. (1948a). Aggressiveness in Psychoanalysis. In: *Écrits* (pp. 82–101), B. Fink (Trans.). New York: W. W. Norton and Company, 2006.

Lacan, J. (1948b). Les facteurs psychiques: Essai sur les réactions psychiques de l'hypertendu. In: S. Blondin, A. Weiss, C. Rouvillois and J. Lacan, *Le traitement chirurgical de l'hypertension artérielle, 51e Congrès Français de Chirurgie, Actes du Congrès*, 171–176.

Lacan, J. (1949a). The Mirror Stage as Formative of the I Function as Revealed in Psychoanalytic Experience. In: *Écrits* (pp. 75–81), B. Fink (Trans.). New York: W. W. Norton and Company, 2006.

Lacan, J. (1949b). Intervention sur l'exposé de S. A. Shentoub: « Remarques méthodologiques sur la socio-analyse ». In: *Revue Française de Psychanalyse*, XIII (2), 319.

Lacan, J. (1950a). Prémisses à tout développement possible de la criminologie. In: *Autres Écrits* (pp. 121–125). Paris: Seuil, 2001.

Lacan, J. (1950b). Intervention au 1er Congrès mondial de psychiatrie. In: *Autres Écrits* (pp. 127–130). Paris: Seuil, 2001.

Lacan, J. (1950c). A Theoretical Introduction to the Functions of Psychoanalysis in Criminology. In: *Écrits* (pp. 102–122), B. Fink (Trans.). New York: W. W. Norton and Company, 2006.

Lacan, J. (1951). Some Reflections on the Ego. In: *International Journal of psychoanalysis*, 34, 11–17.

Lacan, J. (1952a). Sur l'homme aux loups. In: *Aux confins du séminaire* (pp. 9–43). Paris: Navarin, 2021.

Lacan, J. (1952b). The Neurotic's Individual Myth. In: *The Psychoanalytic Quarterly*, 48 (3), 405–425, 1979.

Lacan, J. (1953–1954). *The Seminar of Jacques Lacan. Book I. Freud's Papers on Technique*, J. Forrester (Trans.). New York: W.W. Norton and Company, 1991.

Lacan, J. (1953a). Discours de Rome. In: *Autres Écrits* (pp. 133–164). Paris: Seuil, 2001.

Lacan, J. (1953b). The Symbolic, the Imaginary, and the Real. In: *On the Names-of-the-Father* (pp. 1–52), B. Fink (Trans.). Cambridge: Polity Press, 2011.

Lacan, J. (1953c). The Function and Field of Speech and Language in Psychoanalysis. In: *Écrits* (pp. 197–268), B. Fink (Trans.). New York: W. W. Norton and Company, 2006.

Lacan, J. (1954–1955). *The Seminar of Jacques Lacan. Book II. The Ego in Freud's Theory and in the Technique of Psychoanalysis*, S. Tomaselli (Trans.). New York: W. W. Norton and Company, 1991.

Lacan, J. (1954). Introduction to Jean Hyppolite's Commentary on Freud's "Verneinung". In: *Écrits* (pp. 308–317), B. Fink (Trans.). New York: W. W. Norton and Company, 2006.

Lacan, J. (1955–1956). *The Seminar of Jacques Lacan. Book III. The Psychoses*, R. Grigg (Trans.). New York: W. W. Norton and Company, 1997.

Lacan, J. (1955). The Freudian Thing or the Meaning of the Return to Freud in Psychoanalysis. In: *Écrits* (pp. 334–363), B. Fink (Trans.). New York: W. W. Norton and Company, 2006.

Lacan, J. (1956–1957). *The Seminar of Jacques Lacan. Book IV. The Object Relation*, A. Price (Trans.). Cambridge: Polity Press, 2021.

Lacan, J. (1956). On a Question Prior to Any Possible Treatment of Psychosis. In: *Écrits* (pp. 445–488), B. Fink (Trans.). New York: W. W. Norton and Company, 2006.

Lacan, J. (1957–1958). *The Seminar of Jacques Lacan. Book V. Formations of the Unconscious*, R. Grigg (Trans.). Cambridge: Polity Press, 2017.

Lacan, J. (1957a). The Instance of the Letter in the Unconscious or Reason Since Freud. In: *Écrits* (pp. 412–441), B. Fink (Trans.). New York: W. W. Norton and Company, 2006.

Lacan, J. (1957b). Psychoanalysis and Its Teaching. In: *Écrits* (pp. 364–383), B. Fink (Trans.). New York: W. W. Norton and Company, 2006.

Lacan, J. (1958–1959). *The Seminar of Jacques Lacan. Book VI. Desire and its Interpretation*, B. Fink (Trans.). Cambridge: Polity Press, 2019.

Lacan, J. (1958a). La psychanalyse vraie, et la fausse. In: *Autres Écrits* (pp. 165–174). Paris: Seuil, 2001.

Lacan, J. (1958b). The Direction of the Treatment and the Principles of Its Power. In: *Écrits* (pp. 489–541), B. Fink (Trans.). New York: W. W. Norton and Company, 2006.

Lacan, J. (1959–1960). *The Seminar of Jacques Lacan. Book VII. The Ethics of Psychoanalysis*, D. Porter (Trans.). New York: W. W. Norton and Company, 1992.

Lacan, J. (1959). In Memory of Ernest Jones: On His Theory of Symbolism. In: *Écrits* (pp. 585–601), B. Fink (Trans.). New York: W. W. Norton and Company, 2006.

Lacan, J. (1960–1961). *The Seminar of Jacques Lacan. Book VIII. Transference*, B. Fink (Trans.). Cambridge: Polity Press, 2015.

Lacan, J. (1960a). Discourse to Catholics. In: *The Triumph of Religion, preceded by Discourse to Catholics* (pp. 2–53), B. Fink (Trans.). Cambridge: Polity Press, 2013.

Lacan, J. (1960b). Remarks on Daniel Lagache's Presentation: "Psychoanalysis and Personality Structure". In: *Écrits* (pp. 543–574), B. Fink (Trans.). New York: W. W. Norton and Company, 2006.

Lacan, J. (1960c). Position of the Unconscious. In: *Écrits* (pp. 703–721), B. Fink (Trans.). New York: W. W. Norton and Company, 2006.

Lacan, J. (1961–1962). *Le Séminaire. Livre IX. L'identification*. Unpublished.

Lacan, J. (1961). Maurice Merleau-Ponty. In: *Autres Écrits* (pp. 175–184). Paris: Seuil, 2001.

Lacan, J. (1962–1963). *The Seminar of Jacques Lacan. Book X. Anxiety*, A. R. Price (Trans.). Cambridge: Polity Press, 2014.

Lacan, J. (1962). Guiding Remarks for a Convention on Female Sexuality. In: *Écrits* (pp. 610–620), B. Fink (Trans.). New York: W. W. Norton and Company, 2006.

Lacan, J. (1963). Kant with Sade. In: *Écrits* (pp. 645–669), B. Fink (Trans.). New York: W. W. Norton and Company, 2006.

Lacan, J. (1964–1965). *Le Séminaire. Livre XII. Problèmes cruciaux*. Unpublished.

Lacan, J. (1964a). On Freud's "Trieb" and the Psychoanalyst's Desire. In: *Écrits* (pp. 722–725), B. Fink (Trans.). New York: W. W. Norton and Company, 2006.

Lacan, J. (1964b). *The Seminar of Jacques Lacan. Book XI. The Four Fundamental Concepts of Psychoanalysis*, A. Sheridan (Trans.). New York: W. W. Norton and Company, 1998.

Lacan, J. (1965–1966). *Le Séminaire. Livre XIII. L'objet de la psychanalyse*. Unpublished.

Lacan, J. (1966–1967). *Le séminaire. Livre XIV. La logique du fantasme*. Unpublished.

Lacan, J. (1966a). Réponses à des étudiants en philosophie. In: *Autres Écrits* (pp. 203–212). Paris: Seuil, 2001.

Lacan, J. (1966b). On My Antecedents. In: *Écrits* (pp. 51–57), B. Fink (Trans.). New York: W. W. Norton and Company, 2006.

Lacan, J. (1966c). Science and Truth. In: *Écrits* (pp. 726–745), B. Fink (Trans.). New York: W. W. Norton and Company, 2006.

Lacan, J. (1966d). Of Structure as the Inmixing of an Otherness Prerequisite to Any Subject Whatever. In: R. Macksey and E. Donato (Ed.), *The languages of Criticism and the Sciences of Man: The Structuralist Controversy* (pp. 186–200). Baltimore: Johns Hopkins Press, 1970.

Lacan, J. (1966e). Psychanalyse et Médecine. In: *Lettres de l'École freudienne*, (1), 34–51.

Lacan, J. (1966f). On a Purpose. In: *Écrits* (pp. 303–307), B. Fink (Trans.). New York: W. W. Norton and Company, 2006.

Lacan, J. (1967–1968). *Le Séminaire. Livre XV. L'acte*. Unpublished.

Lacan, J. (1967a). Proposition du 9 octobre 1967 sur le psychanalyste de l'École. In: *Autres Écrits* (pp. 243–260). Paris: Seuil, 2001.

Lacan, J. (1967b). *My Teaching*, D. Macey (Trans.). London: Verso, 2008.

Lacan, J. (1967c). *Conférence sur le psychanalyse et la formation du psychiatre à Sainte-Anne le 10 novembre 1967*. Unpublished.

Lacan, J. (1967d). *Conférence à la Faculté de Médecine de Strasbourg*. Unpublished.

Lacan, J. (1967e). *De la psychanalyse dans ses rapports avec la réalité*. In: *Autres Écrits* (pp. 351–360). Paris: Seuil, 2001.

Lacan, J. (1967f). Discours à l'E.F.P. In: *Scilicet* (2/3), 9–29.

Lacan, J. (1968–1969). *Le Séminaire. Livre XVI. D'un Autre à l'autre*. Paris: Seuil, 2006.

Lacan, J. (1969–1970). *The Seminar of Jacques Lacan. Book XVII. The Other Side of Psychoanalysis*, R. Grigg (Trans.). New York: W. W. Norton and Company, 2007.

Lacan, J. (1970a). Préface à une thèse. In: *Autres Écrits* (pp. 393–402). Paris: Seuil, 2001.

Lacan, J. (1970b). Radiophonie. In: *Autres Écrits* (p. 407–448). Paris: Seuil, 2001.

Lacan, J. (1971–1972). *The Seminar of Jacques Lacan. Book XIX. ...or Worse*, A. Price (Trans.). Cambridge: Polity Press, 2018.

Lacan, J. (1971a). Lituraterre. In: *Autres écrits* (pp. 11–20). Paris: Seuil, 2001.

Lacan, J. (1971b). *Le Séminaire. Livre XVIII. D'un discours qui ne serait pas du semblant*. Paris: Seuil, 2006.

Lacan, J. (1971c). *Talking to Brick Walls. A Series of Presentations in the Chapel at Sainte-Anne Hospital*, A. Price (Trans.). Cambridge: Polity Press, 2017.

Lacan, J. (1972–1973). *The Seminar of Jacques Lacan. Book XX. Encore*, B. Fink (Trans.). New York: W.W. Norton and Company, 1999.

Lacan, J. (1972a). L'etourdit. In: *Autres Écrits* (pp. 449–496). Paris: Seuil, 2001.

Lacan, J. (1972b). Interventions sur l'exposé de P. Mathis: « Remarques sur la fonction de l'argent dans la technique analytique ». In: *Lettres de l'École freudienne*, (9), 195–205.

Lacan, J. (1972c). La mort est du domaine de la foi. Conférence à Louvain. In: *Quarto*, (3), 5–20.

Lacan, J. (1973–1974). *Le Séminaire. Livre XXI. Les Non-Dupes Errent*. Unpublished.

Lacan, J. (1973a). Télévision. In: *Autres Écrits* (pp. 509–545). Paris: Seuil, 2001.

Lacan, J. (1973b). Intervention dans une réunion organisée par la Scuola freudiana. In: *Lacan in Italia* (pp. 78–97). Milan: La Salamandra, 1978.

Lacan, J. (1973c). Introduction à l'édition allemande d'un premier volume des Écrits (Walter Verlag). In: *Scilicet*, (5), 11–17.

Lacan, J. (1973d). Note italienne. In: *Autres Écrits* (pp. 307–312). Paris: Seuil, 2001.

Lacan, J. (1974–1975). *Le Séminaire. Livre XXII. RSI*. Unpublished.

Lacan, J. (1974a). La troisième. In: *La cause freudienne*, (79), 11–33, 2011.

Lacan, J. (1974b). Freud Forever: An Interview with Panorama, P. Dravers (Trans). In: *Hurly-Burly*, (12), 13–21, 2015.

Lacan, J. (1975–1976). *The Seminar of Jacques Lacan. Book XXIII. The Sinthome*, A. Price (Trans.). Cambridge: Polity Press, 2016.

Lacan, J. (1975a). Conférences dans les universités nord-américaines: le 2 décembre 1975 au Massachusetts Institute of Technology. In: *Scilicet*, (6–7), 53–63.

Lacan, J. (1975b). Conférences dans les universités nord-américaines: le 25 novembre 1975 au Columbia University, Auditorium School of International Affairs. In: *Scilicet*, (6–7), 42–45.

Lacan, J. (1976–1977). *Le Séminaire. Livre XXIV. L'insu que sait de l'une-bévue s'aile à mourre*. Unpublished.

Lacan, J. (1976). *Journées des cartels de l'École freudienne de Paris. Maison de la chimie. Lettre de l'École freudienne*, (18), 263–270.

Lacan, J. (1977–1978). *Le Séminaire. Livre XXV. Le moment de conclure*. Unpublished.

Lacan, J. (1978). Conclusion. 9e Congrès de l'École Freudienne de Paris sur « La transmission ». In: *Lettres de l'École*, II (25), 219–220.

Laclau, E. (1990). *New Reflections on the Revolution of Our Time*. London: Verso.

Laclau, E. and Mouffe, C. (1985). *Hegemony and Socialist Strategy. Towards a Radical Democratic Politics*. London: Verso.

Landman, P. and Lippi, S. (Eds.) (2013). *Marx, Lacan: l'acte révolutionnaire et l'acte analytique*. Paris: Erès.

Lavoie, P. (2012). Claude Lévi-Strauss et les mathématiques. In: *Bulletin AMQ*, 52 (2), 1–25.

Le Gaufey, G. (2001). *El lazo especular. Un estudio transversal de la unidad imaginaria*, G. Leguizamón (Trans.). Mexico: Epeele.

Le Gaufey, G. (2020). *Lacan and the Formulae of Sexuation*. London: Routledge.

Lefort, C. (1986). *The Political Forms of Modern Society. Bureaucracy, Democracy, Totalitarianism*. Cambridge: MIT Press.

Lévi-Strauss, C. (1955). The Structural Study of Myth. In: *The Journal of American Folklore*, 68 (270), 428–444.

Lévi-Strauss, C. (1956). *Les mathématiques de l'homme*. In: *Esprit*, 243 (10), 525–538.

Lévi-Strauss, C. (1962). *Wild Thought*, J. Mehlman and J. Leavitt (Trans.). Chicago: The University of Chicago Press.

Lévi-Strauss, C. (1963). *Structural Anthropology*, C. Jacobson (Trans.). New York: Basic Books.

Lévi-Strauss, C. (1964). *The Raw and the Cooked. Introduction to a Science of Mythology*: I, J. Weightman and D. Weightman (Trans.). New York: Harper and Row Publishers, 1975.

Lévi-Strauss, C. (1969). *The Elementary Structures of Kinship*, J. Harle Bell (Trans.). Boston: Beacon Press.

Lévi-Strauss, C. (1987). *Introduction to the Work of Marcel Mauss*. London: Routledge and Kegan Paul.

Lippi, S. (2012). *Transgressions. Bataille, Lacan*. Paris: Érès.

Locke, J. (1689). *The Second Treatise of Civil Government*. Oxford: Basil Blackwell, 1946.

Lombardi, G. (2015). *La libertad en psicoanálisis*. Buenos Aires: Paidós.

Lowie, R. (1936), *Traité de sociologie primitive*, E. Métraux (Trans.). Paris: Payot.

Luchelli, J. P. (2016). Le premier Lacan: cinq lettres inédites de Lacan à Kojève. In: *Cliniques méditerranéennes*, 94 (2), 297–308.
Luchelli, J. P. (2017). *Lacan. De Wallon à Kojève*. Paris: Michele.
Lukács, G. (1978). *Marx's Basic Ontological Principles*, D. Fernbach (Trans.). London: Merlin Press.
Marcuse, H. (1956). *Eros and Civilization. A Philosophical Inquiry into Freud*. London: Routledge, 2005.
Marcuse, H. (1960). *Reason and Revolution. Hegel and the Rise of Social Theory*. London: Routledge.
Marcuse, H. (1964). *One-Dimensional Man. Studies in the Ideology of Advanced Industrial Society*. London: Routledge, 2002.
Marini, M. (1992). *Jacques Lacan: the French Context*, A. Tomiche (Trans.). New Brunswick: Rutgers University Press.
Marx, K. (1843a). *Critique of Hegel's Philosophy of Right*, J. O'Malley (Trans.). Oxford: Oxford University Press, 1970.
Marx, K. (1843b). Carta de Marx a Ruge. In: *Escritos de juventud* (pp. 441–442), W. Roces (Trans.). Mexico: Fondo de Cultura Económica.
Marx, K. (1844). *Economic and Philosophic Manuscripts of 1844*, M. Milligan (Trans.). New York: Prometheus Books, 1998.
Marx, K. (1858). *Grundrisse. Foundations of the Critique of Political Economy*, M. Nicolaus (Trans.). London: Penguin, 1973.
Marx, K. (1867a). *Capital. A Critique of Political Economy*, Vol. I, B. Fowkes (Trans.). London: Penguin, 1990.
Marx, K. (1867b). *Capital. A Critique of Political Economy*, Vol. II, D. Fernbach (Trans.). London: Penguin, 1990.
Marx, K. (1867c). *Capital. A Critique of Political Economy*, Vol. III, D. Fernbach (Trans.). London: Penguin, 1990.
Marx, K. and Engels, F. (1846). *The German Ideology*. New York: Prometheus Books, 1998.
Marx, K. and Engels, F. (1848). *Communist Manifesto*. New York: Prometheus Books, 1988.
Masotta, O. (1976). *Ensayos lacanianos*. Barcelona: Anagrama.
Maurras, C. (1937). *Mes idées politiques*. Paris: Albatros, 1983.
Mauss, M. (1924). Rapports réels et pratiques de la psychologie et de la sociologie. In: *Sociologie et anthropologie* (pp. 281–310). Paris: Presses Universitaires de France, 1966.
Mauss, M. (1954). *The Gift. The Form and Reason for Exchange in Archaic Societies*, W. D. Halls (Trans.). London: Routledge, 2002.
McDougall, J. (1978). *Théâtres du corps. Le psychosoma en psychanalyse*. Paris: Gallimard.
McGowan, T. (2013). *Enjoying What We Don't Have: The Political Project of Psychoanalysis*. Lincoln: University of Nebraska Press.
McGowan, T. (2020). Superego and the Law. In: Y. Stavrakakis (Ed.), *Routledge Handbook of Psychoanalytic Political Theory* (pp. 139–150). London: Routledge.
Merani, A. (1976). *Historia crítica de la psicología*. Barcelona: Grijalbo.
Merleau-Ponty, M. (1964). *Signs*, R. McCleary (Trans.). Evanston: Northwestern University Press.
Miller, J.-A. (1966). La Suture: Éléments de la logique du signifiant. In: *Cahiers pour l'analyse*, I, 37–49.

Miller, J.-A. (1968). Action de la structure. In: *Cahiers pour l'analyse*, IX, 93–105.

Miller, J.-A. (2005). *Lecture critique des «complexes familiaux» de Jacques Lacan*. In: *La Cause Freudienne*, 60 (2), 31–51.

Milner, J.-C. (1995). *L'œuvre claire. Lacan, la science, la philosophie*. Paris: Seuil.

Milner, J.-C. (2001). De la lingüística a la lingüistería. In: J. Auber*et al.* (Eds.). *Lacan, el escrito, la imagen*, (pp. 19–40), J. Utrilla (Trans.). Mexico: Siglo XXI.

Milner, J.-C. (2011a). *Pour une politique des êtres parlants. Court traité politique 2*. Paris: Verdier.

Milner, J.-C. (2011b). *Clartés de tout. De Lacan à Marx, d'Aristote à Mao*. Paris: Verdier.

Milner, J.-C. (2013). *El periplo estructural*. Buenos Aires: Amorrortu.

Moncayo, R. (2018). *Knowing, Not-Knowing, and Jouissance: Levels, Symbols, and Codes of Experience in Psychoanalysis*. Londres: Springer.

Moretti, F. (2014). *El burgués. Entre la historia y la literatura*, L. Mosconi (Trans.). Buenos Aires: Fondo de Cultura Económica.

Morgan, L. (1877). *Ancient Society*. Calcutta: K. P. Bagchi, 1982.

Neil, C. (2011). *Lacanian Ethics and the Assumption of Subjectivity*. London: Palgrave Macmillan.

Neil, C. (2018). The excluded in identification. In: L. Auestad (Ed.), *Psychoanalysis and Politics. Exclusion and the Politics of Representation*. London: Routledge.

Nobus, D. (2017). *The Law of Desire. On Lacan's 'Kant with Sade'*. Cham: Palgrave Macmillan.

Ogilvie, B. (1987). *Lacan. La formation du concept de sujet (1932–1949)*. Paris: Presses Universitaires de France.

Parker, I. (2007). *Revolution in Psychology: Alienation to Emancipation*. London: Pluto Press.

Parker, I. (2011). *Lacanian Psychoanalysis. Revolutions in Subjectivity*. London: Routledge.

Parker, I. and Pavón-Cuéllar, D. (2017). *Marxismo, psicología y psicoanálisis*. Mexico: Paradiso.

Parker, I. and Pavón-Cuéllar, D. (2021). *Psychoanalysis and Revolution. Critical Psychology for Liberation Movements*. London: 1968.

Pavón-Cuéllar, D. (2006). *Le révolutio-m'être: notions lacaniennes appliquées à l'analyse de discours en psychologie sociale*. Paris: Psychophores.

Pavón-Cuéllar, D. (2010). La conception lacanienne de la société, entre désagrégation névrotique et protestation homosexuelle. In: *Oxymoron*, (1), 1–10.

Pavón-Cuéllar, D. (2013). *Lacan, lecteur de Marx* [Doctoral thesis]. Université de Rouen.

Pavón-Cuéllar, D. (2016). *Marxism and Psychoanalysis: In or Against Psychology?* London: Routledge.

Pavón-Cuéllar, D. (2017). *Elementos políticos de marxismo lacaniano*. Mexico: Paradiso.

Pavón-Cuéllar, D. (2019). Lacanizing Marxism: the Effects of Lacan in Readings of Marx and Marxist Thinkers. In: *Crisis and Critique. Jacques Lacan: Psychoanalysis, Politics, Philosophy*, 6 (1), 262–289.

Pavón-Cuéllar, D. (2021). Engels y Freud ante el origen: entre el comunismo primitivo y la horda primordial. In: J. Ortega and G. Ambriz (Eds.). *El espíritu pensante: Engels en su bicentenario* (pp. 23–35). Quito: Religación Press.

Pavón-Cuéllar, D. (2022). *Sobre el vacío. Puentes entre el marxismo y el psicoanálisis.* Mexico: Paradiso.
Peirce, Ch. (1958). *The Collected Papers of Charles Sanders Peirce.* Cambridge: Harvard University Press.
Pélissier, Y., Bénabou Le Gaufey, G., Abribat, J.-P., and Cornaz, L. (2002). *789 Néologismes de Jacques Lacan.* Paris: EPEL.
Pessoa, F. (2010). *El primer Fausto/Todavía más allá del océano*, F. Cervantes (Trans.). Mexico: Fondo de Cultura Económica.
Pichon, E. (1939). La famille devant M. Lacan. In: *Revue française de psychanalyse*, XI (1), 107–135.
Piers, G. and Singer, M. (1953). *Shame and Guilt. A Psychoanalytic and a Cultural Study.* Springfield: Charles C. Thomas.
Plato (2000). *The Republic*, T. Griffith (Trans.). Cambridge: Cambridge University Press.
Pluth, E. (2007). *Signifiers and Acts. Freedom in Lacan's Theory of the Subject.* New York: SUNY Press.
Politzer, G. (1972). *Crítica de los fundamentos de la psicología*, F. Gallach (Trans.). Madrid: Martínez Roca.
Poulantzas, N. (1975). *Political Power and Social Classes*, T. O'Hagan (Trans.). London: NLB.
Preciado, P. B. (2016). El método Marx. *El Estado, Mental*, October 23. Retrieved from https://t.ly/CB42
Rabaté, J. M. (2009). 68+1: Lacan's année érotique. In: *Parrhesia*, (6), 28–45.
Radcliffe-Brown, A. (1952). *Structure and Function in Primitive Society.* Glencoe: The Free Press.
Ragland, E. (1995). *Essays on the Pleasures of Death. From Freud to Lacan.* New York: Routledge.
Raynaud, P. (2004). Society. In: B. Cassin (Dir.). *Vocabulaire européen des philosophies. Dictionnaire des intraduisibles* (pp. 1212–1216). Paris: Le Robert/Seuil.
Recalcati, M. (2008). *Clínica del vacío: anorexias, dependencias, psicosis.* Madrid: Síntesis.
Regnault, F. (2005). Le Marx de Lacan. In: *La Lettre Mensuelle de l'ECF*, (242), 4–6.
Reich, W. (1972). *Dialectical Materialism and Psychoanalysis.* London: Socialist Reproduction.
Revueltas, J. (1941). *Los muros de agua.* Mexico: Ediciones Era, 2013.
Rose, N. (1999). *Governing the Soul. The Shaping of the Private Self.* London: Free Association Books.
Roudinesco, E. (1986). *Histoire de la psychanalyse en France. La bataille de cent ans, 1925–1985* (t. 2). Paris: Seuil.
Roudinesco, E. (1997). *Jacques Lacan*, B. Bray (Trans.). New York: Columbia University Press.
Roudinesco, E. (2003). The Mirror Stage: An Obliterated Archive. In: J.-M. Rabaté (Ed.), *The Cambridge Companion to Lacan* (pp. 25–34). Cambridge: Cambridge University Press.
Rouse, H. and Arribas, S. (2011). *Egocracy. Marx, Freud and Lacan.* Zürich: Diaphanes.
Rousseau, J.-J. (1792). *Du contrat social, ou, Principes du droit politique* (Vol. 1). Lyon: De l'Imprimerie d'Amable Le Roy.

Sade, M. de (1795). *Philosophy in the Bedroom*, R. Seaver and A. Wainhouse (Trans.). New York: Grove Press, 1965.

Safatle, V. (2023). *Maneras de transformar mundos. Lacan, política y emancipación*. Buenos Aires: Prometeo.

Samuels, R. (2000). Homosexualities from Freud to Lacan. In: K. Ror Malone and S. Friedlander (Eds.), *The Subject of Lacan. A Lacanian Reader for Psychologists* (pp. 111–121). New York: SUNY Press.

Sauret, M.-J. (2000). *Psychanalyse et politique. Huit questions de la psychanalyse au politique*. Toulouse: Presses Universitaires du Mirail.

Sauret, M.-J. (2009). *Malaise dans le capitalisme*. Toulouse: Presses Universitaires du Mirail.

Saussure, F. de (1916). *Course in General Linguistics*, W. Baskin (Trans.). New York: Philosophical Library, 1959.

Schneider, M. (1979). *Neurosis y lucha de clases. Crítica materialista del psicoanálisis para constituirlo en fuerza liberadora*, V. Romano (Trans.). Madrid: Siglo XXI.

Sebag, L. (1964). *Marxisme et structuralisme*. Paris: Payot.

Sève, L. (1973). Psychanalyse et matérialisme historique. In: C . Clément, *Pour une critique marxiste de la théorie psychanalytique* (pp. 193–270). Paris: Éditions sociales.

Sierra Rubio, M. A. (2021). *Lacan, autor de tesis*. Rennes: CPSY.

Simondon, G. (1989). *L'individuation psychique et collective à la lumière des notions de forme, information, potentiel et métastabilité*. Paris: Aubier.

Smith, S. (2015). *Women and Socialism: Class, Race, and Capital*. Chicago: Haymarket Books.

Soler, C. (2014). *Lacan. The Unconscious Reinvented*, E. Faye and S. Schwartz (Trans.). London: Karnac.

Soto van der Plas, C., Juárez-Salazar, E., Gómez Camarena, C., and Pavón-Cuéllar, D. (Eds.) (2022). *The Marx Through Lacan Vocabulary. A Compass for Libidinal and Political Economies*. London: Routledge.

Soueix, A. (Ed) (1992). *Marx et Lénine, Freud et Lacan. Actes du 2e Colloque de La Découverte Freudienne*. Toulouse: Mirail.

Stalin, J. (1950). *Marxism and Problems of Linguistics*. Moscow: Foreign Languages Publishing House.

Stavrakakis, Y. (1999). *Lacan and the Political*. London: Routledge.

Stavrakakis, Y. (2007). *The Lacanian Left. Psychoanalysis, Theory, Politics*. Edinburgh: Edinburgh University Press.

Sutter, L. de (2018). *Narcocapitalism: Life in the Age of Anaesthesia*. Cambridge: Polity Press.

Taylor, C. (1979). *Hegel and Modern Society*. Cambridge: Cambridge University Press.

Tomšič, S. (2015). *The Capitalist Unconscious: Marx and Lacan*. London: Verso.

Tomšič, S. (2016). Baroque Structuralism: Deleuze, Lacan and the Critique of Linguistics. In: B. Nedoh and A. Zevnik (Eds.), *Lacan and Deleuze: A Disjunctive Synthesis*. Edinburgh: Edinburgh University Press.

Tomšič, S. (2019). *The Labour of Enjoyment. Towards a Critique of Libidinal Economy*. Cologne: August Verlag.

Tomšič, S. (2024). The Antisociality of Capitalism (Some Preliminary Reflections). In: B. Gook (Ed.), *Libidinal Economies of Crisis Times* (pp. 89–108). Bielefeld: Transcript Verlag.

Tönnies, F. (1887). *Community and Civil Society*, J. Harris and M. Hollis (Trans.). Cambridge: Cambridge University Press, 2001.
Toole, J. K. (1980). *A Confederacy of Dunces*. Baton Rouge: Louisiana State University Press, 2000.
Tutt, D. (2022). *Psychoanalysis and the Politics of the Family: The Crisis of Initiation*. Cham: Palgrave Macmillan.
Von Uexküll, J. (1934). *A Foray into the Worlds of Animals and Humans*, J. O'Neil (Trans.). Minneapolis: University of Minnesota Press.
Wapeemukwa, W. (2022). Oedipal Empire: Psychoanalysis, Indigenous Peoples, and the Oedipus Complex in Colonial Context. In: S. George and D. Hook (Eds.), *Lacan and Race. Racism, Identity, and Psychoanalytic Theory* (pp. 83–101). London: Routledge.
Wheen, F. (1999). *Karl Marx: A Life*. New York: W. W. Norton and Company.
Wilson, S. (2008). *The Order of Joy. Beyond the Cultural Politics of Enjoyment*. New York: SUNY Press.
Wujin, Y. (2006). Thing, Value, Time, and Freedom: A Consideration of Some Key Concepts in Marx's Philosophical System. In: *Frontiers of Philosophy in China*, 1 (1), 114–123.
Yamamoto, O. (1987). *A crise e as alternativas da psicologia*. Sao Paulo: Edicon.
Zafiropoulos, M. (2002). *Lacan y las ciencias sociales. La declinación del padre*, H. Pons (Trans.). Buenos Aires: Nueva Visión.
Zafiropoulos, M. (2010). *Lacan and Lévi-Strauss or The Return to Freud (1951–1957)*. London: Karnac.
Zafiropoulos, M. (2016). Ce que Lacan disait de Totem et Tabou. In: *Research in Psychoanalysis*, 1 (21), 117–125.
Zafiropoulos, M. (2017). *Les mythologiques de Lacan. La prison de verre du fantasme: Œdipe roi, Le diable amoureux, Hamlet*. Paris: Érès.
Zevnik, A. (2016a). Kant avec Sade: Ethics Entrapped in Perversions of Law and Politics. In: S. Tomšič and A. Zevnik (Eds.), *Jacques Lacan. Between Psychoanalysis and Politics* (pp. 217–232). London: Routledge.
Zevnik, A. (2016b). *Lacan, Deleuze and World Politics. Rethinking the Ontology of the Political Subject*. London: Routledge.
Žižek, S. (1989). *The Sublime Object of Ideology*. London: Verso.
Žižek, S. (1993). *Tarrying with the Negative: Kant, Hegel, and the Critique of Ideology*. Durham: Duke University Press.
Žižek, S. (1997). *The Plague of Fantasies*. London: Verso, 2008.
Žižek, S. (1998). Kant and Sade: The ideal couple. In: *Lacanian Ink* (13), 13–25.
Žižek, S. (2005). *The Puppet and the Dwarf. The Perverse Core of Christianity*. Cambridge: MIT Press.
Žižek, S. (2006). *How to Read Lacan*. New York: W. W. Norton and Company.
Žižek, S. (2012). *Organs without Bodies. On Deleuze and Consequences*. London: Routledge.

Index

Note: Locators followed by "n" refer end notes.

FSC
www.fsc.org
MIX
Papier | Fördert
gute Waldnutzung
FSC® C083411

Kolibri 360 GmbH
Ferdinand-Jühlke-Straße 7
99095 Erfurt, Deutschland
produktsicherheit@kolibri360.de